CUET

(UG) & Integrated PG

2022

Chemistry

DU | BHU | JNU | JMI | TISS & etc.

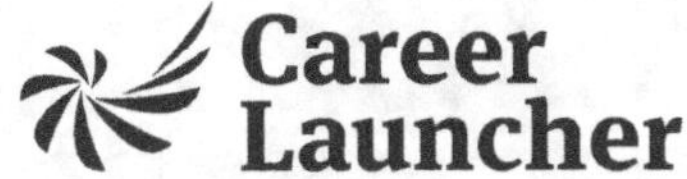

Career Launcher

Title : CUET 2022 : Chemistry

Language : English

Editor's Name : Awdhesh Dubey

Copyright © : 2022 CLIP

Typeset & Published by :

Career Launcher Infrastructure (P) Ltd.

A-45, Mohan Cooperative Industrial Area, Near Mohan Estate Metro Station, New Delhi - 110044

Marketed by :

G.K. Publications (P) Ltd.

Plot No. 9A, Sector-27A, Mathura Road, Faridabad, Haryana-121003

ISBN : 978-93-95101-27-1

For product information :

Visit *www.gkpublications.com* or email to *gkp@gkpublications.com*

CONTENTS

About CUET

A year ago, it would have been unimaginable that cut-offs in Delhi University would skyrocket to 100% for some of the undergraduate courses! While DU has always been known for its high cut-offs, there are several other universities where the story is no different.

However, the National Education Policy 2020 (NEP) aims to do away with the tyranny of the ever-rising cut-offs by introducing a Common Entrance Test for all the Central Universities in the country. NEP not only proposes a holistic approach in evaluating the students by giving them the option to select subjects based on their interest, but it also aims to simplify the process of admission to higher-education institutes.

To start with, there would be a Common Entrance Test for all the Central Universities, which would be conducted twice a year from 2022. While this might sound like a new concept to many, the fact is, there is already a CUET, which is conducted for the Central Universities established in or after 2009. As many as 14 of them already admit students based on their performance in the entrance test. The CUET scores are also accepted by four state universities of the country.

The proposed CUET aims to assess conceptual understanding and application of knowledge; and also, to lessen the burden of appearing in multiple tests.

CUET Eligibility

Getting into a premier University is every student's dream. The brand value of the University not only facilitates securing a seat in a master's program in a national/international institute, but also helps in getting job offers through campus placements.

Entry to a Central University, in most cases earlier, was based on merit, i.e., marks secured in Class XII Board exams. However, from the academic year 2021, all Central Universities will also consider the CUET score for admissions into their Undergraduate programs.

CUET 2022: Eligibility Criteria

While the official criteria will be learnt once the CUET 2021 notification is released, the stipulations are not expected to change much from those of previous years.

- A candidate must have passed Class XII (10+2) or equivalent from a recognized education Board.
- If the respective Board awards grades (or CGPA), the conversion factor given by the Board must be used to compute the percentage of marks.
- Candidates, who have completed their Class XII in 2021, and have passed the Board exams, will also be eligible to apply for CUET 2022.

Eligibility: Class XII Students

While CUET is for students who have passed the Class XII (or equivalent) Board exams, any student who is appearing for the Class XII Board exam in 2022 is also eligible to apply for CUET 2021. The candidate would be required to produce the marksheets and relevant certificates as mandated by the participating Central University, and follow the timelines provided for admissions.

Key Points

- Each participating Central University is free to decide its own eligibility criteria for admissions.

- The weightages for CUET and Class XII Board exam results(if, applicable) will be at the sole discretion of the Central University, to which admission is being sought.

- As of date, CUET does not have an age limit. However, Central Universities can fix minimum & maximum age limit for admissions to all (or any) of the programs on offer.

Reservation of Seats

As CUET is an entrance exam for admissions to Undergraduate courses at the Central Universities, which have been established under an Act of the Parliament, each Central University must follow the norms set by the Government of India, with respect to intake and reservation of seats.

Generally, the following break-up is followed:

Category	Reservation
Scheduled Castes	15%
Scheduled Tribes	7.5%
Other Backward Classes (Non-Creamy)	27%
Persons with Disability	5%

Some institutions might even have provisions for the Economically Weaker Sections, which can account for 10% of the total seats. These EWS seats are carved out from the Open Category.

To avail of the reservation benefit based on caste (or any other category as specified), a candidate must be able to produce valid documents/certificates to support such claims.

Conclusion

It is essential for every candidate to check the validity of their candidature for CUET, as well as the Central University he/she is applying to. The candidate should be aware of the documents that might be required while applying for the exam, or during the admissions.

CUET 2022 notification is expected in March 2022, and registration is also going to start then.

CUET: Exam Pattern

Examination Structure for CUET (UG) -2022:

CUET (UG) –2022 will consist of the following 4 Sections:

> **Section IA** –13 Languages
>
> **Section IB** –19 Languages
>
> **Section II** –27 Domain specific Subjects
>
> **Section III** –General Test

Choosing options from each Section is not mandatory. Choices should match the requirements of the desired University.

Broad features of CUET (UG) -2022 are as follows:

Section	Subjects/ Tests	Questions to be Attempted	Question Type	Duration
Section IA – Languages	There are 13* different languages. Any of these languages may be chosen.	40 questions to be attempted out of 50 in each language	Language to be tested through Reading Comprehension (based on different types of passages–Factual, Literary and Narrative, [Literary Aptitude and Vocabulary]	45 Minutes for each language
Section IB – Languages	There are 19** Languages. Any other language apart from those offered in Section I A may be chosen.			
Section II - Domain	There are 27*** Domains specific subjects being offered under this Section. A candidate may choose a maximum of Six (06) Domains as desired by the applicable University/Universities.	40 Questions to be attempted out of 50	• Input text can be used for MCQ Based Questions • MCQs based on NCERT Class XII syllabus only	
Section III- General Test	For any such undergraduate programme/ programmes being offered by Universities where a General Test is being used for admission.	60 Questions to be attempted out of 75	• Input text can be used for MCQ Based Questions • General Knowledge, Current Affairs, General Mental Ability, Numerical Ability, Quantitative Reasoning (Simple application of basic mathematical concepts arithmetic/algebra geometry/mensuration/s tat taught till Grade 8), Logical and Analytical Reasoning	

* **Languages (13):** Tamil, Telugu, Kannada, Malayalam, Marathi, Gujarati, Odiya, Bengali, Assamese, Punjabi, English, Hindi and Urdu

** **Languages (19):** *French, Spanish, German, Nepali, Persian, Italian, Arabic, Sindhi, Kashmiri, Konkani, Bodo, Dogri, Maithili, Manipuri, Santhali, Tibetan, Japanese, Russian, Chinese.*

*** **Domain Specific Subjects (27):** 1. Accountancy/ Book Keeping 2. Biology/ Biological Studies/ Biotechnology/Biochemistry 3. Business Studies 4. Chemistry 5. Computer Science/ Informatics Practices 6. Economics/ Business Economics 7. Engineering Graphics 8.Entrepreneurship 9. Geography/Geology 10. History 11. Home Science 12.Knowledge Tradition and Practices of India 13. Legal Studies 14. Environmental Science 15. Mathematics 16. Physical Education/ NCC /Yoga 17.Physics 18.Political Science 19. Psychology 20. Sociology 21. Teaching Aptitude 22. Agriculture 23. Mass Media/ Mass Communication 24. Anthropology 25. Fine Arts/Visual Arts (Sculpture/ Painting)/Commercial Arts, 26. Performing Arts – (i) Dance (Kathak/ Bharatnatyam/Oddisi/ Kathakali/Kuchipudi/ Manipuri (ii) Drama- Theatre (iii) Music General (Hindustani/ Carnatic/ RabindraSangeet/ Percussion/ Non-Percussion), 27. Sanskrit *[For all Shastri (Shastri 3 years/ 4 years Honours) Equivalent to B.A./B.A. Honours courses i.e. Shastri in Veda, Paurohitya (Karmakand), Dharamshastra, Prachin Vyakarana, Navya Vyakarana, Phalit Jyotish, Siddhant Jyotish, Vastushastra, Sahitya,Puranetihas, Prakrit Bhasha,Prachin Nyaya Vaisheshik, Sankhya Yoga, Jain Darshan, Mimansa, AdvaitaVedanta, Vishihstadvaita Vedanta, Sarva Darshan, a candidate may choose Sanskrit as the Domain].*

- A Candidate can choose a maximum of **any 3 languages** from Section IA and Section IB taken together. (One of the languages chosen needs to be in lieu of Domain specific subjects)
- Section II offers 27 Subjects, out of which a candidate may choose a **maximum of 6 Subjects.**
- Section III comprises **General Test.**
- For choosing Languages (upto 3) from Section IA and IB and a maximum of 6 Subjects from Section II and General Test under Section III, the Candidate must refer to the requirements of his/her intended University.

Mode of the Test	Computer Based Test-CBT
Test Pattern	Objective type with Multiple Choice Questions
Medium	13 languages (*Tamil, Telugu, Kannada, Malayalam, Marathi, Gujarati, Odiya, Bengali, Assamese, Punjabi, English, Hindi and Urdu)*
Syllabus	**Section IA & IB:** Language to be tested through Reading Comprehension (based on different types of passages–Factual, Literary and Narrative [Literary Aptitude & Vocabulary]
	Section II : As per NCERT model syllabus as applicable to Class XII only
	Section III : General Knowledge, Current Affairs, General Mental Ability, Numerical Ability, Quantitative Reasoning (Simple application of basic mathematical concepts arithmetic/algebra geometry/mensuration/stat taught till Grade 8), Logical and Analytical Reasoning

Level of questions for CUET (UG) -2022:

All questions in various testing areas will be benchmarked at the level of Class XII only. Students having studied Class XII Board syllabus would be able to do well in CUET (UG) – 2022.

Number of attempts:

If any University permits students of previous years of class XII to take admission in the current year also, such students would also be eligible to appear in CUET (UG) – 2022.

Choice of Languages and Subjects:

Generally the languages/subjects chosen should be the ones that a student has opted in his latest Class XII Board examination. However, if any University permits any flexibility in this regards, the same can be exercised under CUET (UG) -2022 also. Candidates must carefully refer to the eligibility requirements of various Central Universities in this regard. Moreover, if the subject to be studied in the Undergraduate course is not available in the list of **27 Domain Specific Subject** being offered, the Candidate may choose the Subject closest to his choice for e.g. For Biochemistry the candidate may choose Biology.

Candidates are advised to visit the NTA CUET (UG)-2022 official website **https://cuet.samarth.ac.in/** for latest updates regarding the Examination.

CUET Syllabus

Before you start your preparation for any entrance exam, it is important to understand the syllabus. Otherwise, your prep will be directionless, and you might be left wondering where things might have gone wrong!

With more than 1.68 lakh seats on offer for the undergraduate courses at the 54 Central Universities, CUET is one the most competitive examinations. For this very reason, while preparing for the exam, you will need to adopt a structured approach. And in doing that, understanding the syllabus is a critical step.

CUET 2022 Overview

CUET 2022 will be a Computer-Based Test (CBT), commonly referred to as an online exam. However, there is a difference between the two terms: CBT and online. In CBT, the questions are kept constant and simply presented in an online format; whereas in an Online Test, questions are stored as a bank, and the system decides which questions are to be presented to the candidate, based on a pre-defined logic.

CUET 2022 is likely to be a General Ability Test, with focus on English Language, Numerical Ability, Logical & Analytical Reasoning, along with General Awareness and Current Affairs.

CUET 2022 Syllabus

The CUET 2022 exam pattern gives a good idea about what is in store for the candidate and how one needs to prepare for the exam.

- **English Language:** The questions in this section will test one's proficiency in the language, based on comprehension passages, fundamentals of grammar, and vocabulary. In the Comprehension section, candidates will be evaluated on their understanding of a passage and its central theme, meanings of words used therein, etc. The Grammar section entails correcting grammatically incorrect sentences, filling of blanks in sentences with appropriate words, etc. Questions on synonyms & antonyms will check one's command over English vocabulary.
- **Numerical Ability:** Questions on Numerical Ability will test the candidate's knowledge of elementary mathematics. Areas like arithmetic, number system, basics of algebra, and modern maths will be central to these types of questions.
- **Logical & Analytical Reasoning:** This section tests the candidate's ability to identify patterns & logical links, and rectify illogical arguments. It can include a variety of Logical Reasoning questions, such as those on syllogisms, logical sequences, analogies, etc., along with Analytical Reasoning questions on series, directions, clocks & calendars, arrangements, and puzzles to name a few.
- **General Awareness and Current Affairs:** The General Awareness section includes static general knowledge, while questions on Current Affairs will gauge a candidate's knowledge of national & international current affairs.

CUET 2022 may or may not have a section on subject knowledge. Once the exam notification is out in March, there will be more clarity on this matter.

While there is no syllabus explicitly mentioned by CUET, the broad idea is always presented. One must look at the previous years' papers and solve the sample papers available to form a basic understanding.

About University of Delhi

University of Delhi (commonly known as DU) was established in 1922 and is one of the largest Universities in the country. With 16 faculties, 86 academic departments, 90 colleges and 540 programs on offer, Delhi University is no doubt one of the sought-after University in the country.

With 1, 96,000 students enrolled in UG programs, Delhi University is a valued university and constantly ranked among the top in the country. DU bagged 11th Rank in NIRF 2020 and ranked 6th in QS India Rankings 2020. The University has two Campuses: North and South.

DU UG Programs

Delhi University offers several programs at the undergraduate level. With more than 60 constituent colleges, the Delhi University offers many undergraduate courses.

Please refer to the table below for the important undergraduate courses offered by the DU and the intake across each program.

Program	Intake
B. A (Pass)	11249
B. A (Hons) Geography	788
B. A (Hons) Economics	2754
B. A (Hons) History	2791
B. A (Hons) Political Science	3657
B. A (Hons) Sociology	596
B. A (Hons) Psychology	670
B. A (Hons) Applied Psychology	252
B. A (Hons) Social Work	133
B. A (Hons) Philosophy	783
B. A (Hons) English	2886
B. A (Hons) Hindi	2829
B. A (Hons) Sanskrit	1407
B. A (Hons) Punjabi	214
B. A (Hons) Urdu	207
BA(Hons) French	49

Program	Intake
BA(Hons) German	49
BA(Hons) Spanish	49
BA(Hons) Italian	49
B. Com (Hons)	7953
B.Com (Pass)	7854
Program	Intake
B.Sc. (H) Biomedical Science	162
B.Sc. (H) Botany	937
B.Sc. (H) Chemistry	1487
B.Sc. (H) Computer Science	1265
B.Sc. (H) Electronics	624
B.Sc. (H) Mathematics	2428
B.Sc. (H) Physics	1659
B.Sc. (H) Zoology	944
B.Sc. Life Sciences	1515
B.Sc. Physical Science with Chemistry	703
B.Sc. Physical Science with Computer Science	553
B.Sc. Physical Science with Electronics	247
B. Sc (Hons.) Statistics	476
B. Sc. (Prog.) Applied Physical Science Industrial Chemistry	96
B.Sc. (Hons.) Home Science	900
B. Sc. (Hons.) Psychology	57
B.Sc. (H) Food Technology	179
B.Sc. (H)Instrumentation	99
B.Sc. (H) Microbiology	238
B.Sc. (H) Polymer Science	59
B.SC. Mathematical Science	224
B.SC. (Hons.) Biochemistry	146
B.SC. Industrial Chemistry	78
B.Sc. (Prog.) Physical Science	940
B.SC. (Hons.) Geology	98

DU UG Programs Eligibility:

As the University offers multiple programs and separate intake for male and female candidates, it is important to check the university official website regularly to keep oneself updated about the eligibility for each program, which can change.

DU UG Admissions:

Until 2021, Delhi University admitted students on the basis of class XII marks. From the academic year 2022, admissions to UG programs offered Delhi University will be based on CUET. CUET will be a common entrance for admissions to UG programs offered by all the Central Universities in the country.

Delhi University UG Programs Reservation:

DU being a Central University offers reservations in admissions according to central government rules.

Schedule Caste (SC): 15% of the total seats are reserved for students who belong to SC category.

Schedule Tribe (ST): 7.5% of the total seats are reserved for students belonging to ST Category.

Other Backward Classes (OBC): 27% of the total intake is reserved for students from Other Backward Classes (OBC), excluding those from creamy layer.

Economically Weaker Section (EWS): The University has reserved 10% seats for EWS category, in accordance with the directive of Ministry of Education.

Persons with Disability (PWD): 5% of the seats are reserved on horizontal basis for students from PWD category.

About BHU

Banaras Hindu University (BHU), situated in the holy city of Varanasi, was founded by Pandit Madan Mohan Malviya in cooperation with Dr. Annie Besant, in 1916 under the act of Parliament-B.H.U Act, 1915. BHU, which is a Central University, comprises of 6 Institutes, 14 Faculties, 144 academic departments, and 4 Inter-disciplinary centers, spread over 1300 acres. The University consists of 15,000 students, 1700 teachers and 8000 non-teaching staff.

BHU was ranked 3rd among the Universities in India in 2020. According to university submissions for NIRF 2021, BHU has 10, 585 students pursuing UG programs, of which 236 students are foreign nationals.

BHU UG Programs

BHU offers a host of undergraduate programs including medical and engineering. Through its various faculties, BHU offers a range of programs which caters to students learning abilities. The University along with its main campus, also offers the undergraduate courses from the following colleges: Mahila Mahavidyalaya (MMV); Arya Mahila Post Graduate College (AMPGC), Vasant Kanya Mahavidyalaya (VKM); Vasanta College for Women (VCW); DAV Post Graduate College (DAVPGC) and Rajiv Gandhi South Campus (RGSC).

Please refer to the table below for the important undergraduate courses offered by BHU and the intake across each program/campuses.

Faculty of Arts				
Course	Campus	Intake	Status	Duration
B.A (Hons) Arts	Faculty of Arts	765	Co-Ed	3 Years
	Mahila Mahavidyalaya	286	Women	3 Years
	Arya Mahila Post Graduate College	383	Women	3 Years
	Vasant Kanya Mahavidyalaya	286	Women	3 Years
	Vasanta College for Women	412	Women	3 Years
	DAV Post Graduate College	309	Co-Ed	3 Years
Faculty of Social Sciences				
Course	Campus	Intake	Status	Duration
B.A (Hons) Social Sciences [incl. B. A (Hons) Economics]	Faculty of Social Sciences	573	Co-Ed	3 Years
	Mahila Mahavidyalaya	193	Women	3 Years
	Arya Mahila Post Graduate College	383	Women	3 Years
	Vasant Kanya Mahavidyalaya	249	Women	3 Years
	Vasanta College for Women	210	Women	3 Years
	DAV Post Graduate College	326	Co-Ed	3 Years

Faculty of Commerce				
Course	Campus	Intake	Status	Duration
B. Com (Hons)	Faculty of Commerce	286	Co-Ed	3 Years
	Vasant Kanya Mahavidyalaya	96	Women	3 Years
	Arya Mahila Post Graduate College	96	Women	3 Years
	DAV Post Graduate College	227	Co-Ed	3 Years
	Rajiv Gandhi South Campus, Mirzapur	114	Co-Ed	3 Years
B. Com (Hons) Financial Markets Management	Faculty of Commerce	62	Co-Ed	3 Years
	Rajiv Gandhi South Campus, Mirzapur	62	Co-Ed	3 Years

Institute of Science				
Course	Campus	Intake	Status	Duration
B.Sc (Hons) Maths Group	Faculty of Science	573	Co-Ed	3 Years
	Mahila Mahavidyalaya	96	Women	3 Years
B.Sc (Hons) Bio Group	Faculty of Science	383	Co-Ed	3 Years
	Mahila Mahavidyalaya	193	Women	3 Years

Faculty of Visual Arts				
Course	Campus	Intake	Status	Duration
B.F.A (Bachelor of Fine Arts)	Faculty of Visual Arts	96	Co-Ed	4 Years
Faculty of Arts				
Bachelor of Vocation (Retail and Logistics Management)	Rajiv Gandhi South Campus	62	Co-Ed	3 Years
Bachelor of Vocation (Hospitality & Tourism Management)	Rajiv Gandhi South Campus	62	Co-Ed	3 Years
Bachelor of Vocation (Fashion Designing and Event Management)	Rajiv Gandhi South Campus	62	Co-Ed	3 Years
Bachelor of Vocation (Modern Office Management)	Rajiv Gandhi South Campus	62	Co-Ed	3 Years
Bachelor of Vocation (Food Processing & Management)	Rajiv Gandhi South Campus	62	Co-Ed	3 Years
Bachelor of Vocation (Medical Lab. & Technology)	Rajiv Gandhi South Campus	62	Co-Ed	3 Years

BHU UG Programs Eligibility:

Each of the courses have different eligibility for admissions. To be eligible for admissions, one must fulfil all the criteria as laid down by the respective faculties of the University.

B.A (Hons) Arts/ B.A (Hons) Social Sciences: Candidate must not be more than 22 years of age and must have passed class XII or equivalent with minimum 50% marks in aggregate.

B.A (Hons) Economics: Candidate must not be more than 22 years of age and must have passed class XII or equivalent with minimum 50% marks in aggregate along with mathematics as one of the papers.

B. Com (Hons)/B. Com (Hons) Financial Markets Management: Candidate must not be more than 22 years of age and must have passed class XII or equivalent with minimum 50% marks in aggregate with Commerce/ Economics/Maths/Computer Science/Finance/Financial Markets Management as one of the subjects.

B. Sc (Hons) Maths Group: Candidate must not be more than 22 years of age and must have passed class XII or equivalent with minimum 50% marks in aggregate in the subjects Physics, Maths plus any one of the following: Chemistry, Statistics, Geology, Computer Science, Information Technology and Geography and must have passed in each of the concerned three subjects.

B. Sc (Hons) Bio Group: Candidate must not be more than 22 years of age and must have passed class XII or equivalent with minimum 50% marks in aggregate in the subjects Physics, Chemistry plus any one of the following: Biology, Geology and Geography and must have passed in each of the concerned three subjects.

B. F. A (Bachelor of Fine Arts): Candidate must not be more than 22 years of age and must have passed class XII or equivalent with minimum 50% marks in aggregate.

Bachelor of Vocation: Candidate must have passed class XII or equivalent in any stream (Science for Food Processing and Medical Lab Technology) or level 4 NSQF certificate.

BHU UG Admissions:

Until 2021, admissions to BHU UG courses were based on Undergraduate Entrance Test (UET) conducted by the University. From the academic year 2022, admissions to UG programs offered by BHU will be based on CUET, which will replace the UET. CUET will be a common entrance for admissions to UG programs offered by all the Central Universities in the country.

BHU UG Programs Reservation:

BHU being a Central University offers reservations in admissions according to central government rules.

Schedule Caste (SC): 15% of the total seats are reserved for students who belong to SC category.

Schedule Tribe (ST): 7.5% of the total seats are reserved for students belonging to ST Category.

Other Backward Classes (OBC): 27% of the total intake is reserved for students from Other Backward Classes (OBC), excluding those from creamy layer.

Economically Weaker Section (EWS): The University has reserved 10% seats for EWS category, in accordance with the directive of Ministry of Education.

Persons with Disability (PWD): 5% of the seats are reserved on horizontal basis for students from PWD category.

About JNU

Ever wondered which University, the cadets from National Defence Academy (NDA) graduate from? Yes. It is Jawaharlal Nehru University (JNU). JNU started in the year 1969, three years after the act of Parliament in 1966. With several academic centres of JNU declared "Centres of Excellence" by the University Grants Commission, JNU has been ranked No. 1 by National Assessment and Accreditation Council (NAAC). JNU has been ranked No. 2 by National Institutional Ranking Framework (NIRF) 2020 and has been awarded the Best University Award by the President of India in 2017. The European Commission has awarded the Jean Monnet Centre of Excellence for European Union Studies in India (CEEUSI) to Jawaharlal Nehru University in 2018. This is one of the highest international recognition for any European Studies programme.

JNU was the first University to start integrated five-year Master of Arts in Language Courses. JNU actively collaborates with National and International Universities for student and faculty exchange programs.

According to university submissions for NIRF 2020, JNU has 1,048 students pursuing UG programs, of which 46 are foreign nationals.

JNU UG Programs

JNU offers a limited program at the undergraduate level, unlike other universities. The focus at undergraduate has been largely on language courses. In 2018, JNU started two programs in engineering and plans to add a few more specializations in future.

Please refer to the table below for the important undergraduate courses offered by JNU and the intake across each program.

School	Program	Intake	Duration
School of Language, Literature and Cultural Studies	B. A (Hons) Pashto	19	3 Years
	B. A (Hons) Persian	39	3 Years
	B. A (Hons) Arabic	39	3 Years
	B. A (Hons) Japanese	48	3 Years
	B. A (Hons) Korean	39	3 Years
	B. A (Hons) Chinese	44	3 Years
	B. A (Hons) French	48	3 Years
	B. A (Hons) German	48	3 Years
	B. A (Hons) Russian	68	3 Years
	B. A (Hons) Spanish	39	3 Years

School of Sanskrit and Indic Studies	B. Sc - M. Sc Integrated Program in Ayurveda Biology	20	5 Years
School of Engineering	B. Tech in Computer Science and Engineering & MS/M. Tech in Social Sciences/Humanities/Science/Technology	25	5 Years
	B. Tech in Electronics and Communication Engineering & MS/M. Tech in Social Sciences/Humanities/Science/Technology	25	5 Years

JNU UG Programs Eligibility:

Each of the courses have different eligibility for admissions. To be eligible for admissions, one must fulfil all the criteria as laid down by the respective faculties of the University.

B.A (Hons) Language Courses: Candidate must not be less than 17 years of age and must have passed Senior School Certificate (10+2) or equivalent examination with minimum of 45% marks.

B. Sc - M. Sc Integrated Program in Ayurveda Biology: Candidate must not be less than 17 years of age and must have passed Senior School Certificate (10+2) or equivalent examination with minimum of 45% marks.

B. Tech-M. Tech: Based on JEE Mains

JNU UG Admissions:

Until 2021, admissions to JNU UG courses were based on JNU Entrance Examination (JNUEE) conducted by the National Testing Agency (NTA). From the academic year 2022, admissions to UG programs offered by JNU will be based on CUET, which will replace the JNUEE. CUET will be a common entrance for admissions to UG programs offered by all the Central Universities in the country.

JNU UG Programs Reservation:

JNU being a Central University offers reservations in admissions according to central government rules.

Schedule Caste (SC): 15% of the total seats are reserved for students who belong to SC category.

Schedule Tribe (ST): 7.5% of the total seats are reserved for students belonging to ST Category.

Other Backward Classes (OBC): 27% of the total intake is reserved for students from Other Backward Classes (OBC), excluding those from creamy layer. Also, Central List of Caste to be followed.

Economically Weaker Section (EWS): The University has reserved 10% seats for EWS category, in accordance with the directive of Ministry of Education.

Persons with Disability (PWD): 5% of the seats are reserved on horizontal basis for students from PWD category.

About Jamia Milia Islamia

Jamia Milia Islamia (JMI) was founded in 1920 in Aligarh and became a Central University in 1988 by the act of Parliament. Jamia in Urdu stands for University and Milia means National, making Jamia Milia Islamia a National University. Jamia Milia Islamia moved to Delhi in 1925 and shifted to its present campus in Okhla in 1935.

Jamia Milia Islamia is a NAAC accredited University with grade "A" and was placed 10th in NIRF Rankings 2020. According to submissions made by University for NIRF 2021, Jamia Milia Islamia has a total of 5,911 students pursuing undergraduate courses at the University, of which 105 are foreign nationals. The University also manage to place a total of 681 UG students with an average salary ranging 4.2 Lacs-6.0 Lacs.

JMI UG Programs

Jamia Milia Islamia (JMI) offers a host of undergraduate programs for students. Through its various faculties, JMI offers a range of programs which caters to students learning abilities.

Please refer to the table below for the important undergraduate courses offered by Jamia Milia Islamia and the intake across each program.

Faculty	Course	Intake	Duration
Faculty of Humanities and Language	B. A (Hons) English	60	3 Years
	B. A (Hons) Hindi	40	3 Years
	B. A (Hons) Mass Media-Hindi	40	3 Years
	B. A (Hons) History	60	3 Years
	Bachelor of Hotel Management (BHM)	40	3 Years
	Bachelor of Tourism and Travel Management	40	3 Years
	B. Voc (Food Production)	40	3 Years
Faculty of Social Sciences	Bachelor of Arts (B. A)	68	3 Years
	B. Com (Hons)	55	3 Years
	BBA (Bachelor of Business Administration)	44	3 Years
	B. A (Hons) Economics	53	3 Years
	B. A (Hons) Sociology	42	3 Years
	B. A (Hons) Political Science	42	3 Years
	B. A (Hons) Psychology	42	3 Years
Faculty of Natural Sciences	B. Sc (Bachelor of Science)	50	3 Years
	B. Sc Biosciences	40	3 Years
	B. Sc Biotechnology	35	3 Years
	B. Sc (Hons) Chemistry	40	3 Years
	B. A/B. Sc (Hons) Geography	60	3 Years
	B. Sc (Hons) Mathematics	45	3 Years
	B. Sc (Hons) Applied Mathematics	45	3 Years
	B. Sc (Hons) Physics	45	3 Years
Faculty of Fine Arts	Bachelor of Fine Arts (Applied Art)	30	4 Years
	Bachelor of Fine Arts (Art Education)	20	4 Years
	Bachelor of Fine Arts (Painting)	20	4 Years
	Bachelor of Fine Arts (Sculpture)	10	4 Years

JMI UG Programs Eligibility:

Each of the courses have different eligibility for admissions. To be eligible for admissions, one must fulfil all the criteria as laid down by the respective faculties of the University.

B. Com (Hons) /BBA /B. A (Hons) Economics: Candidate must have passed class XII or equivalent with a minimum of 50% marks in five subjects.

BHM/BTTM/B. Voc (Food Production): Candidate must have passed class XII or equivalent with a minimum of 45% marks in five subjects.

B. A (Hons) Mass Media/B. A (Hons) Hindi: Candidate must have passed class XII or equivalent with a minimum of 45% marks in five subjects.

B. Sc/B. Sc (Hons): Candidate must have passed class XII or equivalent with minimum 50% marks in each of the science subjects i.e. Physics, Chemistry and Mathematics and 50% marks in aggregate of best 5-subjects.

JMI UG Admissions:

Until 2021, admissions to JMI UG courses were based on Entrance Test (JMI-ET) conducted by the University. From the academic year 2022, admissions to UG programs offered by JMI will be based on CUET, which will replace the JMI-ET. CUET will be a common entrance for admissions to UG programs offered by all the Central Universities in the country.

JMI UG Programs Reservation:

JMI is a minority reservation-based University and accordingly, seats are reserved for candidates as per the norms laid down by the University.

Muslim Minority: 30% of the total seats are reserved for Muslim applicants; 10% of the total seats are reserved for women applicants who are Muslim; 10% of the total intake is for OBC-NC candidates who are Muslims.

Persons with Disability (PWD): 5% of the seats are reserved for students from PWD category.

Jamia Students: 5% seats in all Undergraduate Programs shall be filled by internal students of Jamia who have passed their qualifying examination of the concerned programme (X or XII) from Jamia Schools as regular students.

In addition, Jamia Milia Islamia has supernumerary seats for Kashmiri Migrants and students from Jammu and Kashmir.

About Aligarh Muslim University

Aligarh Muslim University also referred as AMU was established by Sir Syed Ahmad Khan in 1875. The University started as Muhammadan Anglo-Oriental College and became a University (AMU) in 1920. The university has been ranked 801–1000 in the QS World University Rankings of 2021 and 17 in India by the National Institutional Ranking Framework in 2020.

Aligarh Muslim University is institution of national importance, under the seventh schedule of the Constitution of India.

AMU UG Programs

Aligarh Muslim University offers several programs at the undergraduate level. With 7 constituent colleges, the Aligarh Muslim University offers many undergraduate courses.

Please refer to the table below for the important undergraduate courses offered by the AMU and the intake across each program.

Course	Intake	Duration
B. Sc (Hons) Home Science	30*	3 Years
B.Sc (Hons) Agriculture	40	4 Years
B. A (Hons) Arabic	20+10*	3 Years
B. A (Hons) Communicative English	15+20*	3 Years
B. A (Hons) English	40+35*	3 Years
B. A (Hons) Hindi	40+25*	3 Years
B. A (Hons) Geography	50+20*	3 Years
B. A (Hons) Linguistics	20+25*	3 Years
B. A (Hons) Persian	15+25*	3 Years
B. A (Hons) Philosophy	20+10*	3 Years
B. A (Hons) Quaranic Studies	10+10*	3 Years
B. A (Hons) Sanskrit	15+10*	3 Years
B. A (Hons) Urdu	40+50*	3 Years
Bachelor of Fine Arts	15+15*	3 Years
B. Com (Hons)	180+100*	3 Years
B. Voc Production Technology	50	3 Years
B Voc Polymer and Coating Technology	50	3 Years
B. Voc Fashion Design and Garment Technology	50	3 Years
B. A (Hons) Chinese	20	3 Years
B. A (Hons) French	20	3 Years
B. A (Hons) German	20	3 Years

Program	Intake	Duration
B. A (Hons) Russian	20	3 Years
B. A (Hons) Spanish	20	3 Years
B. Sc (Hons) Biochemistry	30+30*	3 Years
B. Sc (Hons) Botany	60+40*	3 Years
B. Sc (Hons) Zoology	60+45*	3 Years
B. Sc (Hons) Physics	120+35*	3 Years
B. Sc (Hons) Chemistry	120+65*	3 Years
B. Sc (Hons) Mathematics	120+40*	3 Years
B. Sc (Hons) Geography	45+30*	3 Years
B. Sc (Hons) Geology	100+30*	3 Years
B. Sc (Hons) Statistics	60+30*	3 Years
B. Sc (Hons) Industrial Chemistry	20+10*	3 Years
B. Sc (Hons) Computer Applications	40+20*	3 Years

AMU UG Programs Eligibility:

As the University offers multiple programs and separate intake for male and female candidates, it is important to check the university official website regularly to keep oneself updated about the eligibility for each program, which can change.

AMU UG Admissions:

Until 2021, AMU conducted its own entrance test to admit students for the UG programs. From the academic year 2022, admissions to UG programs offered by Aligarh Muslim University will be based on CUET. CUET will be a common entrance for admissions to UG programs offered by all the Central Universities in the country.

University of Allahabad UG Programs Reservation:

Allahabad University being a Central University offers reservations in admissions according to central government rules. Kindly check the university website for further details.

CHEMISTRY

CHAPTER 1

Solid State

Classification of Solids, Crystal Lattices and Unit Cells, Close Packed Structures

Substances which have a definite shape, mass and volume.

General Characteristics of solids:

* Very less intermolecular space and strong intermolecular force.
* The constituents particles (atoms, molecules or ions) can only oscillate about their mean position.
* High boiling and melting point.
* Solids have rigidity, low compressibility and high density.

Types of solid:

* Crystalline solid: Particles with definite shapes and made of huge number of small crystals arranged in order.
  * ➢ Molecular solid
    Non-polar molecular solids
    Polar molecular solids
    Hydrogen bonded molecular solids
  * ➢ Covalent solid
  * ➢ Metallic solids
  * ➢ Ionic solids

Types of Crystalline Solid	Constituent particles	Bonding/ Attractive forces	Examples	Physical Nature	Electrical Conductivity	Melting Point
• Molecular solids	Molecules					
➢ Non-polar		Dispersion or London forces	Ar, CCl_2, H_2, I_2, CO_2	Soft	Insulator	Very low
➢ Polar		Dipole-Dipole interaction	HCl, SO_2	Soft	Insulator	Low
➢ Hydrogen bonded		Hydrogen bonding	H_2O (ice)	Hard	Insulator	Low
• Ionic solids	Ions	Coulombic or Electrostatic	$NaCl$, MgO, Zns, CaF	Hard but brittle	Insulators in solid state but conductors in molten state and aqueous solutions	High

| Metallic solids | Positive ions in a sea of delocalized electrons | Metallic bonding | Fe, Cu Ag, Mg | Hard but malleable and ductile | Conductors in solid state as well as in molten state | Fairly high |
| Covalent or network solids | Atoms | Covalent bonding | SiO_2(quartz), SiC, C(diamond), AlN $C_{Graphite}$ | Hard

Soft | Insulators Conductor (exception) | Very high |

- Amorphous solid: They lack ordered arrangement.

Properties of solid:

- Anisotropy: When the properties of a material vary with different direction in same crystal.
- Isotropy: When the properties of a material are the same in all directions.

Crystal lattice: The symmetrical three-dimensional arrangement of atoms in a crystal.

Unit cell: Smallest three-dimensional unit of crystal lattice.

Types of Unit Cell:

- Primitive unit cell
- Non- primitive unit cell

Types of Non- primitive unit cell:

- Face-centered: Particles at corners and at centre of all faces
- Body-centered: Particles at corners and at centre in the body
- End centered::Particles at corners and at centre of two opposite end faces.

System	Lengths and Angles	Number of Lattices
Cubic	$a = b = c;$ $\alpha = \beta = \gamma = 90°$	3
Tetragonal	$a = b \neq c;$ $\alpha = \beta = \gamma = 90°$	2
Orthorhombic	$a \neq b \neq c;$ $\alpha = \beta = \gamma = 120°$	4
Rhombohedral	$a = b = c;$ $\alpha = \beta = 90°, \gamma = 120°$	1
Monoclinic	$a \neq b \neq c;$ $\alpha = \gamma = 90°, \neq \beta$	2
Triclinic	$a \neq b \neq c;$ $\alpha \neq \gamma \neq \beta$	1
Hexagonal	$a = b \neq c;$ $\alpha = \beta = 90°, \gamma = 120°$	1

Number of atoms in a unit cell:

- Simple cubic: Z = 1
- bcc: Z = 2
- fcc: Z = 4
- ecc: Z = 2

Closed packed structures:

- Close packing in one dimension: Spheres touch each other in a row.
- Close packing in two dimensions: Square close packing: each sphere is in touch with four other

Close packing in three dimensions:

- Cubic Close packed (ccp):In such packing, the spheres of molecules are adjacent to each other in a way that each row is a repetition of the previous row. Lattice of this cubic close packed is simple cubic and its unit cell is primitive cubic unit cell.
- Hexagonal Close packed (hcp):In such packing, the spheres of a row in a particular dimension fit into depressions between adjacent spheres of the previous row

Coordination number:

The number of spheres which are touching a particular sphere.Coordination number for hcp and ccp is 12 and for bcc it is 8.

Packing Efficiency, Calculations Involving Unit Cell Dimensions

Atomic radius:

Half the space between the nuclei of two identical neighboring atoms in its solid form.

Relationship between radius of atom (r) and unit cell edge length (a):

The following formulas show how the sphere (atom) radius, r, is related to the unit cell edge length, a:

Simple Cubic	Body Centered Cubic	Face-Centered Cubic
$a = 2r$	$a = \sqrt{\dfrac{16}{3}}r$	$a = \sqrt{8}r$

	Radius	Atoms/ unit cell	Packing density	# Neighbors
Simple cubic	$\dfrac{a}{2}$	1	$\dfrac{\pi}{6} = 52\%$	6
Body-centered cubic	$\dfrac{\sqrt{3}a}{4}$	2	$\dfrac{\pi\sqrt{3}}{8} = 68\%$	8
Face-centered cubic	$\dfrac{\sqrt{2}a}{4}$	4	$\dfrac{\pi\sqrt{2}}{6} = 74\%$	12
Diamond	$\dfrac{\sqrt{3}a}{8}$	8	$\dfrac{\pi\sqrt{3}}{16} = 34\%$	4

Voids:

The vacant space between the particles in a closed packed structure.

- Triangular voids: It is the two dimensional void.
- Tetrahedral voids: In cubic close packed structure, spheres of the second layer lie above the triangular voids of the first layer. The number of tetrahedral voids is two times the number of spheres.
- Octahedral voids: The vacant space formed by combining the triangular voids of the first layer and that of the second layer. The number of tetrahedral voids is same as the number of spheres.

Packing efficiency:

Packing efficiency is defined as the percentage of total space occupied by the particles packed inside the lattice.

$$\text{Packing efficiency of } hcp = \frac{\text{Volume occupied by four spheres in the unit cell}}{\text{Total volume of the unit cell } (a^3)} \times 100 = 74\%$$

$$\text{Packing efficiency of bcc} = \frac{\text{Volume occupied by two spheres in the unit cell}}{\text{Total volume of the unit cell } (a^3)} \times 100 = 68\%$$

$$\text{Packing efficiency of simple cubic lattice} = \frac{\text{Volume occupied by one spheres in the unit cell}}{\text{Total volume of the unit cell } (a^3)} \times 100 = 52.4\%$$

Imperfections in Solids, Electrical and Magnetic Properties

Defects in solids:

Points defects:

> Stoichiometric defects

  Vacancy defect: vacant lattice sites

  Interstitial defect

  Frenkel defect

  Schottky defect

> Impurity defects

> Non-stoichiometric defects

Metal excess defect

1. Metal excess defect due to anion vacancies
2. F-centers
3. Metal excess defect due to interstitial cation

Metal deficiency defect.

Types of solid based on its conductivity:

- Conductor
- Semi-conductor
- 13-15 compound
- 12-16 compound
- Doping
- N-type
- P-type
- Insulators

Classification on the basis of magnetic properties:

- Parametric: weakly attracted, unpaired electrons
- Diamagnetic: weakly repelled, paired electrons
- Ferromagnetic: All the domains in same direction
- Anti-Ferromagnetic: Equal and opposite domains
- Ferrimagnetic: Unequal domains

EXERCISE

1. Which of the following is non-crystalline solid?
   - (a) $CsCl$
   - (b) $NaCl$
   - (c) CaF_2
   - (d) Glass

2. The lustre of a metal is due to
   - (a) Its high density
   - (b) Its high polishing
   - (c) Its chemical inertness
   - (d) Presence of free electrons

3. A crystalline solid have
   - (a) Long range order
   - (b) Short range order
   - (c) Disordered arrangement
   - (d) None of these

4. Crystalline solids are
   - (a) Glass
   - (b) Rubber
   - (c) Plastic
   - (d) Sugar

5. Davy and Faraday proved that
   - (a) Diamond is a form of carbon
   - (b) The bond lengths of carbon containing compounds are always equal
   - (c) The strength of graphite is minimum compared to platinum
   - (d) Graphite is very hard

6. Which one of the following metal oxides is antiferromagnetic in nature?
   - (a) MnO_2
   - (b) TiO_2
   - (c) VO_2
   - (d) CrO_2

7. In graphite, carbon atoms are joined together due to
   - (a) Ionic bonding
   - (b) Vander Waal's forces
   - (c) Metallic bonding
   - (d) Covalent bonding

8. Which of the following is not correct for ionic crystals.
   - (a) They possess high melting point and boiling point
   - (b) All are electrolyte
   - (c) Exhibit the property of isomorphism
   - (d) Exhibit directional properties of the bond

9. Which of the following is a molecular crystal?
   - (a) SiC
   - (b) $NaCl$
   - (c) Graphite
   - (d) Ice

10. Quartz is a crystalline variety of
    - (a) Silica
    - (b) Sodium silicate
    - (c) Silicon carbide
    - (d) Silicon

11. Which type of solid crystals will conduct heat and electricity?
    - (a) Ionic
    - (b) Covalent
    - (c) Metallic
    - (d) Molecular

12. Which of the following is an example of covalent crystal solid?
    - (a) Si
    - (b) NaF
    - (c) Al
    - (d) Ar

13. Which of the following is an example of ionic crystal solid?
    - (a) Diamond
    - (b) LiF
    - (c) Li
    - (d) Silicon

14. Silicon is
    - (a) Semiconductor
    - (b) Insulator
    - (c) Conductor
    - (d) None of these

15. Which of the following statements about amorphous solids is incorrect?
    - (a) They melt over a range of temperature
    - (b) They are anisotropic
    - (c) There is no orderly arrangement of particles
    - (d) They are rigid and incompressible

16. The ability of a given substance to assume two or more crystalline structure is called
    - (a) Amorphism
    - (b) Isomorphism
    - (c) Polymorphism
    - (d) Isomerism

17. Glass is
    - (a) Supercooled liquid
    - (b) Crystalline solid
    - (c) Amorphous solid
    - (d) Liquid crystal

18. For cubic coordination the value of radius ratio is
    - (a) $0.732 - 1.000$
    - (b) $0.225 - 0.414$
    - (c) $0.000 - 0.225$
    - (d) $0.414 - 0.732$

19. How many space lattices are obtainable from the different crystal systems?
    - (a) 7
    - (b) 14
    - (c) 32
    - (d) 230

20. Example of unit cell with crystallographic dimensions $a \neq b \neq c$, $\alpha = \gamma = 90°$, $\beta \neq 90°$ is
    - (a) Calcite
    - (b) Graphite
    - (c) Rhombic sulphur
    - (d) Monoclinic sulphur

21. In a face-centered cubic lattice, a unit cell is shared equally by how many unit cells?

    (*a*) 8   (*b*) 4

    (*c*) 2   (*d*) 6

22. The maximum radius of sphere that can be fitted in the octahedral hole of cubical closed packing of sphere of radius r is

    (*a*) $0.732\ r$ (*b*) $0.414\ r$

    (*c*) $0.225\ r$ (*d*) $0.155\ r$

23. The unit cell of a $NaCl$ lattice

    (*a*) Is body centred cube

    (*b*) Has 3 Na^+ ions

    (*c*) Has 4 $NaCl$ units

    (*d*) Is electrically charged

24. For tetrahedral coordination number, the radius ratio $\dfrac{r_{c^+}}{r_{a^-}}$ is

    (*a*) $0.732 - 1.000$ (*b*) $0.414 - 0.732$

    (*c*) $0.225 - 0.414$ (*d*) $0.155 - 0.225$

25. What type of lattice is found in potassium chloride crystal?

    (*a*) Face centred cubic   (*b*) Body centred cubic

    (*c*) Simple cubic   (*d*) Simple tetragonal

Answer Keys

1. (*d*)	2. (*d*)	3. (*a*)	4. (*d*)	5. (*a*)	6. (*a*)	7. (*d*)	8. (*d*)	9. (*d*)	10. (*a*)
11. (*c*)	12. (*a*)	13. (*b*)	14. (*a*)	15. (*b*)	16. (*c*)	17. (a,c)	18. (*a*)	19. (*b*)	20. (*d*)
21. (*d*)	22. (*b*)	23. (*c*)	24. (*c*)	25. (*a*)					

Solutions

1. Glass is an amorphous solid.

3. Crystalline solids have regular arrangement of constituent particles, sharp melting points and are anisotropic.

4. Sugar is a crystalline solid while glass, rubber and plastic are amorphous solids.

6. MnO_2 is antiferromagnetic.

7. Graphite is sp² hybridised and a covalent crystal.

8. Ionic crystals exhibit non-directional properties of the bond.

9. Ice is a molecular crystal in which the constituent units are molecules and the interparticle forces are hydrogen bonds.

10. Quartz is a covalent crystal having a framework of silicates or silica, *i.e.* a three dimensional network when all the four oxygen atoms of each of SiO_4 tetrahedron are shared.

11. Metallic crystals are good conductor of heat and current due to free electrons in them.

12. Silicon is a covalent crystal in which constituent particles are atoms.

13. LiF is an example of ionic crystal solid, in which constituent particles are positive (Li^+) and negative (F^-) ions.

14. Silicon is a semiconductor because it is a thermal active and its conductivity increased with increasing temperature.

15. Amorphous solids are isotropic, because of these substances show same properties in all directions.

16. Polymorphism is a ability of a substances which show two or more crystalline structure.

17. (AC) Amorphous solids neither have ordered arrangement (*i.e.* no definite shape) nor have sharp melting point like crystals, but when heated, they become pliable until they assume the properties usually related to liquids. It is therefore they are regarded as super-cooled liquids.

18. For body centred cubic arrangement co-ordination number is 8 and radius ratio (r_+/r_-) is $0.732 - 1.000$.

19. There are 14 Bravais lattices (space lattices).

20. Monoclinic sulphur is an example of Monoclinic crystal system.

23. Each unit cell of $NaCl$ contains 4 $NaCl$ units.

24. For tetrahedral arrangement co-ordination number is 4 and radius ratio (r_+/r_-) is $0.225 - 0.414$.

25. Face-centred cubic lattice found in KCl and $NaCl$.

CHAPTER 2

Solutions

Types of Solutions, Expressing Concentration of Solutions and Solubility

- **Solution:** A homogeneous mixture of two (or more) substances.
- **Binary solution:** A solution consisting of two components. The component which is present in larger quantity is called **solvent** and the component which is small in quantity is called **solute.**

Solute	Solvent	Example
Gas	Gas	Air
Gas	Liquid	Aerated water
Gas	Solid	Hydrogen in palladium
Liquid	Liquid	Alcohol in water, benzene in toluene
Liquid	Solid	Mercury in zinc amalgam
Liquid	Gas	CO_2 dissolved in water
Solid	Liquid	Sugar in water, common salt in water
Solid	Gas	Smoke
Solid	Solid	Various alloys

Types of solutions:

- **Unsaturated solution:** A solution in which more solute can be dissolved without raising temperature.
  - **Saturated solution:** A solution in which no solute can be dissolved any more at a given temperature.
  - **Supersaturated solution:** A solution which contains more solute than that would be required to do saturation at a given temperature.
  - **Aqueous solution:** In this type of solution, water is present as solvent. For example, salt solution.
  - **Non-aqueous solution:** In this type of solution, there is another solvent apart from water. For example, iodine dissolved in alcohol.
- **Solubility:** The maximum amount of a solute that can be dissolved in a given amount of solvent at a given temperature.

The solubility of a solute in a solvent depends upon the following:

* Nature of the solute
* Nature of the solvent
* **Temperature of the solution:** If the dissolution process is endothermic, solubility of solid in liquid increases with increase in temperature, and in endothermic process, solubility decreases.
* **Pressure (in case of gases):** Solubility of gases increase with increase in pressure but it has no effect on solids in liquids.

Methods of Expressing Concentration of Solutions:

- **Mass Percentage (W / w)**

$$W/w\% = \frac{\text{Mass of solute}}{\text{Total mass of solution}} \times 100$$

- **Percentage by volume (V / v%)**

$$V/v\% = \frac{\text{Volume of solute}}{\text{Total volume of solution}} \times 100$$

- **Mass by volume percentage (w/v)**

$$w/v\% = \frac{\text{Mass of solute}}{\text{Volume of solution}} \times 100$$

- **Mole fraction (x):** It is defined as the ratio of the number of moles of a component to the total number of moles of all the components. For a binary solution, if the number of moles of A and B are n_A and n_B respectively, the mole fraction of A will be

$$\chi_A = \frac{n_A}{n_A + n_B}, \chi_B = \frac{n_B}{n_A + n_B}$$

- **Parts per million (ppm):** It is defined as the parts of a component per million parts of the solution.

$$ppm = \frac{\text{number of parts of the component}}{\text{total number of parts of all the components}} \times 10^6$$

It can be expressed in different ways like mass to mass, volume to volume and mass to volume.

$$ppm(\text{mass to mass}) = \frac{\text{Mass of a component}}{\text{Total mass of solution}} \times 10^6$$

$$ppm(\text{volume to volume}) = \frac{\text{Volume of a component}}{\text{Total volume of solution}} \times 10^6$$

$$ppm(\text{mass to volume}) = \frac{\text{Mass of a component}}{\text{Volume of solution}} \times 10^6$$

- **Molarity (M):** It is the number of moles of solute present in 1L (dm^3) of the solution.

$$M = \frac{\text{Number of moles of solute}}{\text{Volume of solution}} = \frac{W_B \times 1000}{M_B \times V(ml)}$$

- **Molality (m):** It is the number of moles of solute per kilogram of the solvent.

$$m = \frac{\text{Number of moles of solute}}{\text{Mass of solvent}} = \frac{W_B \times 1000}{W \times W_A}$$

- **Normality (N):** The number of gram equivalents of solute present in 1 L of solution.

$$\text{Normality} = \frac{\text{Number of gram equivalent of solute}}{\text{Volume of solution in L}}$$

Number of gram equivalents of solute

$$= \frac{\text{Mass of solute in gram}}{\text{Equivalent weight}}$$

- **Relationship between Molarity and Molality:**

$$m = \frac{1000M}{M \times M_B - 1000d}$$

- **Henry's law:** The partial pressure of a gas in vapour phase (p) is proportional to the mole fraction of the gas (χ) in a solution. It is a special case of Raoult's law.

$$\rho = K_H \chi, \quad K_H \text{ is the Henry's constant}$$

Higher the value of K_H, lower the solubility of gas in the liquid.

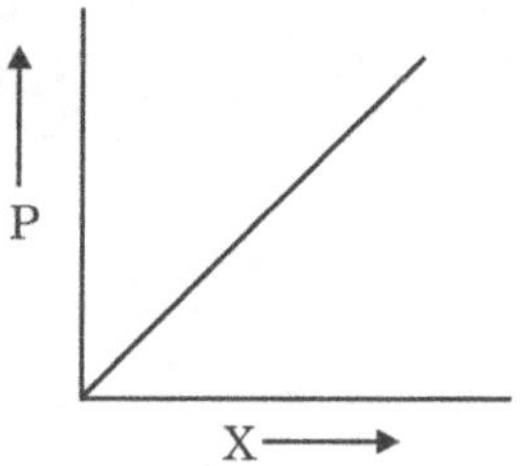

Slope of the line gives the value of K_H

- **Limitations of Henry's law:** This law is applicable only when

  * The law does not apply for gases which undergo association or dissociation in the solution.
  * This law is not applied for gases at high pressure and low temperature.
  * The law does not apply for gases which undergo any chemical change.

- **Applications of Henry's law:**

  * At high altitudes, low blood oxygen makes people weak and cause a problem called anoxia.
  * Bottles of soft drinks are sealed under high pressure to increase the solubility of CO_2
  * Scuba divers use air diluted with helium, nitrogen and oxygen to avoid toxic effects of nitrogen in blood.

Vapour Pressure of Liquid Solutions, Ideal and Non-ideal Solutions

- **Vapour Pressure:** Vapour pressure of a liquid solution is the amount of pressure that the vapours exert on the liquid solvent when they are in equilibrium and at a fixed temperature. It changes with the temperature of the surroundings and the nature of the liquid.

- **Raoult's Law:** The law states that the partial pressure is directly proportional to the mole fraction of the solute component. So, according to Raoult's Law, the partial pressure of A will be

$$P_A \propto x_A$$

$$P_A = P_A^0 x_A$$

Where P_A^0 is the vapour pressure of pure liquid component A.

Similarly partial pressure of B will be

$$P_B \propto x_B$$

$$P_B = P_B^0 x_B$$

Where $P_B^{\,0}$ is the vapour pressure of pure liquid component B. The total pressure (P_{total}) of the solution placed in a container is the sum of partial pressures of its respective components. That is

$$P_{total} = P_A + P_B$$

$$P_{total} = P_A^{\,0} x_A + P_B^{\,0} x_B$$

- **Raoult's Law as a Special Case of Henry's Law:**

  According to Raoult's law, vapour pressure of volatile component is given by, $p_i = x_i p_i^{\,o}$

  According to Henry's law, the gaseous component is volatile that it exist as a gas and solubility depends on Henry's law:

  $$p_A = K_H x_A$$

- **Positive and negative deviation from Raoult's law:**

  Positive deviation leads to increase in vapour pressure. In positive deviation, A-B interactions are weaker than interaction between B-B or A-B. Examples: Acetic acid and toluene, Methanol and chloroform, etc.

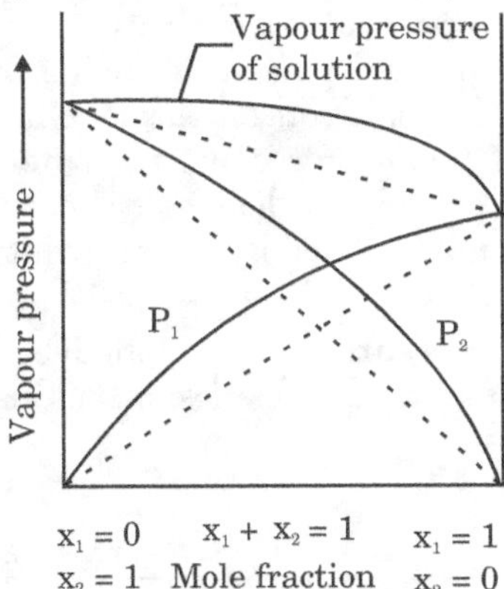

Negative deviation leads to decrease in vapour pressure. In negative deviation, A-A and B-B intermolecular forces are weaker than interaction between A-B. Examples: Chloroform and benzene, chloroform and methyl acetate, etc.

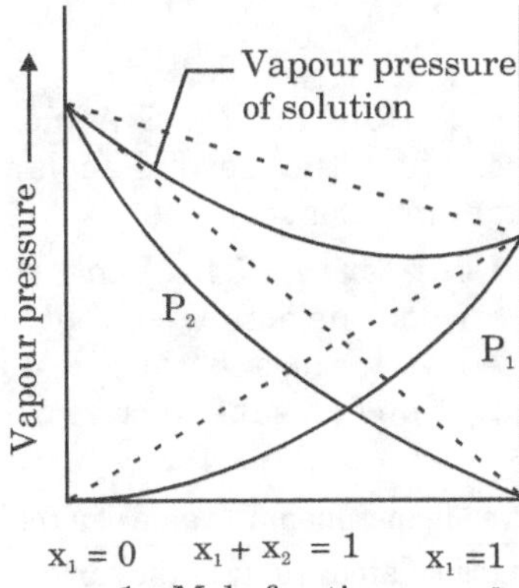

- **Ideal Solution:** These are the solutions which obey Raoult's law over the entire range of concentration.

  Two properties of Raoult's law:

  $$\Delta H_{mix} = 0 \text{ and } \Delta V_{mix} = 0$$

  Examples of ideal solutions are: Ethyl bromide and ethyl chloride, benzene and toluene.

- **Non-ideal Solutions:** These solutions do not obey Raoult's law over the range of concentration.

  If the vapour pressure of such a solution is higher, then the solution exhibits positive deviation and if it is lower, then the solution exhibits negative deviation.

- **Azeotropes:** Binary mixtures which have same composition in liquid and vapour phase and boil at constant temperature are called azeotropes.

- **Minimum boiling azeotrope:** Solutions which show large positive deviation from Raoult's law. For example: Ethanol-water mixture.

- **Maximum boiling azeotrope:** Solutions which show large negative deviation from Raoult's law. For example: Nitric acid and water.

Colligative Properties, Determination of Molecular Mass and Abnormal Molar Mass

Colligative properties depend on the number of solute particles but do not depend on its chemical identity. When a non volatile solute is added to volatile solvent, vapour pressure decreases. The properties of such solutions are:

- **Relative lowering of vapour pressure of solvent:** A relation between vapour pressure of solution, mole fraction and vapour pressure of the solvent is as follows:

  $$p_i = x_i p_i^{\,o}$$

  Reduction in vapour pressure of solvent is given by:

  $$\Delta p_i = \left(1 - x_i\right) p_i^{\,o} = x_j p_i^{\,o}$$

  $$\frac{\Delta p_i}{p_i^{\,o}} = \frac{p_i^{\,o} - p_i}{p_i^{\,o}} = x_j$$

  This expression is called relative lowering of vapour pressure which equals mole fraction of the solute.

- **Elevation of boiling point:** Boiling point of a solution is always higher than the boiling point of the pure solvent. The elevation of boiling point depends on the number of solute molecules.

  The difference between the boiling point of solution and boiling point of pure solvent gives the elevation of boiling point.

  $$\Delta T_b = T_b - T_b^{\,o}$$

For dilute solutions, $\Delta T_b = K_b m$, where K_b is called Boiling Point Elevation Constant, and m is molality.

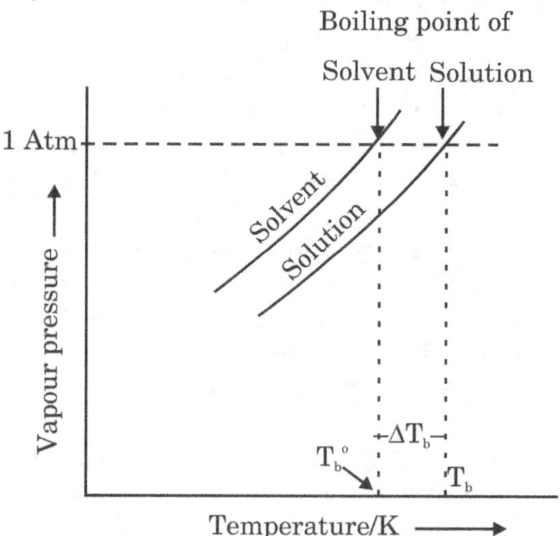

ΔT_b denotes elevation of boiling point of solvent

- **Depression of freezing point:** Lowering of vapour pressure causes depression of freezing point. The difference between the freezing point of pure solvent and freezing point of solvent when non volatile solute is dissolved in it gives the depression in freezing point.

$\Delta T_f = T_f^o - T_f$

For dilute solutions, $\Delta T_f = K_f m$, where K_f is the freezing point depression constant

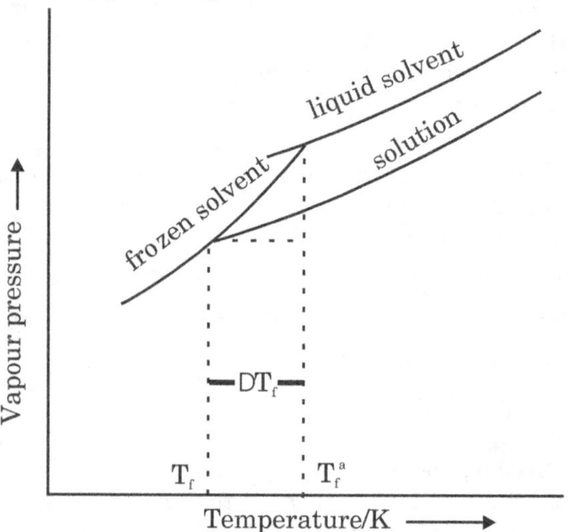

- **Osmosis:** The flow of solvent molecules from pure solvent to solution is called osmosis. Some extra pressure applied which just stops the flow of solvent is called osmotic pressure.

Osmotic pressure of solution

$\pi = \dfrac{n}{VRT}$, where $\pi = CRT$ as the osmotic pressure

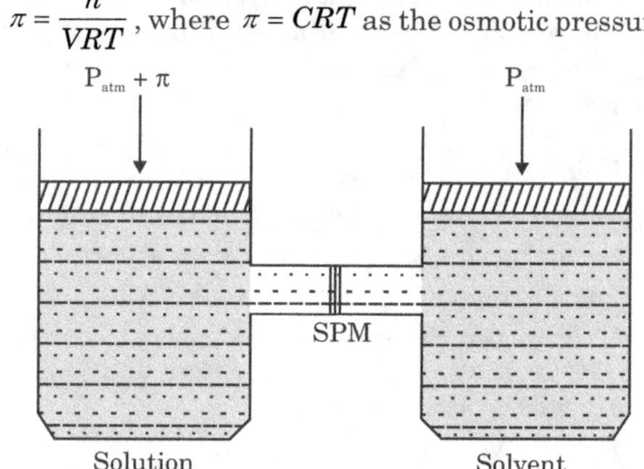

Excess pressure is equal to the osmotic pressure

- **Isotonic solutions:** Any two solutions having same osmotic pressure are called isotonic solutions. No osmosis occurs between such solutions which are separated by semi permeable membrane.

- **Hypertonic and hypotonic solutions:** When cells shrink due to water flowing out of the cell due to more salt concentration, then the solution is called hypertonic solution. When water flows into the cell due to less salt concentration, then the solution is called hypotonic solution.

- **Reverse Osmosis:** Pressure larger than the osmotic pressure when applied on the solution side causes reverse osmosis. It is used for water purification.

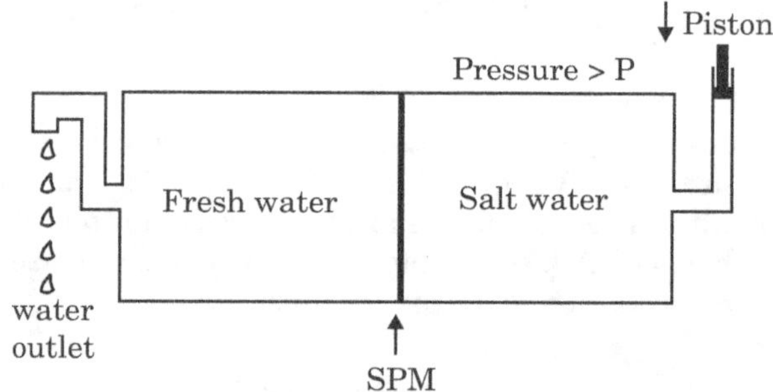

- **Abnormal Molar Mass:** A molar mass higher or lower than the normal molar mass is called abnormal molar mass.

- **Van't Hoff factor:** The Van't Hoff factor is the ratio between the actual concentration of particles produced when the substance is dissolved, and the concentration of a substance as calculated from its mass.

$$i = \dfrac{\text{observed (experimental) value of a colligative property}}{\text{Normal (calculated) value of the same colligative property}}$$

EXERCISE

1. The solubility of a gas in water depends on
   - (a) Nature of the gas
   - (b) Temperature
   - (c) Pressure of the gas
   - (d) All of the above.

2. The solution of sugar in water contains
   - (a) Free atoms
   - (b) Free ions.
   - (c) Free molecules
   - (d) Free atom and molecules.

3. The amount of anhydrous Na_2CO_3 present in 250 ml of 0.25 M solution is
   - (a) 6.225 g
   - (b) 66.25 g
   - (c) 6.0 g
   - (d) 6.625 g

4. The molarity of 0.006 mole of NaCl in 100 ml solution is
   - (a) 0.6
   - (b) 0.06
   - (c) 0.006
   - (d) 0.066

5. Which of the following has maximum number of molecules
   - (a) 16 gm of O_2
   - (b) 16 gm of NO_2
   - (c) 7 gm of N_2
   - (d) 2 gm of H_2

6. Molarity is expressed as.
   - (a) Gram/litre
   - (b) Moles/litre
   - (c) Litre/mole
   - (d) Moles/1000 gms.

7. 10 litre solution of urea contains 240 g urea. The active mass of urea will be
   - (a) 0.04
   - (b) 0.02
   - (c) 0.4
   - (d) 0.2

8. The sum of the mole fraction of the components of a solution is
   - (a) 0
   - (b) 1
   - (c) 2
   - (d) 4

9. When mercuric iodide is added to the aqueous solution of potassium iodide, the
   - (a) Freezing point is raised
   - (b) Freezing point is lowered
   - (c) Freezing point does not change
   - (d) Boiling point does not change

10. An aqueous solution of methanol in water has vapour pressure
    - (a) Equal to that of water
    - (b) Equal to that of methanol
    - (c) More than that of water
    - (d) Less than that of water

11. Which has maximum vapour pressure
    - (a) HI
    - (b) HBr
    - (c) HCl
    - (d) HF

12. 18 g of glucose ($C_6H_{12}O_6$) is added to 178.2 g of water. The vapour pressure of water for this aqueous solution at $100°$ C is
    - (a) 759.00 Torr
    - (b) 7.60 Torr
    - (c) 76.00 Torr
    - (d) 752.40 Torr

13. Which one of the following mixtures can be separated into pure components by fractional distillation
    - (a) Benzene-toluene
    - (b) Water-ethyl alcohol
    - (c) Water-nitric acid
    - (d) Water-hydrochloric acid

14. All form ideal solutions except
    - (a) C_2H_5Br and C_2H_5I
    - (b) C_6H_5Cl and C_6H_5Br
    - (c) C_6H_6 and $C_6H_5CH_3$
    - (d) C_2H_5I and C_2H_5OH

15. Which of the following is not current for ideal solution.
    - (a) $\Delta S_{mix} = 0$
    - (b) $\Delta H_{mix} = 0$
    - (c) It Obeys Raoult's law
    - (d) $\Delta V_{mix} = 0$

16. Which of the following is a colligative property
    - (a) Osmotic pressure
    - (b) Boiling point
    - (c) Vapour pressure
    - (d) Freezing point

17. Which of the following is not a colligative property
    - (a) Osmotic pressure
    - (b) Elevation in B.P.
    - (c) Vapour pressure
    - (d) Depression in freezing point

18. Which of the following solutions is water possesses the lowest vapour pressure.
    - (a) 0.1 (M) NaCl
    - (b) 0.1 (N) $BaCl_2$
    - (c) 0.1 (M) KCl
    - (d) None of these

19. When benzoic acid dissolve in benzene, the observed molecular mass is.
    - (a) 244
    - (b) 61
    - (c) 366
    - (d) 122

20. Which of the following compounds corresponds van't Hoff factor 'i' to be equal to 2 for dilute solution.

    (a) K_2SO_4 (b) $NaHSO_4$

    (c) Sugar   (d) $Mg\,SO_4$

21. The Van't Hoff factor 'i' for a 0.2 molal aqueous solution of urea is

    (a) 0.2   (b) 0.1

    (c) 1.2   (d) 1.0

22. Acetic acid dissolved in benzene shows a molecular weight of

    (a) 60   (b) 120

    (c) 180   (d) 240

23. Which of the following aqueous solutions containing 10 gm of solute in each case has highest B.P.

    (a) NaCl solution   (b) KCl solution

    (c) Sugar solution   (d) Glucose solution

Answer Keys

1. (d)   2. (c)   3. (d)   4. (b)   5. (d)   6. (b)   7. (c)   8. (b)   9. (b)   10. (c)

11. (c)   12. (d)   13. (a)   14. (d)   15. (a)   16. (a)   17. (c)   18. (b)   19. (a)   20. (d)

21. (d)   22. (b)   23. (a)

Solutions

1. The solubility of a gas in water depends on nature of the gas, temperature and pressure of the gas.

2. The solution of sugar in water contains free molecules.

3. $M = \dfrac{w}{m \times V(I)} \Rightarrow 0.25 = \dfrac{w}{106 \times 0.25}$

    $\Rightarrow w = 0.25 \times 106 \times 0.25 = 6.625$ g.

4. $M = \dfrac{n}{V} = \dfrac{0.006}{0.1} = 0.06$

5. 2 gm Hydrogen has maximum number of molecules than others.

6. Molarity is expressed as moles/litre.

7. $\because$ 10 litre of urea solution contains 240 gm of urea

    $\therefore$ Active mass $= \dfrac{240}{60 \times 10} = 0.4$

8. The sum of the mole fraction of the components of a solution is always 1.

9. HgI_2 although insoluble in water but shows complex formation with KI and freezing point is decreased.

10. Methanol has low boiling point than H_2O lower is boiling point of solvent more is vapour pressure.

11. The lower is boiling point more is vapour pressure; boiling point order, HCl < HBr < HI < HF

12. $X_{solute} = \dfrac{P_0 - P}{P_0}$

    $= \dfrac{\dfrac{18}{180}}{\dfrac{18}{180} + \dfrac{178.2}{18}} = \dfrac{760 - P}{760}$

    $\therefore$ P = 752.40 Torr

13. Aromatic compound generally separated by fractional distillation e.g. Benzene + Toluene.

14. C_2H_5I and C_2H_5OH do not form ideal solution.

15. For the ideal solution ΔS_{mix} is not equal to zero.

    $\therefore \Delta S_{mix} = 0$

16. Osmotic pressure is a colligative property.

17. Vapour pressure is not a colligative property.

18. $BaCl_2$ gives maximum ion hence it shows lowest vapour pressure.

19. Benzoic acid in benzene undergoes association through intermolecular hydrogen bonding.

    $\therefore$ The observed molecular mass is 244.

20. $MgSO_4$ dissociates to give 2 ions.

21. Urea does not give ion in the solution.

22. Molecular weight of CH_3COOH = 60

    Hence the molecular weight of acetic acid in benzene = 2 × 60 = 120

23. NaCl contain highest boiling point than others compound.

CHAPTER 3

Electrochemistry

Electrochemical Cells, Galvanic cells and Nernst Equation

- **Electrolytic conduction:** The conduction of an electrical current by the movement of ions.
- **Electrolyte:** A substance that dissociates into ions in solution and hence conducts electricity.
- **Degree of ionization:** The ratio of the number of ions of a solute to the total number of molecules of that solute in a solution.
- **Specific resistivity:** It is the resistance offered by a material or solution occupying one cm^3 volume.
- **Specific conductance or conductivity (κ):** It is the conductance of a material between two electrodes of cross sectional area 1 cm^2, separated by 1 cm distance.
- **Electrochemical cell:** It is a device that generates a potential difference between electrodes using redox reactions.
- **Galvanic cell or voltaic cell:** The Galvanic Cell is a device which transforms chemical energy into electric energy.
- **Daniel cell:** A galvanic cell in which one electrode is Zn plate in $ZnSO_4$ (or Zn^{++} ion) solution and the other is Cu plate in $CuSO_4$ (or Cu^{++} ion) solution. Following diagram shows a Daniel cell:

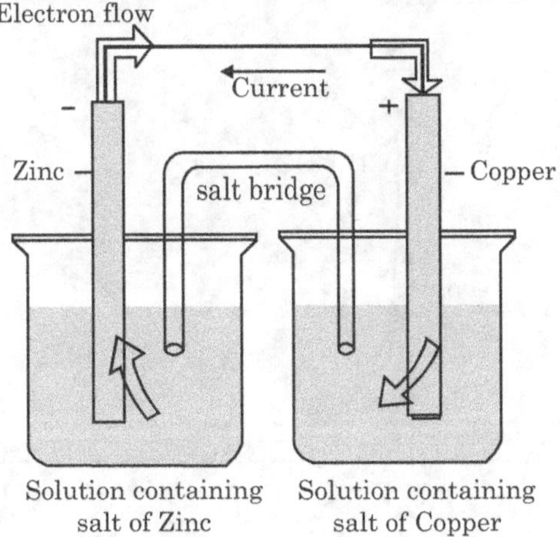

Solution containing salt of Zinc   Solution containing salt of Copper

- **Salt Bridge:** A salt bridge is a combination of two noncovalent interactions i.e. electrostatic interactions and hydrogen bonding. Since, noncovalent interactions are weak interactions, formation of salt bridges provide an additional level of stabilizing interactions that can add important contribution to the overall stability of a molecule.
- **Standard electrode potential (E°):** It is defined by measuring the potential relative to a standard hydrogen electrode using 1 mol solution at 25 °C and 1 bar pressure.
- Emf of a cell can also be defined as the work done or required for transforming a unit positive charge from negative to positive terminal within the cell.

$$E_{cell} = E_{cathode} - E_{anode}$$

- The standard reduction potentials of a number of electrodes are measured using standard hydrogen electrode as the reference electrode. These various electrodes can be arranged in increasing order of their reduction potentials which is called electrochemical series.

Application of electrochemical series:

- Calculation of the standard EMF of the cell
- Predicting the feasibility of a redox reaction
- Comparison of the reactivities of metals.

Debye-Huckel-Onsagar equation:

It is for a strong electrolyte

$$\Lambda = \Lambda^0 - AC^{\frac{1}{2}}$$

Λ = Equivalent conductivity at given concentration.

Λ^0 = Equivalent conductivity at infinite dilution.

C = Concentration and A is a constant

- **Redox reaction:** When both reduction and oxidation reactions go side-by-side, it is known as a redox reaction.
- **Redox couple:** It is defined as having together the oxidized and reduced form of a substance taking part in and oxidation or reduction half reaction.

Nernst Equation:

It is used when the concentration of species in the electrode reaction is not equal to $1M$.

$$aA + bB \xrightarrow{ne^-} mM + nN$$

The Nernst equation at 298 K can be written as

$$E_{cell} = E^0{}_{cell} - \frac{0.059}{n} \log \frac{[M]^m [N]^n}{[A]^a [B]^b}$$

- **Gibb's Energy:**

$$\Delta G^0 = -nFE^0{}_{cell}$$

For spontaneous cell reaction, ΔG must be negative.

$$\Delta G^0 = -2.303 RT \log K$$

Conductance of Electrolytic Solutions or Ionic Solution and its Measurement

Conductance

- The electrical resistance of an object is given by $R = \rho \dfrac{l}{A}$ where l is the length and the area of cross section is A. ρ is called as resistivity.

- Conductance (G): It is the tendency of a material to allow current through it. It is the reciprocal of resistance. It depends on the following factors

  - Temperature
  - Nature an structure of the metal
  - Number of valence electrons per atom

- The conductance of electricity by ions present in thesolutions is called electrolytic or ionic conductance. The conductivity of electrolytic (ionic) solutions depends on following factors

  - Temperature
  - Concentration of electrolyte
  - The nature of electrolyte added
  - The nature of solvent and its viscosity
  - Size of ions produced and their solvation

Measurement of conductivity of Ionic Solutions

Measuring resistance of ionic solution using Wheatstone bridge faces two problems

- A solution cannot be connected to the bridge like a metallic wire. This problem is solved by using a specially designed vessel which is called conductivity cell.

- The composition of the solution is changed by passing direct current. This problem is solved by using alternating current source of power.

Cell constant (G*): The ratio of the distance between the electrodes to the cross sectional area of the electrodes is known as cell constant.

$$G^* = \frac{l}{A} = R\kappa$$

After determining the cell constant, it is used for measurement of resistance or conductivity of the solution using the circuit shown below:

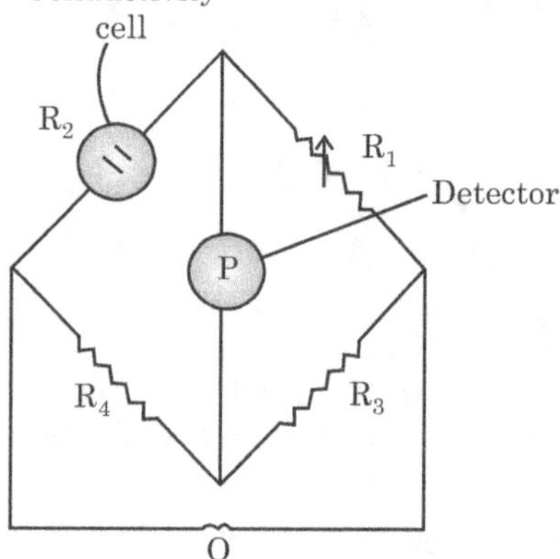

Unknown Resistance $\quad R_2 = \dfrac{R_1 R_4}{R_3}$

Variation of conductivity and molar conductivity with concentration

- **Strong Electrolytes**

  - On dilution, the number of ions per unit volume that carry the current in a solution decreases. Hence, conductivity and molar conductivity decreases with decrease in concentration for strong and weak electrolytes.

  - Molar conductivity increases with decrease in concentration as the total volume of solution containing one mole of electrolyte also increases.

  - Λ increases with dilution and is shown as

    $$\Lambda_m = E_m{}^o - Ac^{\frac{1}{2}}$$ where $E_m{}^o$ is limiting molar conductivity.

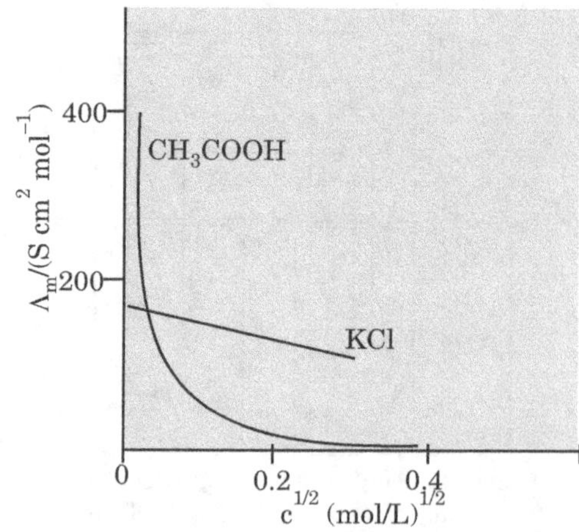

- **Kohlrausch's law of independent migration of ions.**

  Limiting molar conductivity of an electrolyte at infinite dilution is expressed as the sum of contributions from the individual ions.

  $\Lambda_m{}^{\infty} = v_+\lambda_+{}^{\infty} + v_-\lambda_-{}^{\infty}$ where v_+, v_- are the number of cations and anions per formula of electrolyte.

Application of Kohlrausch's law

  - Calculation of limiting conductivities of weak electrolytes
  - Determination of degree of ionization (α) of weak electrolyte

- **Weak Electrolytes**
  - Weak electrolytes have lower degree of dissociation at higher concentrations and hence for such electrolytes, the change in Λ_m with dilution is due to increase in the degree of dissociation and consequently the number of ions in total volume of solution that contains 1 mol of electrolyte. For weak electrolyte is obtained using Kohlrausch's Law.

  - $K_a = \dfrac{c\Lambda_m{}^2}{\Lambda_m{}^o\left(\Lambda_m{}^o - \Lambda_m\right)}$

Electrolysis, Batteries, Fuel Cells and Corrosion

- Electrolysis is the passage of electricity through an electrolyte, in which cations move to the cathode to get reduced, and anions move towards the anode to get oxidized.
- Faraday's Laws of Electrolysis
  - Faraday's First Law of Electrolysis

    The mass of the substance (m) which occurs at any electrode is directly proportional to the quantity of electricity or charge (Q) passed.

    $m = ZIt$, where Z = Electrochemical equivalent
  - Faraday's second Law of Electrolysis

    When the same quantity of electricity is passed through different electrolytes, the masses of different ions liberated at the electrodes are directly proportional to their chemical equivalents (Equivalent weights)

    $$\frac{w}{E_1} = \frac{w}{E_2}$$

- The product of electrolysis depends on the types of electrode used and the physical state of the material.

- **Batteries:** It is a source of electrical energy where one or more cells are connected in series.
  - **Primary Battery:** They are non-chargeable batteries like Dry cell and Lechlanche Cell.

Dry cell

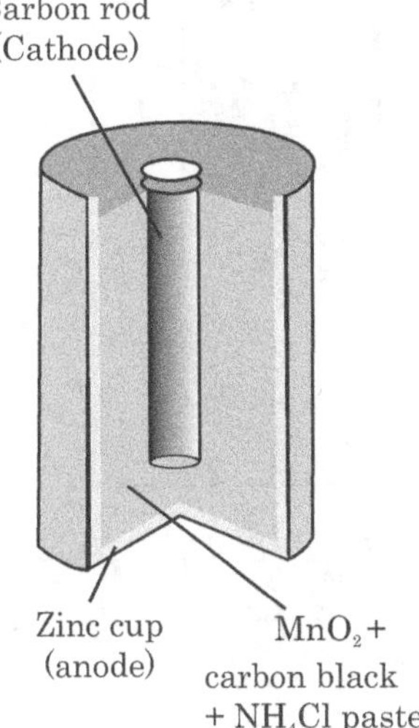

At anode: $Zn_{(s)} \rightarrow Zn^{2+}{}_{(aq)} + 2e^-$

At cathode:

$MnO_{2(s)} + NH_4^+{}_{(aq)} + 2e^- \rightarrow Mn(OH)_2 + NH_3$

The net reaction:

$Zn + MnO_{2(s)} + NH_4^+{}_{(aq)} \rightarrow Zn^{2+} + Mn(OH)_2 + NH_3$

- **Secondary Battery:** These are the chargeable cells like lead storage battery and nickel-cadmium cells.

Lead storage battery:

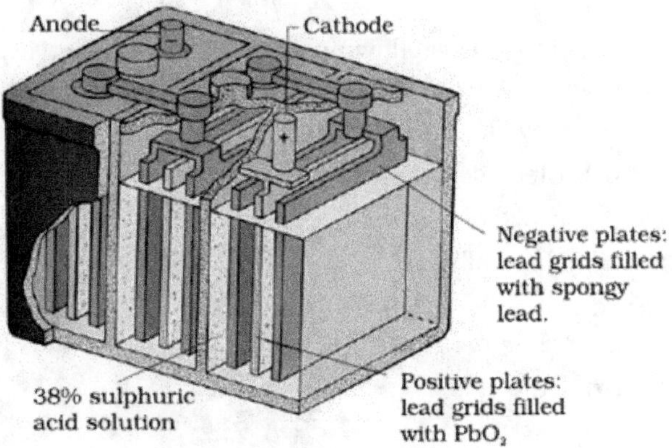

Anode: Spongy lead

Cathode: Lead packed with lead dioxide

Electrolyte: Aqueous solution of H_2SO_4

At anode: $Pb_{(S)} + SO_4{}^{2-}{}_{(aq)} \rightarrow PbSO_{4(S)} + 2e^-$

At cathode: $PbSO_{4(S)} + 2e^- \rightarrow Pb_{(S)} + SO_4{}^{2-}{}_{(aq)}$

- **Fuel cell:** These are the cells which convert energy from fuels like methane, hydrogen into electrical energy. Following diagram shows a fuel cell.

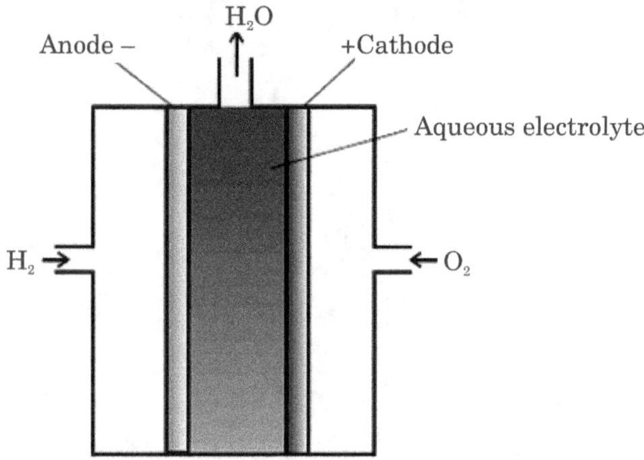

Anode: $\left[H_{2(g)} + 2OH_{(aq)}^- \rightarrow 2H_2O_{(l)} + 2e^- \right] \times 2$

Cathode: $O_{2(g)} + 2H_2O_{(l)} + 4e^- \rightarrow 4OH^-_{(aq)}$

Net reaction: $O_{2(g)} + 2H_{2(g)} \rightarrow 2H_2O_{(l)}$

- **Corrosion:** The conversion of metals into undesirable compounds (usually oxides) on reaction with moisture and other gases.

Rusting of Iron:

$$Fe_{(S)} + 2H^+_{(aq)} + \frac{1}{2}O_{2(g)} \rightarrow Fe^{2+}_{(aq)} -+ H_2O_{(l)}$$

$$2Fe^{2+}_{(S)} + \frac{1}{2}O_{2(g)} + 2H_2O_{(l)} \rightarrow Fe_2O_{3(S)} + 4H^+$$

$$Fe_2O_{3(S)} + xH_2O_{(l)} \rightarrow Fe_2O_3 \cdot xH_2O$$

Corrosion can be prevented using following measures

- ➢ Alloying
- ➢ Barrier protection by covering the surface with paint.
- ➢ Sacrificial protection by galvanization

EXERCISE

1. In charging the lead accumulator battery
   - (a) PbO_2 dissolves
   - (b) H_2SO_4 is reproduced
   - (c) $PbSO_4$ deposits on lead electrode
   - (d) Pb deposits on lead electrodes.

2. When colourless gas evolves, when NH_4Cl reacts with zinc in a dry cell battery
   - (a) NH_4
   - (b) N_2
   - (c) H_2
   - (d) Cl_2

3. A cell from the following which converts electrical energy into chemical energy
   - (a) Dry cell
   - (b) Electrochemical cell
   - (c) Electrolytic cell
   - (d) None of these

4. In the cell $Zn/Zn^{2+} \| Cu^{2+}/Cu$, the negative electrode is
   - (a) Cu
   - (b) Cu^{2+}
   - (c) Zn
   - (d) Zn^{2+}

5. Which one of the following statement is true for a electrochemical cell.
   - (a) H_2 is cathode and Cu is anode
   - (b) H_2 is anode and Cu is cathode
   - (c) Reduction occurs at H_2 electrode
   - (d) Oxidation occurs at Cu electrode

6. Which of the following statements about galvanic cell is incorrect.
   - (a) Anode is positive
   - (b) Cathode is positive
   - (c) Reduction occurs at cathode
   - (d) All are incorrect

7. Standard electrode potential of SHE at 298 K is
   - (a) 0.05 V
   - (b) 0.1 V
   - (c) 0.00 V
   - (d) 0.11 V

8. $E^° = \dfrac{RT}{nF} \ln Keq$. This is called
   - (a) Gibb's equation
   - (b) Gibb's Helmholtz equation
   - (c) Nernst's equation
   - (d) Vander wall's equation

9. If the conductance and specific conductance of a solution is one then its cell constant would be
   - (a) 1
   - (b) 0
   - (c) 0.5
   - (d) 4

10. Saturated solution of KNO_3 is used to make 'salt-bridge' because
    - (a) Velocity of K^+ is greater than that of NO_3^-
    - (b) Velocity of NO_3^- is greater than that of K^+
    - (c) Velocities of both K^+ and NO_3^- are nearly the same
    - (d) KNO_3 is highly soluble in water.

11. When Zn piece is kept in $CuSO_4$ solution, the copper get precipitated due to standard potential of zinc is

(a) > Copper   (b) < Copper

(c) > Sulphate   (d) < Sulphate

12. Which of the following metal does not react with the solution of copper sulphate

(a) Mg   (b) Fe

(c) Zn   (d) Ag

13. If an iron rod is dipped in $CuSO_4$ solution

(a) Blue colour of the solution turns green

(b) Brown layer is deposited on iron rod

(c) Blue colour of the solution vanishes

(d) None of the above

14. Which of the following metal can displace copper from copper sulphate solution.

(a) Hg   (b) Fe

(c) All   (d) Platinum

15. Which of the following will not conduct electricity in aqueous solution.

(a) Copper sultphate   (b) Sugar

(c) Common salt   (d) None of these

16. Which one of the following metals could not be obtained on electrolysis of aqueous solution of its salts

(a) Ag   (b) Mg

(c) Cu   (d) Cr

17. The addition of a polar solvent to a solid electrolyte results in

(a) Polarization

(b) Association

(c) Ionization

(d) Non-liberation of heat

18. Hydrogen-oxygen fuel cell are used in space-craft to supply.

(a) Power for heat and light

(b) Power for pressure

(c) Water

(d) both (b) and (c)

19. A depolarizer used in dry cell batteries is

(a) Ammonium chloride

(b) Manganese dioxide

(c) Potassium hydroxide

(d) Sodium phosphate

20. When a lead storage battery is discharged

(a) SO_2 is evolved

(b) Lead sulphate is consumed

(c) Lead is formed

(d) Sulphuric acid is consumed

21. Rusting of iron is catalysed by which of the following

(a) Fe   (b) O_2

(c) Zn   (d) H^+

22. Which of the following is a highly corrosive salt

(a) $FeCl_2$ (b) $PbCl_2$

(c) Hg_2Cl_2 (d) $HgCl_2$

Answer Keys

1. (b)	2. (c)	3. (c)	4. (c)	5. (b)	6. (a)	7. (c)	8. (c)	1. (a)	2. (c)
11. (b)	12. (d)	13. (b)	14. (b)	15. (b)	16. (b)	17. (c)	18. (d)	19. (b)	20. (d)
21. (d)	22. (d)								

Solutions

1. Reactions taking place during charging, i.e. when electrical energy is supplied to it from an external field.

$$2Pb\,SO_4 + 2H_2O \longrightarrow Pb + PbO_2 + 4H^+ + 2SO_4{}^{2-}$$

2. $2NH_4Cl + Zn \longrightarrow 2NH_3 + Zn\,Cl_2 + H_2\uparrow$

3. In the electrolytic cell electrical energy change into chemical energy.

4. In the cell $Zn\,|\,Zn^{2+}\,||\,Cu^{2+}\,|\,Cu$ the negative electrode (anode) is Zn. In electrochemical cell representation anode is always written on left side while cathode on right side.

5. In electrochemical cell H_2 releases at anode and Cu is deposited at cathode.

6. Anode has negative polarity.

7. At 298 K standard electrode potential of SHE electrode is 0.00 V.

8. Actually the equation is derived from Nernst equation assuming equilibrium condition is a cell reaction, when E = 0

9. $\because \dfrac{K}{C} = Cell\ Cons\tan t$

   $\therefore$ Cell constant would be one

10. Velocities of both K^+ and NO_3^- are nearly the same in KNO_3 So it is used to make salt-bridge

11. Standard potential of zinc < copper

12. Ag (Silver) does not react with the solution of copper sulphate.

13. Brown layer is deposited on iron road because Cu has greater reduction potential than that of Fe^{2+}.

14. Cu^{++} will be reduced and Fe will be oxidized.

   $Cu^{++} + Fe \longrightarrow Cu^{2+} + 2Ag.$

15. Sugar solution does not form ion. Hence it does not conduct electricity in solution.

16. The reduction potential of Mg is less than that of water. Hence their ions in the aqueous solution cannot be reduced instead water will be reduced.

   $$2H_2O + 2e^- \longrightarrow H_2 + 2OH^-$$

17. When polar solvent added in to solid electrolyte than it ionised.

18. Fuel-cells are used to provide power and drinking water to astronauts in space programme.

19. MnO_2 (Manganese dioxide) is used in dry batteries cell

20. $Pb + PbO_2 + 2H_2SO_4 \xrightleftharpoons[\text{Recharge}]{\text{Discharge}} 2PbSO_4 + 2H_2O$

   Sulphuric acid is consumed on discharged.

21. Rusting of iron is catalysed by H^+

22. $HgCl_2$ has corrosive action. It is highly poisonous. It sublimes on heating. It is, therefore, known as corrosive sublimate.

CHAPTER 4

Chemical Kinetics

Rate of a Chemical Reaction and Factors Influencing Rate of a Reaction

- **Chemical Kinetics:** The study of chemical reactions, their rates, effect of various factors on rate of reaction is considered under chemical kinetics.

- **Rate of Reaction:** The change in concentration of reactant or product with respect to time is called the rate of reaction.

  For the reaction, $R \rightarrow P$

  Rate of disappearance of $R = -\dfrac{\Delta[R]}{\Delta t}$;

  Rate of appearance of $P = \dfrac{\Delta[P]}{\Delta t}$

  Units of rate of reaction are concentration $\times$ time^{-1}. Unit of concentration varies according to the state of the reactant. For gases, concentration is expressed as partial pressures, for liquids, concentration is in mol L^{-1}.

- Rate of chemical reaction can be instantaneous or average. Rate of reaction at a particular moment of time is instantaneous rate while the rate of reaction over a time interval is average rate.

- **Factors affecting the rate of a chemical reaction:** There are various factors which affect the rate of reaction.

  - **Pressure of the reaction:** Pressure varies directly with the rate of reaction. As the pressure is increased, volume decreases and concentration increases. Therefore with increase in concentration, rate of reaction increases.

  - **Temperature of the reaction:** Temperature varies directly with the rate of reaction. As the temperature of the reaction increases, rate increases and vice versa.

  - **Concentration of the reaction:** As the concentration of the reactants increases, rate of reaction increases and if the concentration of the reactants is less then rate of reaction decreases.

  - **Surface area of the reactants:** For reactions which takes place on the surface of the reactant, the rate of reaction increases with increase in surface.

  - **Presence of catalyst:** Rate of reaction increases on adding catalyst. It is because the catalyst decreases the activation energy of the reaction.

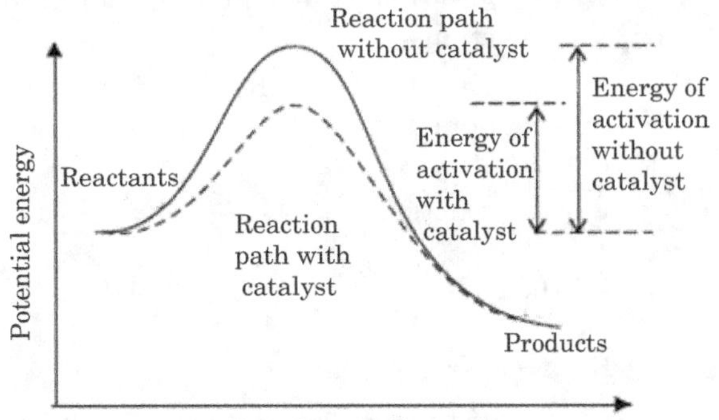

  - **Nature of reactants:** Simpler molecules separate easily and take part in chemical reaction while molecules which are complex take time to separate the bonds and the rate of reaction thus decreases.

- **Rate Law:** It is an expression where rate of chemical reaction is written in terms of concentration of the reactants with each term raised to some power which may or may not be same as the stoichiometric coefficients of the reacting species.

  For example:

  For the reaction,

  $$2NO \, (g) + O_2 \, (g) \rightarrow 2NO_2 \, (g)$$

  Rate $= k \, [NO]^2 \, [O_2]$

  Here k is the rate constant.

- **Molecularity:** It is defined as the number of reacting species (molecules, atoms or ions) in an elementary reaction. It cannot be a non integer or zero.

- **Elementary or complex reactions:** If a reaction takes place in a single step, it is an elementary reaction while a reaction involving series of elementary reactions is called complex reaction.

- **Rate determining step:** The step which takes place slowly is called the rate determining step.

Integrated Rate Equation, Pseudo First Order Reaction

- **Order of reaction:** It is defined as the sum of powers of the concentration of reactants in the rate law expression. It can be zero and even fraction.

  Units of rate constant are different for reactions of different order.

Reaction	Order	Units of rate constant
Zero order reaction	0	$mol\ L^{-1}\ s^{-1}$
First order reaction	1	s^{-1}
Second order reaction	2	$mol^{-1}\ Ls^{-1}$

- **Integrated rate equations:** A relation between directly measured experimental data and rate constant is given by integrated rate equation. There are different rate equations for different order of reactions.

  - *Zero order reaction:* Rate of reaction is independent of the concentration of the reactants.

    For the reaction,

    $$2NH_3(g)\xrightarrow[Pt\ catalyst]{1130K} N_2(g)+3H_2(g)$$

    Rate $= k\ [NH_3]^0 = k$

  - *First order reaction:* Rate of reaction is directly proportional to the first power of the concentration of the reactants.

    For the reaction,

    $$C_2H_4(g)+H_2(g)\rightarrow C_2H_6(g)$$
    Rate $= k\ [C_2H_4]$

    $$k=\frac{2.303}{t}\log\frac{[A_o]}{[A]}$$

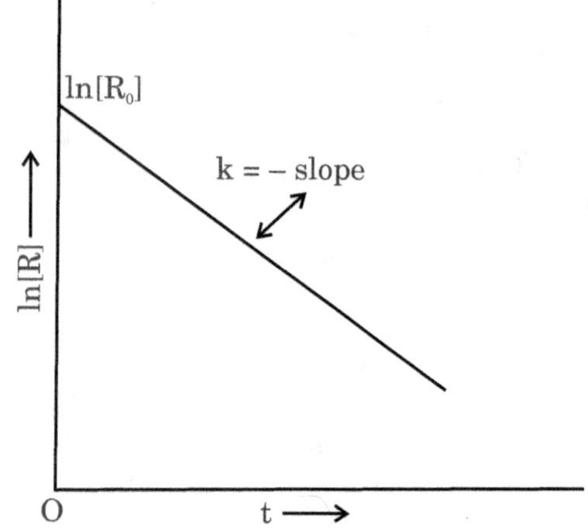

Graph showing the relation between $ln\ [R]$ and t for first order reaction

- **Second order reaction:** In this rate law the sum of powers of concentration terms in rate law is equal to 2.

  For example: $A+B\rightarrow C+D$

  $$\frac{dx}{dt}=k[A]'[B]'$$

- **Pseudo first order reaction:** The reaction is not of first order but certain conditions makes the reaction of first order.

  For example: Reaction of ethyl acetate with water.

  $$CH_3COOC_2H_5+H_2O\xrightarrow{H^+}CH_3COOH+C_2H_5OH$$

  It should be of second order but water is in very less quantity so it is pseudo first order reaction.

- **Half life of a reaction:** The time in which concentration of the reactant reduces to half of the initial concentration is called half-life of a reaction. It is represented as $t_{1/2}$.

  For a zero order reaction, the rate constant at $t_{1/2}$,

  $$k=\frac{[R]_o}{2t_{1/2}}$$

  For a first order reaction, the rate constant at $t_{1/2}$

  $$t_{1/2}=\frac{0.693}{k}$$

Temperature Dependence of the Rate of a Reaction, Collision Theory of Chemical Reactions

Electrostatic potential:

- The rate of a reaction depends on temperature. As the temperature increases, rate of reaction increases.

- **Activation Energy:** It is the energy of reactant molecules so that collision of molecules leads to formation of products. It cannot be negative.

- **Threshold energy:** It is the minimum energy required by the reactants to form products.

- **Arrhenius equation:** The relation between rate of reaction and temperature is given in the Arrhenius equation.

  $$k=Ae^{\frac{-E_a}{RT}}$$

  $$\log\frac{k_2}{k_1}=\frac{E_a}{2.303R}\left[\frac{1}{T_1}-\frac{1}{T_2}\right]$$

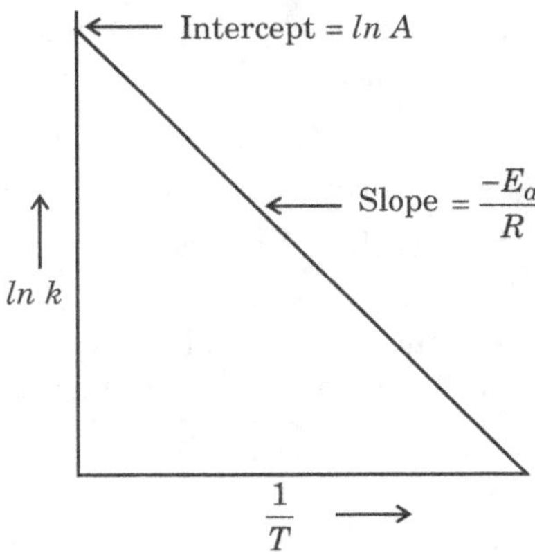

- **Collision Theory:** According to this theory, It is assumed that reactant molecules are hard spheres and reaction occurs when reactant molecules collide with each other.

Number of collisions per second per unit volume gives collision frequency.

$$\text{Rate} = Z_{AB}\, e^{\frac{-E_a}{RT}}$$

Where Z_{AB} is the collision frequency

When molecules collide with sufficient kinetic energy to facilitate breaking of bonds to form products, it is called effective collisions.

Rate of reaction $= f \times z$

Where f is the frequency of effective collisions.

- Collision theory ignores the structural aspect and considers molecules as hard spheres which is a drawback of collision theory.

EXERCISE

1. The rate of a chemical reaction
   - (a) Increases as the reaction proceeds
   - (b) Decreases as the reaction proceeds
   - (c) May increase or decrease during the reaction
   - (d) Remains constant as the reaction proceeds.

2. The rate of a reaction that not involve gases is not dependent on
   - (a) Pressure
   - (b) Temperature
   - (c) Concentration
   - (d) Catalyst

3. The rate at which a substance reacts depends on its
   - (a) Atomic weight
   - (b) Equivalent weight
   - (c) Molecular weight
   - (d) Active mass

4. The concentration of a reactant decreases from 0.2 M to 0.1 M in 10 minutes. The rate of the reaction is
   - (a) 0.01 M
   - (b) 10^{-2}
   - (c) $0.01\ \text{mol dm}^{-3}\,\text{min}^{-1}$
   - (d) $1\ \text{mol dm}^{-3}\,\text{min}^{-1}$

5. Time required for completion of ionic reactions in comparison to molecular reaction is
   - (a) Maximum
   - (b) Minimum
   - (c) Equal
   - (d) None

6. The rate of a reaction depends upon the
   - (a) Volume
   - (b) Force
   - (c) Pressure
   - (d) Concentration of reactant

7. A catalyst increases the rate of a chemical reaction by
   - (a) Increasing the activation energy
   - (b) Decreasing the activation energy
   - (c) Reacting with reactants
   - (d) Reacting with products.

8. Which of these does not influence the rate of reaction.
   - (a) Nature of the react ants
   - (b) Concentration of the reactants
   - (c) Temperature of the reaction.
   - (d) Molecularity of the reaction.

9. The rate constant of a reaction depends on
   - (a) Temperature
   - (b) Mass
   - (c) Weight
   - (d) Time

10. Rate constant for a reaction $H_2 + I_2 \longrightarrow 2HI$ is 49, then rate constant for reaction $2HI \longrightarrow H_2 + I_2$ is
    - (a) 7
    - (b) $\frac{1}{49}$
    - (c) 49
    - (d) 21

11. The value of rate constant $A + B \longrightarrow$ products depends on
    - (a) Concentration of A and B
    - (b) Pressure
    - (c) Temperature
    - (d) All of the above

12. Catalyst decomposition of hydrogen peroxide is a _____ order reaction
    - (a) First
    - (b) Second
    - (c) Third
    - (d) Zero

13. Half life period $t_{\frac{1}{2}}$ for first order reaction is
    - (a) K
    - (b) $\dfrac{1.303 \log 2}{K}$
    - (c) $\dfrac{2.303 \log 2}{K}$
    - (d) $\dfrac{9}{K}$

14. The half life of a first order reaction is 69.35 sec. The value of the rate constant of the reaction is
    - (a) 1.0 sec^{-1}
    - (b) 0.1 sec^{-1}
    - (c) 0.01 sec^{-1}
    - (d) 0.001 sec^{-1}

15. The number of collisions depends upon
    - (a) Pressure
    - (b) Concentration
    - (c) Temperature
    - (d) All of these

16. The minimum energy a molecule should possess in order to enter into a fruitful collision is known as
    - (a) Reaction energy
    - (b) Collision energy
    - (c) Activation energy
    - (d) Threshold energy

17. Activation energy of any reaction depends on
    - (a) Temperature
    - (b) Nature of reactants
    - (c) Number of collisions per unit time
    - (d) Concentration of reactants

18. Consider an endothermic reaction $X \to Y$ with the activation energies E_b and E_f for the backward and forward reactions, respectively, in general
    - (a) $E_b < E_f$
    - (b) $E_b > E_f$
    - (c) $E_b = E_f$
    - (d) There is no definite relation between E_b and E_f

19. Chemical reaction with very high E_a values are generally
    - (a) Very fast
    - (b) Very slow
    - (c) Moderately fast
    - (d) Spontaneous

20. The reactions with low activation energy always.
    - (a) Adiabatic
    - (b) Slow
    - (c) Non-spontaneous
    - (d) Fast

Answer Keys

1. (b)	2. (a)	3. (d)	4. (c)	5. (b)	6. (d)	7. (b)	8. (d)	9. (a)	10. (b)
11. (c)	12. (a)	13. (c)	14. (c)	15. (d)	16. (d)	17. (b)	18. (a)	19. (b)	20. (d)

Solutions

1. Rate of reaction continuously decreases with time.

2. The rate of reaction depends upon conc. of reactant surface area of reactant, temperature, presence of light and catalyst.

3. According to law of mass action.

4. Rate of reaction $\dfrac{dx}{dt} = \left[\dfrac{0.2 - 0.1}{10}\right] = \dfrac{0.1}{10}$

$$= 0.01 \text{ mol dm}^{-3} \text{ min}^{-1}$$

5. Ionic reactions are very fast reactions i.e. take place instantaneously.

6. The rate of a reaction depends upon concentration of reactant.

7. Catalyst increases the rate by decreasing the activation energy.

8. Molecularity of the reaction does not influence the rate of reaction.

9. $K = Ae^{\frac{-E_a}{RT}}$ by this equation it is clear that rate constant of a reaction depends on temperature.

10. For reversible reaction rate constant is also reverse.

11. Rate constant depends on temperature only.

12. It is a first order reaction as is clear from rate law expression, $r = k (H_2O_2)$

13. $t_{\frac{1}{2}} = \dfrac{2.303 \log 2}{K} = \dfrac{0.693}{K}$

14. $K = \dfrac{0.693}{t_{\frac{1}{2}}} = \dfrac{0.693}{69.35} = 9.99 \times 10^{-3} = 0.01 \text{ sec}^{-1}$

15. Number of collision depend upon pressure, concentration and temperature.

16. The definition of threshold energy.

17. The value of activation energy for a chemical reaction is primarily dependent on the nature of reacting species.

18. For endothermic reaction $\Delta H = +Ve$

Then from equation $\Delta H = E_{\propto F.R.} - E_{\propto B.R.}$;

$E_{B.R} < E_{F.R.}$

19. If the activation energy for a reaction is low, the fraction of effective collisions will be large and the reaction will be fast. On the other hand, If the activation energy is high, then fraction of effective collisions will be small and the reaction will be slow.

20. Less is the activation energy faster is the reaction or greater is the activation energy slower is the reaction.

CHAPTER 5

Surface Chemistry

Adsorption

- **Surface chemistry:** The branch of chemistry which deals with the phenomenon that occur at the surfaces or interfaces. This phenomenon is usually studied with the help of adsorption and colloidal state.

Adsorption

- **Adsorption:** The accumulation of molecular species at the surface rather than in the bulk of a solid or liquid is termed adsorption. The surface that adsorbs is known as adsorbent whereas the one that gets adsorbed is known as adsorbate. For example: Silica and aluminium gels are used to adsorb moisture to reduce humidity.

- Types of adsorption:
  - **Physisorption:** It is also known as physical adsorption. When the gas is accumulated on the surface of the solid on account of weak van der Waal's forces, it is known as physical adsorption or physisorption.
  - **Chemisorption:** It is also known as chemical adsorption. When the gas molecules or atoms are held to the solid surface by chemical bonds, it is known as chemical adsorption or chemisorptions.

- **Desorption:** It is a process of removing an adsorbed substance from the surface of an adsorbent.

- In absorption, the substance is uniformly distributed throughout the bulk of the solid. For example: Chalk stick dipped in ink.

- **Sorption:** When adsorption and absorption takes place simultaneously, it is called sorption. For example: Cotton dipped in ink.

- **Enthalpy of adsorption:** Adsorption generally occurs with the release of energy and is exothermic in nature. The enthalpy change for the adsorption of one mole of an adsorbate on the surface of adsorbent is called enthalpy or heat of adsorption.

- Difference between Adsorption and Absorption:

Adsorption	Absorption
It is a surface phenomenon	It concerns with the whole mass of the absorbent.
The concentration of the adsorbate at the surface of adsorbent is much more than that in the bulk.	Absorbed material is uniformly distributed throughout the bulk. Thus, concentration is same throughout.
It is rapid in the beginning and slows down near the equilibrium.	It occurs at a uniform rate.
Example: NH_3 is adsorbed by charcoal.	Example: NH_3 is absorbed in water to form NH_4OH.

- Factors affecting adsorption of gases on solids:
  - Nature of gas
  - Nature of adsorbent
  - Specific area of the solid
  - Pressure of the gas
  - Effect of temperature
  - Activation of adsorbent

- **Adsorption isobar:** A plot of extent of adsorption $\left(\dfrac{x}{m}\right)$ vs. temperature (T) at constant pressure is called adsorption isobar.

- **Adsorption isotherm:** A plot of extent of adsorption $\left(\dfrac{x}{m}\right)$ vs. pressure (P) at constant temperature is called adsorption isotherm, where 'x' is the quantity of the gas adsorbed by unit mass 'm' of the solid adsorbed.

- **Freundlich Adsorption Isotherm:** It gives the relationship between the quantity of gas adsorbed by unit mass of solid adsorbent and pressure at a constant temperature. It is represented by a mathematical equation,

$$\frac{x}{m} = kp^{1/n} \qquad \ldots (1)$$

$$\log \frac{x}{m} = \log k + \frac{1}{n} \log p \quad \ldots (2)$$

A plot of $\log \dfrac{x}{m}$ vs. $\log p$ gives a straight line with slope $\dfrac{1}{n}$ and y intercept $= \log k$.

In case of solution, the isotherm takes the form,

$$\frac{x}{m} = k(C)^{1/n} \, ; \log \frac{x}{m} = \log k + \frac{1}{n} \log C$$

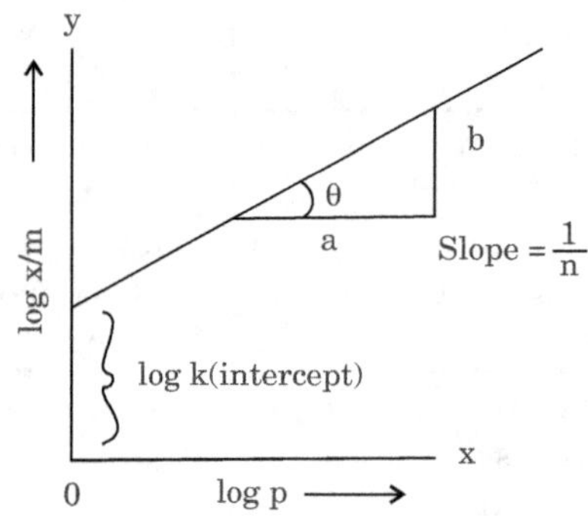

Where x is the amount of adsorbate adsorbed on m gram of adsorbent at pressure p or concentration C of the adsorbate, k and n are constants, $n > 1$.

- **Applications of adsorption:**
  - In the preparation of gas masks using activated charcoal.
  - Froth floatation method used for concentration of sulphide ores.
  - Silica gel is used to remove moisture.
  - Ion exchange method used to soften water.
  - Adsorption chromatography is used to purify and separate pigments, hormones etc.
  - Charcoal powder can remove coloured impurities from sugar.
  - Charcoal is used for making high vacuum.
  - The cleaning action of soaps and detergents.
  - In heterogeneous catalysis.
  - In curing diseases.

Catalysis

- **Catalysis:** Catalyst is a substance that is used to increase the rate of the reaction without changing itself and this process is known as catalysis. For example,

$$C_6H_6 + Cl_2 \xrightarrow{\;AlCl_3\;} C_6H_5Cl + HCl$$

The catalyst remains unchanged with respect to mass and composition. Catalyst does not affect ΔH, ΔS. ΔG and equilibrium constant k.

- **Promoters:** Those substances which increase the activity of the catalysts are called promoters. For example,

  Mo is promoter whereas Fe is catalyst in Haber's process.

$$N_2(g) + 3H_2(g) \underset{Mo}{\overset{Fe}{\rightleftharpoons}} 2NH_3(g)$$

- **Poisons or Inhibitors:** Substances which destroy the activity of the catalyst by their presence are known as poisons or inhibitors. For example,

  Arsenic acts as catalytic poison in the manufacturing of sulphuric acid by contact process.

- Types of catalysis:
  - Homogeneous Catalysis: A catalytic process where the reactants and the catalyst are in the same phase (i.e. liquid or gas). For example, Catalytic oxidation of SO_2 to SO_3 in presence of NO is an example of Homogeneous catalysis.
  - Heterogeneous Catalysis: A catalytic process where the reactants and the catalyst are in different phase. For example, Hydrogenation of vegetable oils in the presence of finely divided nickel as catalyst.

- **Adsorption theory of Heterogeneous Catalysis:** According to modern adsorption theory, there are free valencies on the surface of solid catalyst and mechanism involves following five steps:
  - Diffusion of reactants to the surface of the catalyst.
  - Adsorption of reactant molecules on the surface of the catalyst.
  - Occurrence of a chemical reaction forming an intermediate on the surface.
  - Desorption of the product molecules from the surface.
  - Diffusion of product molecules away from the surface of the catalyst.

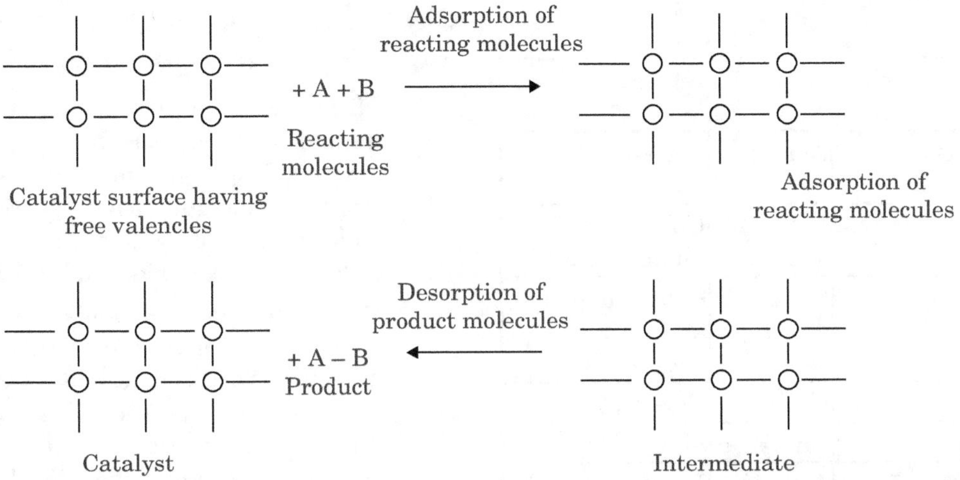

Catalyst surface having free valences

$+ A + B$

Reacting molecules

Adsorption of reacting molecules

Adsorption of reacting molecules

Catalyst

$+ A - B$
Product

Desorption of product molecules

Intermediate

- Important features of solid catalysts:
  - Activity: It is the ability of catalyst to increase the rate of reaction.
  - Selectivity: It is the ability of a catalyst to direct the reaction in such a way, that we get a desired product.
- Shape-selective catalysis by zeolites: It is the catalytic reaction that depends upon the pore structure of the catalyst and the size of the reactant and product molecules. Zeolites are shape selective catalyst having honey comb structures. Zeolite catalyst, ZSM-5 is used in petroleum industry to convert alcohols into gasoline by dehydration.
- Enzyme Catalysis: Enzymes are complex nitrogenous organic compounds produced by living plant and animals which are basically protein molecules but with high molecular mass and form colloidal solution in water. In enzyme catalysis, specific biochemical reactions occur. For example, decomposition of urea into ammonia and carbon dioxide. The enzyme urease catalyses this decomposition.

$$NH_2CONH_2 + H_2O \xrightarrow{Urease} 2NH_3 + CO_2$$
$$(Urea)$$

- Characteristics of enzymes:
  - Enzymes are very active catalysts as they form a colloidal solution in water.
  - Like inorganic catalyst they cannot disturb the final state of equilibrium of a reversible reaction.
  - They are highly specific in nature.
  - They have an optimum temperature range between 25°C–35°C and get deactivated at 70°C. Hence, they are highly specific to temperature.
  - A small quantity of enzyme is sufficient for a large change.
  - They are destroyed by UV rays.

- Their efficiency is decreased in the presence of electrolytes.
- Mechanism of enzyme catalysed reaction: This type of reaction may proceed in two steps,
  - Binding the enzyme to substrate to form an activated complex.

  $$E + S \longrightarrow ES^{\neq}$$

  - Decomposition of the activated complex to form product.

  $$ES^{\neq} \longrightarrow E + P$$

- Co-enzymes: Certain substances, which can increase the activity of enzymes are known as Co-enzymes.

Colloids

- Colloids: A colloid is a heterogeneous system in which one substance is dispersed (dispersed phase) as very fine particles in another substance called dispersion medium. The size of colloidal particles is in the range 1-100 nm.
- Colloidal solution: Colloidal solutions, or colloidal suspensions, are nothing but a mixture in which the substances are regularly suspended in a fluid. It is a heterogeneous system in which a very tiny and small material is spread out uniformly all through another substance called dispersion medium. For example, glue, ink, water etc.
- Dispersed phase: It is a component present in small proportion like solute in solution.
- Dispersion medium: The medium in which the colloidal particles are dispersed is called dispersion medium.
- Crystalloids: The substances whose aqueous solution can pass through a semi-permeable membrane are called crystalloids.

Types of colloidal solutions:

Dispersed phase	Dispersion Medium	Name	Examples
Solid	Gas	Aerosol	Smoke, dust particles
Solid	Liquid	Sol	Gold Sol, starch, muddy water
Solid	Solid	Solid Sol	Coloured gem stones, pearls, ruby glass
Liquid	Solid	Gel	Cheese, butter
Liquid	Liquid	Emulsion	Milk, hair cream
Liquid	Gas	Aerosol	Fog mist, cloud
Gas	Solid	Solid foam	Foam rubber, cork
Gas	Liquid	Foam	Whipped cream, soap lather

Classification based on nature of interaction between:

- **Lyophillic Colloids:** Lyophillic means "liquid loving", thus, lyophillic colloids are colloids mixed with suitable liquid with high force of attraction between the colloids and the solvent. They are also known as intrinsic colloids. For example, gelatin, starch, etc.

- **Lyophobic Colloids:** Lyophobic means "liquid hating", thus, lyophobic colloids consists of the phases which do not interact with each other. Their solution can only be prepared by special methods. They are also known as extrinsic colloids. For example, metals and their sulphides.

Classification based on the type of particles of the dispersal phase:

- **Multimolecular Colloids:** When a large number of dispersed particles (having diameter less than 1nm) combine together in a dispersion medium to form aggregates of many molecules, it is known as multimolecular colloids. For example, sulphur sol, gold sol etc.

- **Macromolecular Colloids:** When certain substances form large molecules whose dimensions are comparable to those of colloidal particles, they are known as macromolecules. When such substances are dispersed in suitable medium, the resulting colloidal solution is known as macromolecular solution. For example, Polythene, nylon etc.

- Associated Colloids (Micelles):

Micelles: Those colloids which behave as normal strong electrolytes at low concentrations, show colloidal properties at higher concentration due to the formation of aggregated particles of colloidal dimensions. Such compounds are also referred to as associated colloids

Mechanism of micelles formation: Molecules having lyophillic as well as lyophobic ends generally form micelles. Such types of molecules are known as surface active molecule. Soap is sodium or potassium salt of a higher fatty acid and may be represented as $RCOONA^+$. When dissolved in water, it breaks down into $RCOO^-$ and NA^+ ions. However, it contains two parts – a long hydrocarbon chain R which is hydrophobic and a polar group COO^-, which is hydrophilic.

Sodium stearate ($C_{12}H_{33}COO^- Na^+$)

Hydrophobic tail
Stearate ion

Hydrophilic head

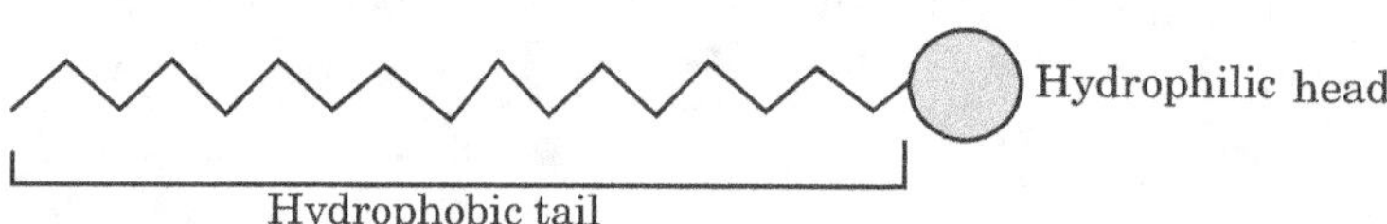

Hydrophobic tail

The $RCOO^-$ ions are present on the surface with their COO^- groups in water and the hydrocarbon chains R staying away from it and remains at the surface. At the critical micelle concentration, the anions are pulled into the bulk of the solution and aggregate to form a spherical shape with their hydrocarbon chains pointing towards the centre of the sphere whereas, the COO^- part remaining outward on the surface of the sphere. The result of this is known as 'ionic micelle'.

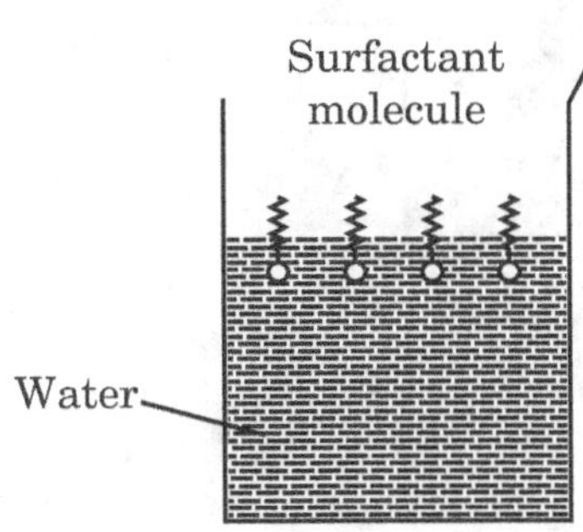

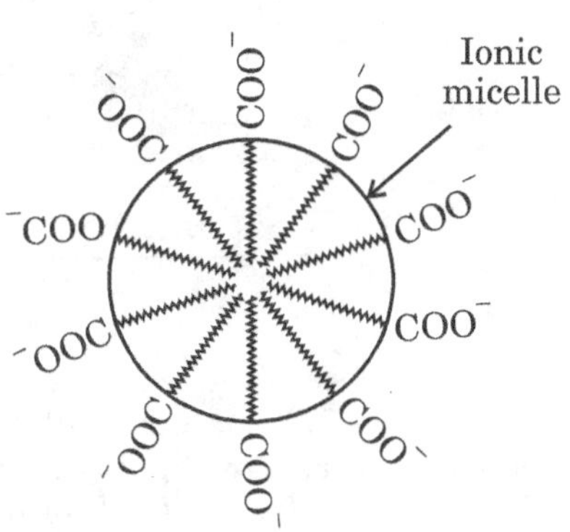

- **Preparation of colloidal solution:** Colloidal solutions can be prepared by following methods:
  - ➢ **Mechanical dispersion:** A suspension of coarsely ground particles prepared in dispersion medium is fed into a colloidal mill and speed of rotation is adjusted so as to get the particles of colloidal size.
  - ➢ **Electrical disintegration or Bredig's Arc method:** This process involves dispersion as well as condensation. In this method, two rods of the metal (Au, Cu, Pt, Ag) are immersed in cold and a direct electric arc is struck between them. This results in the formation of vapours of metal which in turn condense to form particles of colloidal size.

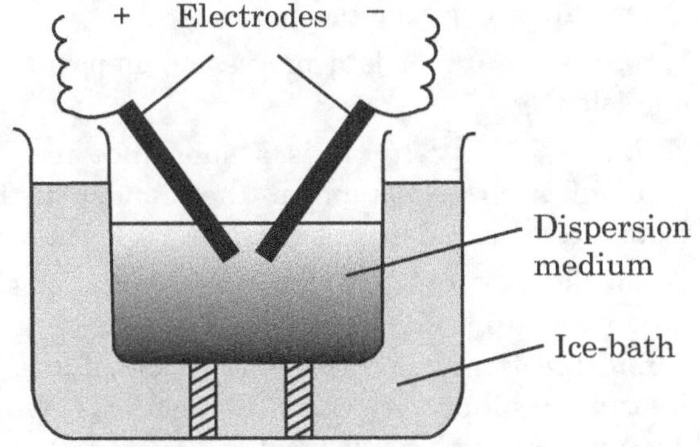

  - ➢ **Chemical Methods:**
    Oxidation: Solutions of non-metals are prepared by this method. For example,

$$2H_2S + 2(O) \xrightarrow{\;HNO_3(Conc.)\;} 2S + 2H_2O$$

    Reduction: Metal sols can be prepared by this method. For example,

$$2AuCl_3 + 3SnCl_2 \longrightarrow 2Au + 3SnCl_4$$

    Hydrolysis: Hydroxides sols are prepared by this method.

$$FeCl_3 + 3H_2S \longrightarrow Fe(OH)_3 + 3HCl$$

    Double decomposition: This method is used to prepare colloids from inorganic salts.

    Exchange of solvent: There are a few substances that form true solution in one solvent but forms colloidal solution in another due to lower solubility. For example, sulphur dissolved in alcohol forms colloidal solution in water.

- **Peptization:** When precipitates are passed into a colloidal solution in presence of an electrolyte, it is known as peptization. The electrolyte used is known as peptizing agent.

- **Purification methods of colloidal solutions:** Colloidal solution can be purified by following methods:
  - ➢ **Dialysis:** In dialysis, a dissolved substance is removed from a colloidal solution by means of diffusion through a suitable membrane. The membrane used is usually a parchment paper or cellophane membrane.
  - ➢ **Electrodialysis:** This method is faster than simple dialysis because in this method, movement of ions across the membrane can be quickened by applying electric potential through two electrodes.

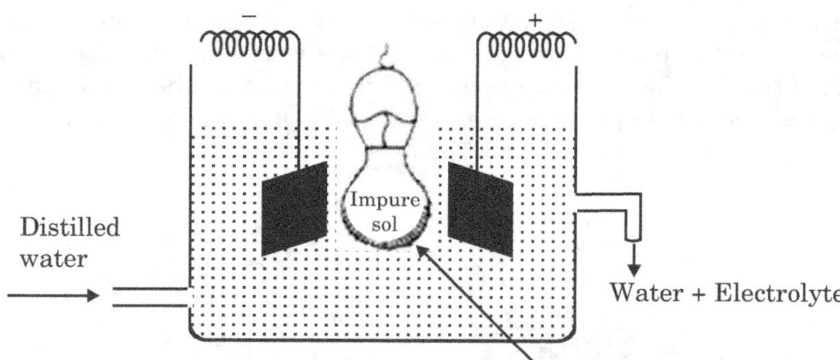

Cellophane bag (Dialysing membrane)

> **Ultrafiltration:** The process of separating colloidal particles by specially prepared filter papers whose pores is reduced by dipping it in a solution made up of 4% of nitrocellulose in mixture of alcohol and ether.

Properties of colloids:

> **Brownian movement:** The haphazard movement of colloidal particles is known as Brownian movement. The movement of particles is observed under a powerful microscope.

> **Tyndall effect:** Scattering of light by colloidal particles is called Tyndall effect.

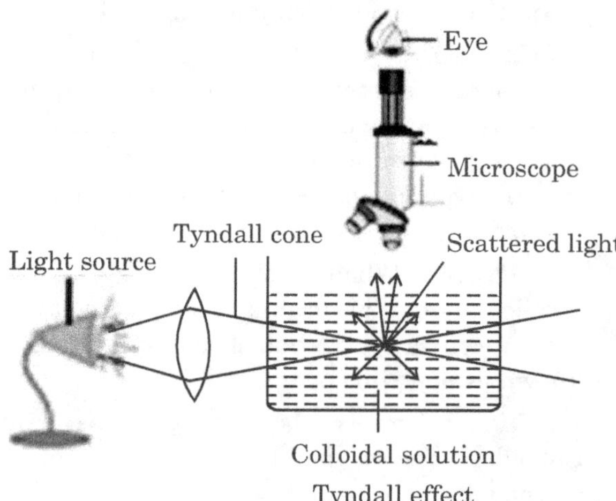

Tyndall effect

> **Electrophoresis:** When electricity is passed through a colloidal solution, the colloidal particles move towards one of the electrodes. This phenomenon is called electrophoresis.

Hardy-Schulze rules:

> Opposite charged ions are effective for coagulation.

> The coagulating power of electrolyte increases with increase in charge on the ions used for coagulation. For example, $Al^{3+} > Ba^{2+} > Na^+$ for negatively charged colloids.

Coagulation value is the inverse of coagulating power, i.e. lower the coagulation value, higher will be coagulating power.

- **Electrokinetic Potential or Zeta Potential:** The potential difference between the fixed layer and diffused layer of opposite charges is called zeta potential.

- **Coagulation:** It is a process by which a liquid changes into a solid or semi-solid state.

- **Coagulating value:** The minimum concentration of an electrolyte which is required to cause the coagulation is known as coagulating value.

$$Coagulation\,Value \propto \frac{1}{Coagulating\,Power}$$

- **Emulsions:** They are the type of colloidal system where the dispersed phase and the dispersion medium both are liquids. There are two types of emulsions:

  > **Oil in water:** In this type of emulsion, oil is the dispersed phase and water is the dispersion medium. For example, milk.

  > **Water in oil:** In this type of emulsion, water is the dispersed phase and oil is the dispersion medium. For example, butter.

- **Emulsification:** It is a process of preparing an emulsion.

- **Emulsifying agent:** It is a substance used in emulsification, to stabilize the emulsion. For example, soap and detergents.

- **Demulsification:** The process of decomposing an emulsion into it's constituent liquids is called demulsification. It is carried out by centrifugation, freezing, boiling or chemical methods which destroy the emulsifying agent.

Applications of colloids:

> Sewage disposal
> Purification of drinking water
> Smoke precipitation
> Medicines
> Tanning
> Rubber industry

Distinction between true solution, colloids and suspension:

True Solution	Colloids	Suspension
It is homogeneous.	It is heterogeneous, though it appears homogeneous.	It is heterogeneous.
Particle size is less than 1nm.	Particle size ranges from 1nm to 100nm.	Particle size is more than 100nm.
It passes through filter paper.	It passes through ordinary filter paper but not through ultrafilters.	It does not pass through filter paper.
It does not show Tyndall effect.	It shows Tyndall effect.	It does not show Tyndall effect appreciably.
It has higher value of colligative property.	It has low value of colligative property.	It has very low value of colligative property.
Its particles cannot be seen even with powerful microscope.	Its particles can be seen by powerful microscope due to scattering of light.	Its particles can be seen even with naked eyes.

EXERCISE

1. When the temperature is raised, the viscosity of liquid decreases, this is because

   (a) Decreased volume of the solution

   (b) Increase in temperature increase the average kinetic energy of molecules, which overcome the attractive force between them.

   (c) Decreased covalent and hydrogen bond forces.

   (d) Increased attraction between molecules.

2. The charge on As_2O_3 sol in due to the adsorbed

   (a) H^+ (b) OH^-

   (c) O^{2-} (d) S^{2-}

3. According to Langmuir adsorption isotherm, the amount of gas adsorbed at very high pressure.

   (a) Reaches a constant limiting value.

   (b) Goes on increasing with pressure

   (c) Goes on decreasing with pressure

   (d) Increases first and decreases later with pressure.

4. In adsorption of oxalic acid on activated charcoal, the activated charcoal is known as.

   (a) Adsorbent   (b) Absorbate

   (c) Adsorber   (d) Absorber

5. Which of the following statement is not applicable to chemisorption.

   (a) It is slow

   (b) It is irreversible

   (c) It is highly specific

   (d) It is independent of temperature

6. Adsorption is always

   (a) Endothermic   (b) Exothermic

   (c) Either (a) or (b)   (d) None of these.

7. Adsorption due to strong chemical forces is called

   (a) Chemisorption

   (b) Physisorption

   (c) Reversible adsorption

   (d) Both (b) and (c)

8. Physical adsorption is inversely proportional to the

   (a) Volume   (b) Concentration

   (c) Temperature   (d) All of these.

9. A catalyst is a substance which

   (a) Alters the equilibrium in a reaction

   (b) Is always in the same phase as the reactants.

   (c) Participates in the reaction and provides easies pathway for the same.

   (d) Does not participate in the reaction but speeds it up.

10. Which of the following types of metals make the most efficient catalysts

   (a) Alkali metals

   (b) Transition metals

   (c) Alkaline-earth metals

   (d) Radioactive metals

11. Which of the following catalyses the conversion of glucose into ethanol

   (a) Zymase   (b) Invertase

   (c) Maltase   (d) Diastase

12. Hydrolysis of ethyl acetate is catalysed by aqueous
    (a) Na_2SO_4 (b) K_2SO_4
    (c) H_2SO_4 (d) $BaSO_4$

13. Which one of the following changes when catalyst is used in a reaction
    (a) Heat of reaction
    (b) Product of reaction
    (c) Equilibrium constant
    (d) Activation energy

14. In the Ostwald's process for the manufacture of HNO_3, the catalyst used is
    (a) Mo   (b) Fe
    (c) Ni   (d) Pt

15. Which of the following statement is incorrect
    (a) Enzymes are in colloidal state
    (b) Enzymes are catalysts
    (c) Enzymes can catalyses any reaction
    (d) Urease in an enzyme

16. Wilhem Ostwald redefined the action of
    (a) Anomers
    (b) Isomers
    (c) Catalyst
    (d) Geometry of monomer's

17. $As_2 S_3$ sol has a negative charge. Capacity to precipitate it is highest in
    (a) $AlCl_3$ (b) Na_3PO_4
    (c) $CaCl_2$ (d) K_2SO_4

18. Sky looks blue due to
    (a) Dispersion effect   (b) Reflection
    (c) Transmission   (d) Scattering

19. A negatively charged suspension of clay in water will need for precipitation the minimum amount of
    (a) Aluminium chloride
    (b) Potassium sulphate
    (c) Sodium hydroxide
    (d) Hydrochloride acid

20. The stability of lyophilic colloids is due to
    (a) Charge on their particles
    (b) A layer of dispersion medium on their particles
    (c) The smaller size of their particles
    (d) The large size of their particles

21. Milk is a colloid in which
    (a) A liquid is dispersed in liquid
    (b) A solid is dispersed in liquid
    (c) A gas is dispersed in liquid
    (d) Some suger is dispersed in water

22. Which one of the following is not a colloidal solution
    (a) Smoke   (b) Ink
    (c) Air   (d) Blood

23. Purification of colloids is done by the process of
    (a) Electrophoresis
    (b) Electrodispersion
    (c) Peptization
    (d) Ultra-filteration

24. According to Graham, colloids are those substances which are
    (a) Insoluble in water
    (b) In solution do not pass through filter paper
    (c) Of definite size of particles
    (d) Separated from crystalloid by parchment paper

Answer Keys

1. (b)   2. (d)   3. (a)   4. (a)   5. (d)   6. (b)   7. (a)   8. (c)   9. (d)   10. (b)
11. (a)   12. (c)   13. (d)   14. (d)   15. (d)   16. (a)   17. (a)   18. (d)   19. (a)   20. (b)
21. (a)   22. (c)   23. (d)   24. (d)

Solutions

1. When the temperature is raised, the viscosity of liquid decreases, this is because increase in temperature increases the average kinetic energy of molecules which overcome the attractive force between them.

2. Charge on As_2S_3 sol is due to the adsorbed sulphide ion.

3. According to Langmuir adsorption isotherm the amount of gas adsorbed at very high pressures reaches a constant limiting volume.

4. According to definition of adsorbent.

5. Chemisorption first increases and then decreases with temperature.

6. Adsorption is an exothermic process.

7. Adsorption due to strong chemical bond is called chemical adsorption or chemisorption or Langmuir adsorption.

8. Physical adsorption decreases with increases of temperature.

9. A catalyst does not take part in the reaction but can speed it up. It can be recovered after the reaction.

10. Transition metals are most efficient catalysts due to half filled d-orbitals.

11. $$C_6H_{12}O_6 \xrightarrow[\text{Enzyme}]{\text{Zymase}} 2C_2H_5OH + 2CO_2$$

    Glucose $\qquad\qquad$ Ethanol

12. $$CH_3COOC_2H_5 + HOH \xrightarrow[\text{Catalyst}]{\text{Conc. } H_2SO_4}$$
    $$CH_3COOH + C_2H_5OH$$

13. Activation energy changes when catalyst is used in a reaction.

14. $$4NH_3 + 5O_2 \xrightarrow[\text{1100K}]{\text{Pt guage}} 4NO \xrightarrow{O_2}$$
    $$4NO_2 \xrightarrow{2H_2O + O_2} 4HNO_3$$

15. Mn^{++} is a product in reaction so it is auto catalyst (according to definition).

16. Generally transition elements act as catalysts. Adam's catalyst is another name of platinum.

17. Negatively charged As_2S_3 sol is coagulated most effectively by $AlCl_3$. This is because oppositely charged Al^{+++} ions have maximum charge.

    $As^{3+} > Ca^{2+} > Na^+$

18. Sky looks blue due to scattering of light by dust particles present in the atmosphere.

19. Negatively charged sols require minimum amount of electrolyte having higher valency of cation.

20. Lyophilic possesses solvent loving nature and thus a thin layer of dispersed phase is formed round sol particles.

21. Milk is a colloid of liquid (H_2O) dispersed in liquid (fat)

22. Air is not a colloidal solution because it is a homogeneous mixture.

23. In purification separation of colloids from crystalloids is done by the process of ultra-filtration.

24. According to Graham, colloids are separated from crystalloids by parchment paper.

CHAPTER 6

General Principles and Processes of Isolation of Elements

- Important terms:
  - **Minerals:** There are many natural occurring chemical substances present in the earth's crust and mining is needed to obtain them.
  - **Ores:** Out of many minerals, the minerals in which we may find metal are known as ores.
  - **Gangue:** The undesired or earthy materials that contaminate the ore is called gangue.
  - **Metallurgy:** The process that involves isolation of the metal from its ores is known as metallurgy.

    Concentration: Removing the unwanted materials from the ore is called concentration.
  - **Flux:** It is a substance which needs to be added in the ore for the conversion of non-fusible gangue into fusible compound.
  - **Slag:** The fusible compound which is converted by flux from gangue is called slag

- Concentration of ore:

  The process to remove the gangue from the ore is carried out by the following methods:
  - **Crushing and Grinding:**

    The process begins with breaking the huge lumps into small pieces in the jaw crushers and then to make the powder, a ball mill or stamp mill is used. This process is alternatively called pulverization.

  - Magnetic separation method:

    The process that involves removal of tungsten ore particles from cassiterite (SnO_2) is called magnetic separation.

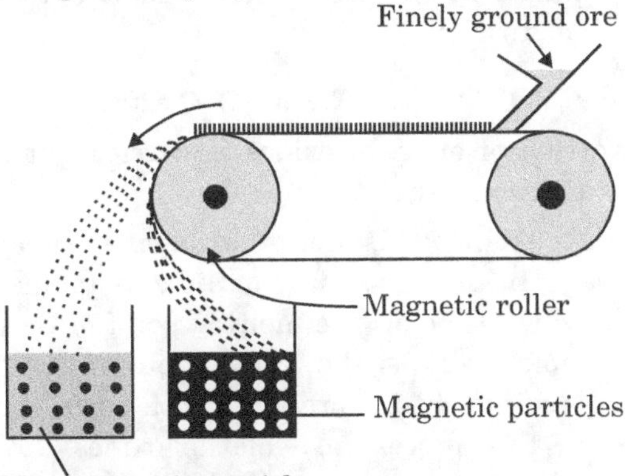

  - Froth floatation process:

    The principal of preferential wetting of solid surfaces is used by this process. This involves the concentration of sulphide ores because the metallic sulphides are more wetted by certain oils and less by water. For example, ores of lead, zinc and copper.

    A blast of air is passed through the mixture to agitate it. The froth which forms in this step then carries the ore particles along with it to the surface and leaves the impurities behind.

    The ore is concentrated by froth floatation process once the froth is scummed off.

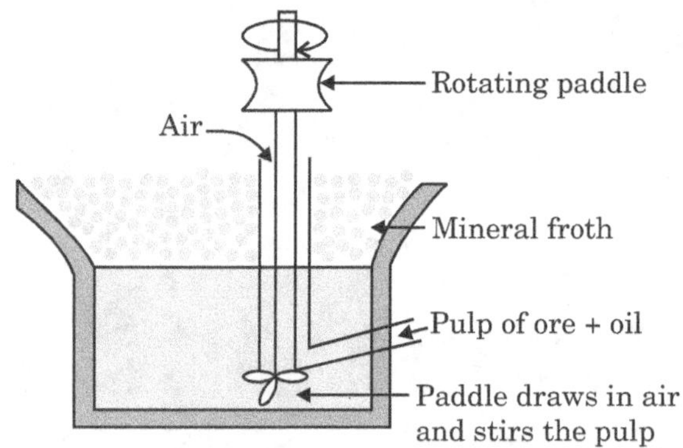

Enlarged view of an air bubble showing mineral particles attached to it

- ➢ **Hydraulic washing:** It entirely depends on the difference in the densities of the gangue particle and the ore. An upward stream of running water is used to wash away the lighter gangue particles from the powdered ore. After this process only the heavier ore stays behind.

- ➢ **Leaching:** If the ore is soluble in a particular reagent then this process is used to make sure that only the ore dissolves in it but not the impurities.

Conversion of ore into oxide:

Conversion of ore into oxides is carried out by the following two methods:

- ➢ **Roasting:** This process involves the heating of ore in regular supply of air at a temperature which is below the melting point of the metal which allows the conversion of the given ore into oxides ore. Impurities are removed in this process as volatile oxides. Roasting allows the conversion of sulphide ores into oxides. Reverberatory furnace is used for this process.

$$2ZnS + 3O_2 \rightarrow 2ZnO + 2SO_2$$

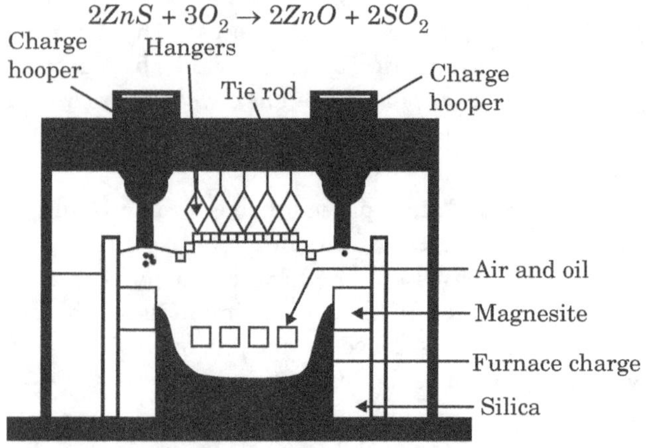

- ➢ **Calcination:** This process involves the heating of ore in the absence of air which allows it to convert carbonate ores into oxides.

$$FeCO_3 \xrightarrow{Heat} FeO + CO_2$$
$$Siderate$$
$$Fe_2O_3 . xH_2O_{(s)} \xrightarrow{Heat} Fe_2O_{3(s)} + xH_2O_{(g)}$$

- • Reduction of oxide to metal: This process involves the heating of metal oxides with some other substance which acts as reducing agent. Carbon, carbon monoxide or any other metal like Al or Mg are some commonly used reducing agents. This process is carried out by following methods:

- ➢ **Auto reduction:**

  This method involves heating the ore in the air to reduce the inactive metals. This method is used for the extraction of copper, lead, antimony, mercury etc. For example,

  $$2CuS + 3O_2 \rightarrow 2Cu_2O + 2SO_2 \uparrow$$
  $$Cu_2S + 2Cu_2O \rightarrow 6Cu + SO_2 \uparrow$$

- ➢ **Smelting:**

  This process allows metal oxide to be reduced to metal C or CO. For example,

  $$Fe_2O_3 + 3C \xrightarrow{>1123K} 2Fe + 3CO \uparrow$$
  $$Fe_2O_3 + 3CO \xrightarrow{1123K} 2Fe + 3CO_2 \uparrow$$
  $$ZnO + C \rightarrow Zn + CO\uparrow$$

- ➢ **Aluminothermic reduction:**

  It allows the reduction of metal oxide by aluminium. Thermite process is used to extract metal like manganese and chromium.

  $$3MnO_4 + 8AI \rightarrow 4AI_2O_3 + 3Mn$$
  $$Cr_2O_3 + 2AI \rightarrow AI_2O_3 + 2Cr$$

- ➢ **Reduction with hydrogen:**

  Hydrogen acts as an efficient reducing agent for metal oxides. The ore obtained from roasting is heated in a current of hydrogen and metal oxides and then reduced to metal. Hydrogen is used to reduce oxides of W, Mo etc.

  $$WO_3 + 3H_2 \rightarrow W + 3H_2O$$

- • **Methods to remove impurities from a metal:**

- ➢ **Distillation:** In this method the impure metal is evaporated to get the pure metal in the form of distillate. This method is used for the purification of metals like zinc and mercury since they have a low boiling point.

> **Electrolytic refining:** In this method the crude metal is used as anode and the same metal in pure form is used as a cathode. A soluble salt of the same metal is used as an electrolyte.

Copper is refined using electrolytic refining method. Impure copper is taken as an anode and pure copper strip as cathode.

Anode: $Cu \rightarrow Cu^{2+} + 2e^-$

Cathode: $Cu^{2+} + 2e^- \rightarrow Cu$

> **Liquation:** In this method a metal with low melting point is made to flow on a surface having a certain slope. Hence, the low melting metal can be separated from higher melting impurities.

> **Chromatographic method:** This method is based on chromatography. Which means that the different components in a mixture are adsorbed differently by an adsorbent. There are several chromatographic techniques such as paper chromatography, column chromatography, gas chromatography, etc.

In column chromatography method the column of Al_2O_3 is prepared in a glass tube and the moving medium containing a solution of the components is in liquid form. The adsorbed components are removed (eluted) by using suitable solvent (eluant).

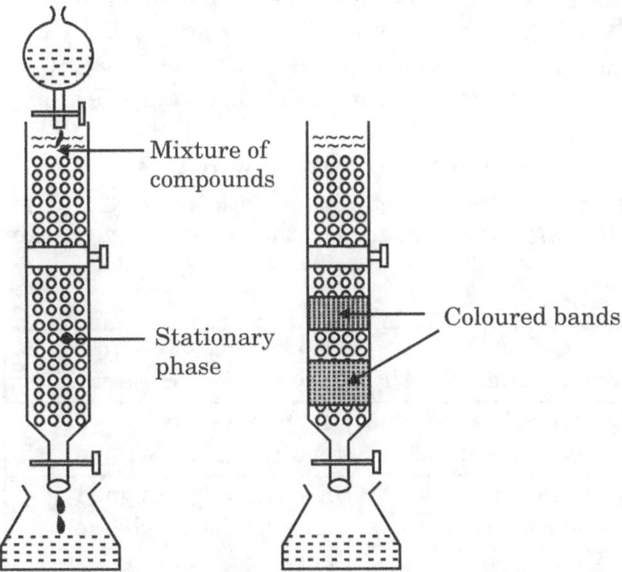

> **Zone refining:** In this method a circular mobile heater is moved along the rod. The metal rod is placed inside a small induction furnace. The molten metal moves along with the heater and the pure metal crystallises out of the molten state while the impurities remain in the adjacent molten zone. When the process is repeated several times, the heater is moved in the same direction and impurities gets

accumulated at the end. The end is removed or cut off. This method is used for the purification of semiconductors.

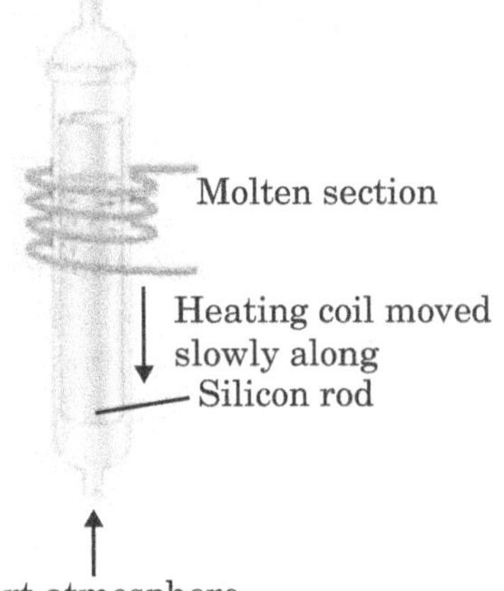

> **Vapour phase refining:** In this method, the pure metal is obtained by decomposing the volatile compound formed by the impure metal. It is shown by two methods:

Mond's process: This process is used for refining nickel. Nickel is heated in a stream of Carbon monoxide and nickel tetracarbonyl is formed as a volatile complex. The carbonyl is heated at a high temperature to obtain pure Nickel.

$$Ni + 4CO \xrightarrow{330-350K} Ni(CO)_4$$

$$\xrightarrow{450-470K} Ni + 4CO$$

Van Arkel Method: This method is used to refine titanium or zirconium. It removes all nitrogen and oxygen present in the metal as impurities. Heat is imparted to the impure metal in an evacuated vessel in presence of Iodine. The metal iodide is then decomposed on an electrically heated tungsten filament.

$$Zr + 2I_2 \rightarrow ZrI_4 \xrightarrow[Tunsten\ filament]{1800K} Zr + 2I_2$$

$$impure \qquad\qquad\qquad Pure$$

• **Ellingham diagram:** H.J.T. Ellingham first used the graphical representation of Gibbs energy. This diagram helped in selecting the suitable reducing agent for the reduction of oxides

The diagram can be used to predict if the ore can be thermally reduced or not. Ellingham diagram consists of graphs which represent the variation of standard free energy with temperature of the formation of oxides of various elements, i.e. of $\Delta_f G^\circ$ vs T. Similar plots can also be plotted for sulphides and halides.

Consider the formation of a metal oxide (M_xO).

$2xM\ (s) + O_2\ (g) \rightarrow 2M_xO\ (s)$

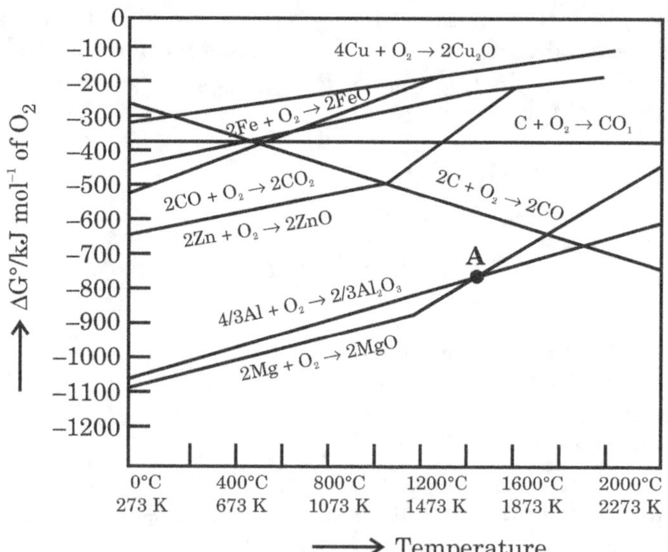

In this reaction, there is decrease in the value of $\Delta S°$ as (M_xO) is solid and O_2 is a gas, i.e., ΔS is negative. Thus, if temperature is increased, $T\Delta S°$ becomes more negative. As in the equation,

$$\Delta S° = \Delta H° - T\Delta S°$$

$T\Delta S°$ is subtracted, therefore, $\Delta G°$ becomes less negative, i.e., $\Delta G°$ is likely to increase with rise in temperature and this trend is confirmed from the curves.

➢ The slope of the curves of the formation of metal oxides is +ve because $\Delta G°$ becomes less negative or increases with the rise in temperature.

➢ Each curve is a straight line except when some change takes place in phase. The temperature at which such a change occurs is indicated by an increase in the slope on the +ve side. For example, in the $Zn–ZnO$ curve, the melting of zinc is indicated by an abrupt increase in the +ve slope at temperature 692 K.

➢ In the case of less reactive metals like silver and mercury, $\Delta G°$ becomes positive at high temperatures. It indicates that both silver oxide (Ag_2O) and mercury oxide (HgO) are unstable and decompose at high temperature.

➢ In the curve of CO, $\Delta G°$ decreases as $\Delta S°$ increases. This is indicated by the downward trend.

➢ Any metal oxide with lower value of $\Delta G°$ is more stable than a metal oxide with higher $\Delta G°$. This implies that the metal oxide placed higher in the diagram can be reduced by the metal involved in the formation of the oxide placed lower in the diagram.

• **Some metal ores and their extractions:**

Aluminium	Bauxite $Al_2O_3.xH_2O$ Cryolite Na_3AlF_6	Electrolysis of Al_2O_3 dissolved in molten Na_3AlF_6	Good source of electricity is required for the extraction.
Iron	Haematite, Fe_2O_3 Magnetite, Fe_3O_4	Oxide is reduced in the Blast furnace with CO and coke.	High temperature is required (2170 K).
Copper	Copper pyrites, $CuFeS_2$ Copper glance, Cu_2S Malachite, $CuCO_3.Cu(OH)_2$ Cuprite, Cu_2O	Sulphides are partially roasted and then reduced.	In a specially designed converter, self-reduction takes place. In hydrometallurgy, H_2SO_4 leaching is also used.
Zinc	Zinc blende or Sphalerite, ZnS Calamine, $ZnCO_3$ Zincite, ZnO	Roasting and reduction with coke.	Purification may be done by fractional distillation.

EXERCISE

1. The most abundant element on earth crust is
   - (a) Hydrogen
   - (b) Oxygen
   - (c) Silicon
   - (d) Carbon

2. Which one of the following is correct
   - (a) A mineral cannot be an ore
   - (b) An ore cannot be a mineral
   - (c) All minerals are ores
   - (d) All ores are minerals

3. Which ore contains both iron and copper.
   - (a) Cuprite
   - (b) Chalcocite
   - (c) Chalcopyrite
   - (d) Malachite

4. Formula of Feldspar is
   - (a) $K_2O. Al_2O_3. 6SiO_2$
   - (b) $K_2O_3. Al_2O_3. 6SiO_2. 2H_2O$
   - (c) $Al_2O_3. 2SiO_2. 2H_2O$
   - (d) $3MgO. 4SiO_2. H_2O$

5. Which of the following is not an ore of iron
   - (a) Magnetite
   - (b) Siderite
   - (c) Smithsonite
   - (d) Limonite

6. Sulphide ores are generally concentrated by
   - (a) Froth floatation process
   - (b) Magnetic separation
   - (c) Gravity separation
   - (d) By hand picking

7. The substance added in water in the froth floatation process is
   - (a) Olive oil
   - (b) Pine oil
   - (c) Coconut oil
   - (d) None of these

8. For which ore of the metal, froth floatation method is used for concentration
   - (a) Horn silver
   - (b) Bauxite
   - (c) Cinnabar
   - (d) Haematite

9. Bauxite ore is concentrated by
   - (a) Froth floation
   - (b) Electromagnetic separation
   - (c) Chemical separation
   - (d) Hydraulic separation

10. Copper pyrites are concentrated by
    - (a) Electromagnetic method
    - (b) Gravity method
    - (c) Froth floatation process
    - (d) All of these

11. Main function of roasting is
    - (a) To remove volatile substances
    - (b) Oxidation
    - (c) Reduction
    - (d) Slag formation

12. Roasting is generally done in case of the following
    - (a) Oxide ores
    - (b) Silicate ores
    - (c) Sulphide ores
    - (d) Carbonate ores

13. When lime stone is heated strongly, it gives off CO_2. In metallurgy this process is known as
    - (a) Calcination
    - (b) Roasting
    - (c) Smelting
    - (d) Ore dressing

14. Which of the following substance can be used for drying gases
    - (a) $CaCO_3$
    - (b) Na_2CO_3
    - (c) $NaHCO_3$
    - (d) CaO

15. During extraction of Fe; slag obtained is
    - (a) FeO
    - (b) $FeSiO_3$
    - (c) $MgSiO_3$
    - (d) $CaSiO_3$

16. General method for the extraction of metal from oxide ore is
    - (a) Carbon reduction
    - (b) Reduction by aluminium
    - (c) Reduction by hydrogen
    - (d) Electrolytic reduction

17. Function of the flux added during smelting is
    - (a) To make ore porous
    - (b) To remove gangue
    - (c) To make reduction easier
    - (d) To precipitate slag

18. Chemical reduction is not suitable for converting
    - (a) Bauxite into aluminium
    - (b) Cuprite into copper
    - (c) Haematite into iron
    - (d) Zinc oxide into zinc

19. Cupellation process is used in the metallugry of
    - (a) Copper
    - (b) Silver
    - (c) Aluminium
    - (d) Iron

20. Of the following, which cannot be obtained by electrolysis of the aqueous solution of their salts
    - (a) Ag
    - (b) Mg and Al
    - (c) Cu
    - (d) Cr

Answer Keys

1. (b)	2. (d)	3. (c)	4. (a)	5. (c)	6. (a)	7. (b)	8. (c)	9. (c)	10. (c)
11. (a)	12. (c)	13. (a)	14. (d)	15. (d)	16. (a)	17. (b)	18. (a)	19. (b)	20. (b)

Solutions

1.

Element	% abundance by weight
O	46.6
Si	27.7
Al	8.3
Fe	5.1
Ca	3.6

2. All minerals are not suitable for the extraction of metals commercially. Thus all ores are minerals, but all minerals are not ores.

3. Among cuprite [Cu_2O], Chalcocite [Cu_2S], Chalcopyrite [$CuFeS_2$] and Malachite [$Cu(OH)_2 \cdot CuCO_3$], only chalcopyrite is an ore which contains both Fe and Cu.

4. Feldspar is $K_2O \cdot Al_2O_3 \cdot 6SiO_2$

5. Magnetite (Fe_3O_4), siderite ($FeCO_3$), Limonite ($Fe_2O_3 \cdot 3H_2O$) and Haematite (Fe_2O_3), are ores of iron. Only smithsonite is not an ore of iron.

6. Froth flotation method is based on the fact that the surface of sulphide ores is preferentially wetted by oil while that of gangue is wetted by water.

7. Pine oil is foaming agent. Now another substance collector such as potassium ethyl xanthate or amyl xanthate are added.

8. Cinnabar (HgS) the ore of mercury is concentrated by froth floation process.

9. Chemical separation or leaching.

In this powdered ore is treated with a suitable reagent which can dissolve the ore but not the impurities.

10. Sulphides ores are always concentrated by froth floatation process.

11. To remove volatile substances

$$S_8 + 8O_2 \longrightarrow 8SO_2 \uparrow; P_4; + 5O_2 \longrightarrow P_4O_{10} \uparrow;$$

$$4As + 3O_2 \longrightarrow 2As_2O_3 \uparrow$$

12. In this process sulphides ores are converted into oxide ores

$$2ZnS + 3O_2 \longrightarrow 2ZnO + 2SO_2 \uparrow$$

13. $CaCO_3 \longrightarrow CaO + CO_2$

Heating the ore in absence of air is calcination.

14. $CaO \longrightarrow$ It is hydroscopic in nature.

15. During extraction of Fe calcium silicate ($CaSiO_3$) slag is obtained.

16. Carbon reduction, $Fe_2O_3 + 3C \longrightarrow 2F + 3CO$

17. Flux + Gangue $\longrightarrow$ Slag

18. Bauxite into aluminium because Al is a strong reducing agent it has strong affinity with oxygen than carbon.

19. Cupellation method is used when the impure metals contain impurity of another metal which forms volatile oxide.

20. Mg and Al can not be obtained by the electrolysis of aqueous solution of their salts because instead of metal H_2 gas is liberated at cathode.

p-Block Elements

Group 15 Elements

- **Electronic configuration:** $ns^2 np^3$
- **Oxidation state:** They exhibit two important oxidation states, + 3 and + 5 but +3 oxidation is favored by heavier elements due to 'inert pair effect'.
- **Ionization Enthalpy:** Decreases from Nitrogen (N) to Bismuth (Bi) due to increase in atomic size.
- Metallic character increases down the group as the ionization energy decreases.
- Boiling point increases down the group.
- Melting point increases up to As and decreases up to Bi.
- Nitrogen differs from rest of the elements of this group due to its small size, high electronegativity, high ionization energy, and non-availability of d-orbitals and formation of pϖ–pϖ multiple bonds with itself and with highly electronegative atom like O or C.
- Dinitrogen is a colourless, odourless, tasteless and non-toxic gas
- Dinitrogen can be prepared in laboratory as well as on industrial scale by following reactions.

$$3CuO + 2NH_3 + heat \rightarrow N_2 + Cu + 3H_2O$$

$$CaOCl_2 + 2NH_3 + heat \rightarrow CaCl_2 + 2H_2O + N_2$$

$$NH_4NO_2 + heat \rightarrow Cr_2O_3 + 3H_2O + N_2$$

- The main use of dinitrogen is in the manufacture of ammonia and other industrial chemicals containing nitrogen, (e.g., calcium cyanamide).
- Nitrogen forms oxides in various oxidation states as $N_2O, NO, N_2O_3, NO_2, N_2O_4 and N_2O_5$. These oxides have resonating structures and have multiple bonds.

- Ammonia is a colourless gas with a pungent odour. Its freezing and boiling points are 198.4 and 239.7 K respectively.
- Ammonia (NH_3) is prepared on large scale by Haber's process.

$$N_2(g) + 3H_2(g) \rightarrow 2NH_3(g)$$

- Ammonia is used to produce various nitrogenous fertilisers (ammonium nitrate, urea, ammonium phosphate and ammonium sulphate) and in the manufacture of some inorganic nitrogen compounds, the most important one being nitric acid. Liquid ammonia is also used as a refrigerant.
- Nitric acid (HNO_3) is a colorless liquid (f.p. 231.4 K and b.p. 355.6 K) and is a powerful oxidizing agent. Metals and non-metals react with HNO_3 under different conditions to give NO or NO_2.
- The major use of nitric acid is in the manufacture of ammonium nitrate for fertilisers and other nitrates for use in explosives and pyrotechnics.
- Phosphorus another important element of group 15 is found in many allotropic forms, the important ones being white, red and black.
- Phosphorus exists as P_4 in elemental form. It forms hydride, PH_3 (phosphine) which is a highly poisonous gas.
- It forms two types of halides as PX_3 and PX_5. PCl_3 is prepared by the reaction of white phosphorus with dry chlorine.

$$P_4 + 6Cl_2 \rightarrow 4PCl_3$$

- While PCl_5 is prepared by the reaction of phosphorus with SO_2Cl_2.

$$P_4 + 10SO_2Cl_2 \rightarrow 4PCl_5 + 10SO_2$$

- Phosphorus forms a number of oxoacids. Depending upon the number of P–OH groups, their basicity varies. The oxoacids which have P–H bonds are good reducing agents.

Group 16 Elements

- **Electronic configuration:** $ns^2\,np^4$
- **Atomic and Ionic radii:** Due to increase in the number of shells, atomic and ionic radii increase from top to bottom in the group. The size of oxygen atom is, however, exceptionally small.
- **Ionization Enthalpy:** Decreases down the group. It is due to increase in size.
- **Electronegativity:** Decreases down the group.
- **Oxidation state:** They show +2, +4, and +6 oxidation states. Only oxygen shows an oxidation state of -2 (except of OF_2 and H_2O_2).
- Dioxygen is a colourless and odourless gas, it directly reacts with nearly all metals and non-metals except some metals (e.g., Au, Pt) and some noble gases.
- Its combination with other elements is often strongly exothermic which helps in sustaining the reaction.
- In laboratory, dioxygen is prepared by heating $KClO_3$ in presence of MnO_2.
- It forms a number of oxides with metals and they are classified on the basis of chemical nature. For example, Metallic oxides (Na_2O, CaO etc), Non-metallic (CO_2, SO_2 etc), amphoteric oxides (SnO_2, Al_2O_3 etc).
- Allotropic form of oxygen is O_3, which is a highly oxidizing agent.
- Sulphur forms a number of allotropes. Of these, α– and β– forms of sulphur are the most important. Sulphur combines with oxygen to give oxides such as SO_2 and SO_3. SO_2 is prepared by the direct union of sulphur with oxygen.
- SO_2 is used in the manufacture of H_2SO_4.
- Sulphur forms a number of oxoacids. Amongst them, the most important is H_2SO_4.
- It is prepared by contact process. It is a dehydrating and oxidizing agent. It is used in the manufacture of several compounds.

Group 17 Elements

- **Electronic configuration:** $ns^2\,np^5$
- **Atomic and Ionic radii:** They have the smallest radii in their respective periods because of increase in nuclear charge. It increases down the group.
- **Ionization Enthalpy:** Decreases down the group.

- **Electronegativity:** Decreases down the group and they are the most electronegative elements in their respective periods.
- **Oxidation state:** Except fluorine, other elements show oxidation states of +1, +3, +5 and +7. Fluorine shows -1 oxidation state.
- **Melting and boiling point:** It increases as we move down the group due to increase in radii and nuclear charge which causes greater van der Waal's forces of attraction.
- These elements are extremely reactive and as such they are found in the combined state only.
- They form oxides, hydrogen halides, interhalogen compounds and oxoacids.
- Acidic strength of Hydrogen halides: $HF < HCl < HBr < HI$.
- Most of the oxides formed by these halogens are unstable and their stability decreases in the order $I > Cl > Br$.
- Acidic strength of oxoacids containing different halogen:

$$HClO > HBrO > HIO$$

- Acidic strength of oxoacids containing the same halogen:

$$HClO < HClO_2 < HClO_3 < HClO_4$$

- Chlorine is conveniently obtained by the reaction of HCl with $KMnO_4$.

$$MnO_2\,4HCl \xrightarrow{\Delta} MnCl_2 + Cl_2 + 2H_2O$$

- **Properties of Chlorine:** Greenish yellow gas with a pungent suffocating smell, soluble in water.
- HCl is prepared by heating NaCl with concentrated H_2SO_4.

$$NaCl + 4H_2SO_4 \xrightarrow{420K} NaHSO_4 + HCl$$

- Halogens combines with one another to form a number of compounds known as interhalogen compounds. General formula are XX', XX_3', XX_5', XX_7' where X is a halogen of larger size and higher electro positivity and of smaller size. For example:

$$Cl_2 + F_2 \xrightarrow{470K} 2ClF$$

Group 18 Elements

- **Electronic configuration:** $ns^2\,np^6$.
- **Atomic and Ionic radii:** They have the largest radii in their respective periods and it increases down the group.

- **Ionization Enthalpy:** Decreases down the group and have highest ionization enthalpy in their respective periods.
- Low melting and boiling points because of weak van der Waal's forces. Increases down the group.
- Due to complete octet of outermost shell, they have less tendency to form compounds. The best characterised compounds are those of xenon with fluorine and oxygen only under certain conditions.
- These gases have several uses. Argon is used to provide inert atmosphere, helium is used in filling balloons for meteorological observations, neon is used in discharge tubes and fluorescent bulbs.

- Xenon forms three binary fluorides, XeF_2, XeF_4 and XeF_6 by following reactions.

$$Xe(g) + F_2(g) \xrightarrow{673K,\ 1bar} XeF_2(s)$$

$$Xe(g) + 2F_2(g) \xrightarrow{873K,\ 7bar} XeF_4(s)$$

$$Xe(g) + 2F_2(g) \xrightarrow{573K,\ 60\text{-}70bar} XeF_6(s)$$

- Xenon trioxide (XeO_3)

$$6XeF_4(g) + 12H_2O \rightarrow 2XeO_3 + 4Xe + 3O_2 + 24HF$$

- Xenon oxyfluorides

$$XeF_4 + H_2O \rightarrow XeOF_2 + 2HF$$

$$XeF_6 + H_2O \xrightarrow[hydrolysis]{partial} XeOF_4 + 2HF$$

$$XeF_6 + OH_2O \xrightarrow[hydrolysis]{complete} XeO_2F_4 + 4HF$$

EXERCISE

1. Metaphosphoric acid has formula
   - (a) H_3PO_4
   - (b) HPO_3
   - (c) H_2PO_3
   - (d) H_3PO_2

2. White phosphorus (P_4) has
   - (a) Six P-P single bonds.
   - (b) Four P-P single bonds
   - (c) PPP angle at 60°
   - (d) both (a) and (c)

3. On heating a mixture of NH_4Cl and KNO_2 we get
   - (a) NH_4NO_3
   - (b) N_2
   - (c) N_2O
   - (d) NO

4. Which of the following oxide of nitrogen is the anhydride of HNO_3.
   - (a) NO
   - (b) N_2O_3
   - (c) N_3O_4
   - (d) N_2O_5

5. Phosphorus is manufactured by heating in an electric furnace a mixture of
   - (a) Bone ash and Coke
   - (b) Boke ash and Silica
   - (c) Bone ash, silica and Coke
   - (d) None of these

6. Which of the following is not hydrolysed
   - (a) $AsCl_3$
   - (b) PF_3
   - (c) $SbCl_3$
   - (d) NF_3

7. Which one of the following elements occur free in nature
   - (a) Nitrogen
   - (b) Phosphorus
   - (c) Arsenic
   - (d) Antimony

8. The strongest base is
   - (a) NH_3
   - (b) PH_3
   - (c) AsH_3
   - (d) SbH_3

9. Industrial name for $H_2S_2O_7$ is
   - (a) Pyrosulphuric acid
   - (b) Marshall's acid
   - (c) Oleum
   - (d) All of these.

10. Oxygen molecule exhibits
    - (a) Paramagnetism
    - (b) Diamagnetism
    - (c) Ferromagnetism
    - (d) Ferrimagnetism

11. Copper turnings when heated with concentrate sulphuric acid will give.
    - (a) SO_2
    - (b) SO_3
    - (c) H_2S
    - (d) O_2

12. When SO_2 is passed through acidified $K_2Cr_2O_7$ solution
    - (a) The solution turns blue
    - (b) The solution is decolorised
    - (c) SO_2 is reduced
    - (d) Green $Cr_2(SO_4)_3$ is formed.

13. Which of the following mixture is chromic acid
    - (a) $K_2Cr_2O_7$ and Conc H_2SO_4
    - (b) $K_2Cr_2O_7$ and HCl
    - (c) K_2SO_4 and Conc H_2SO_4
    - (d) H_2SO_4 and HCl

14. Which of the following gas is used in artificial respiration
    - (a) $O_2 + CO_2$
    - (b) $O_2 + CO$
    - (c) $O_2 + H_2$
    - (d) All of these

15. Carbogen is
    (a) Pure form of carbon
    (b) $COCl_2$
    (c) Mixture of CO and CO_2
    (d) Mixture of O_2 and CO_2
16. Among KO_2, NO_2^-, BaO_2 and NO_2^+ unpaired electron is present in
    (a) NO_2^+ and BaO_2
    (b) KO_2 and BaO_2
    (c) KO_2 only
    (d) BaO_2 only
17. Which of the following has greatest reducing power.
    (a) HI
    (b) HBr
    (c) HCl
    (d) HF
18. Bad conductor of electricity is
    (a) H_2F_2
    (b) HCl
    (c) HBr
    (d) HI
19. Which one of the halogen acids is a liquid
    (a) HF
    (b) HCl
    (c) HBr
    (d) HI
20. Which of the following is the weakest acid
    (a) HF
    (b) HCl
    (c) HBr
    (d) HI
21. Chloride can be manufactured from
    (a) Electrolysis of NaCl
    (b) Electrolysis of brine
    (c) Electrolysis of bleaching powder
    (d) All of the above
22. Br^- is converted into Br_2 by using
    (a) Cl_2
    (b) Conc . HCl
    (c) HBr
    (d) H_2S
23. Hydrogen bonding does not play any role in boiling of
    (a) NH_3
    (b) H_2O
    (c) HI
    (d) C_2H_5OH

24. Argon is used in arc welding because of its
    (a) Low reactivity with metal
    (b) Ability to lower the melting point of metal
    (c) Flammability
    (d) High calorific value
25. Which of the following is monoatomic
    (a) Nitrogen
    (b) Fluorine
    (c) Neon
    (d) Oxygen
26. Among the fluorides below, the one which does not exist is
    (a) XeF_4
    (b) HeF_4
    (c) SF_4
    (d) CF_4
27. XeF_4 on Partial hydrolysis produces.
    (a) XeF_2
    (b) $XeOF_2$
    (c) $XeOF_4$
    (d) XeO_3
28. Which of the following electronic configuration represents noble gas.
    (a) ns^2, np^6
    (b) ns^2, np^5
    (c) ns^2, np^4
    (d) ns^2, np^3
29. Which one of the following noble gases is the least polarizable
    (a) Xe
    (b) Ar
    (c) Ne
    (d) He
30. Which one of the following noble gases is not found in the atmosphere.
    (a) Rn
    (b) Kr
    (c) Ne
    (d) Ar
31. Who among the following first prepared a stable compound of noble gas
    (a) Rutherford
    (b) Rayleigh
    (c) Ramsay
    (d) Neil Bartlett
32. Which of the following gas is/are called rare gas
    (a) Ne
    (b) He
    (c) Kr
    (d) All of these

Answer Keys

1. (b)	2. (d)	3. (b)	4. (d)	5. (c)	6. (d)	7. (a)	8. (a)	9. (c)	10. (a)
11. (a)	12. (d)	13. (a)	14. (a)	15. (d)	16. (c)	17. (a)	18. (a)	19. (a)	20. (a)
21. (a)	22. (a)	23. (c)	24. (a)	25. (c)	26. (b)	27. (b)	28. (a)	29. (d)	30. (a)
31. (d)	32. (d)								

Solutions

1. HPO_3, Metaphosphoric acid

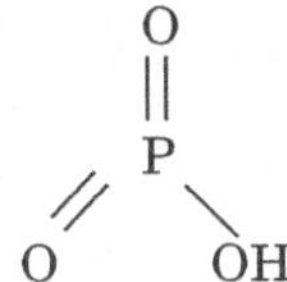

2. P_4 molecule

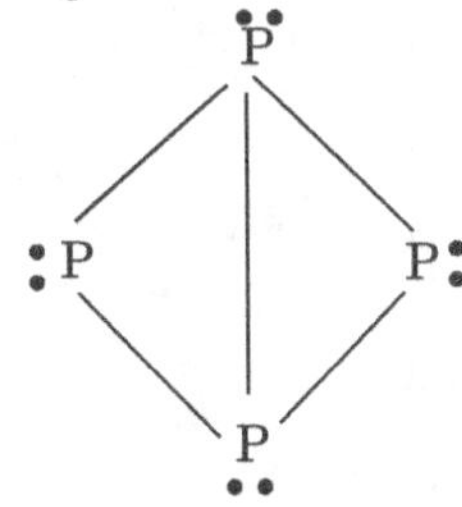

Bond angle = $60°$

Six P-P single bonds

Lone pairs = 4

3. $NH_4Cl + KNO_2 \rightarrow NH_4NO_2 + KCl$
$$\downarrow$$
$$N_2 + 2H_2O$$

4. $2HNO_3 \rightarrow N_2O_5 + H_2O$
Nitric acid

5. $2Ca_3(PO_4)_2 + 6\,SiO_2 \xrightarrow{1770K} 6CaSiO_3 + P_4O_{10}$

$P_4O_{10} + 10C \xrightarrow{1770K} P_4 + 10CO$

   White

6. Due to absence of d-orbitals in N-atom, it cannot accept electrons from H_2O for hydrolysis of NF_3

7. Atmospheric nitrogen is inert and unreactive because of very high bond energy (945/KJ/mole)

8. NH_3 is a strongest base because Lone pair is easily available for donation.

9. $H_2S_2O_7$ (Pyrosulpheric acid) is industrially known as oleum.

10. Paramagnetism because of two unpaired electrons in the antibonding molecular orbitals.

11. $Cu + 2H_2SO_4 \rightarrow CuSO_4 + 2H_2O + SO_2$

12. $K_2Cr_2O_7 + H_2SO_4 + 3SO_2 \rightarrow$
$K_2SO_4 + Cr_2(SO_4)_3 + 3H_2O$
       Green

13. Mixture of $K_2Cr_2O_7$ and Conc. H_2SO_4 is known as chromic acid.

14. Oxygen mixed with helium or carbon dioxide is used for artificial respiration

15. Mixture of O_2 and CO_2

16. KO_2 because in O_2^- (Superoxide ion)
One unpaired electron is present in the antibonding orbital.

17. HI is strongest reducing agent among halogen acids because of lowest bond dissociation energy.

18. Due to H-Bonding free ions are not present in aq. solution. Hence, bad conductor.

19. HF is liquid because of intermolecular H-Bonding

20. HF is the weakest acid, Since it is unable to give H^+ ions which are trapped in H-Bonding.

21. $2NaCl + 2H_2O \xrightarrow{\text{Electrolysis}} 2NaOH + Cl_2 + H_2$
            (aq)   (g)   (g)

22. $Cl_2 + 2\,Br^- \longrightarrow 2Cl^- + Br_2$

23. Hydrogen bonding is absent in HI while it is present in NH_3, H_2O and C_2H_5OH.

24. Argon is used for providing inert atmosphere in the welding of metals or alloys that are easily oxidized as it is very less reactive towards metals.

25. Neon → Ne is monoatomic and others are diatomic N_2, F_2 and O_2.

26. HeF_4 does not exist.

27. Partial hydrolysis,
$XeF_4 + H_2O \rightarrow XeOF_2 + 2HF$
Complete hydrolysis;
$2XeF_4 + 3H_2O \rightarrow Xe + XeO_3 + F_2 + 6HF$

28. Noble gases have fully filled valence shell electronic configuration. Therefore, it represents ns^2, np^6

29. He is least polarizable because of small atomic size

30. Rn, because it is radioactive element obtained by the disintegration of radium.
$$_{88}Ra^{206} \longrightarrow {}_{86}Ra^{202} + {}_{86}He^4$$

31. Neil Bartlett prepared first noble gas compound. Xenon hexafluoroplatinate (IV)

32. He, Ne and Kr all are found in very little amount in atmosphere, so all are called rare gas.

d- and f-Block Elements

d-block elements

- The elements of group 3-12 which have incompletely filled d-orbitals in the ground state are called d- block elements.
- They are also called transitional elements as their properties are in between those of s and p block elements.
- The electronic configuration is given as $(n-1)d^{1-10}ns^{1-2}$.

General properties

- Physical Properties
  - ➤ They are all metals, malleable and ductile(except Hg)
  - ➤ They display high tensile strength, high thermal and electrical conductivity
- Variation in atomic and ionic sizes
  - ➤ With increasing atomic number, ions of the same charge in given series experience decrease in radius as when a new electron enters a d orbital, the nuclear charge increases by unity.
  - ➤ $4f$ orbitals must be filled before $5d$ orbitals which leads to a regular decrease in atomic radii known as Lanthanoid contraction which is responsible for increasing atomic sizes with increasing atomic number.

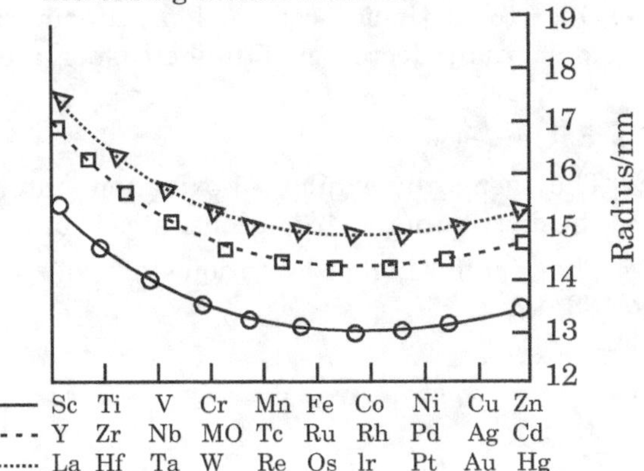

- **Ionisation Enthalpy**

  The ionization enthalpy in a group decreases from $3d$ to $4d$ series and increases from $4d$ to $5d$ series because of Lanthanoid contraction.

- **Oxidation states**
  - ➤ Transition elements show a great variety of oxidation states in their compounds due to incomplete filling of d-orbitals.
  - ➤ Elements in the middle of the group have the maximum number of oxidation states, example: Manganese exhibits oxidation states from +2 to +7.

- **Trends in $\dfrac{M^{2+}}{M}$ electrode potential**

  No regular trend is shown in $E°$ values as ionization and sublimation enthalpy have no regular trend.

- **Magnetic Properties**
  - ➤ The two types of elements are diamagnetic and paramagnetic.
  - ➤ Diamagnetic substances have paired electrons only like Zn whereas paramagnetic substances have atleast one unpaired electron

- **Colored compound formation**

  The transition elements form colored ions as they have unpaired d-electrons.

  When light is absorbed in the visible region, it causes excitation of unpaired d-electrons which causes formation of colored compounds.

- **Alloy Formation**
  - ➤ d- block elements form alloy due to:

    Availability of d-orbitals for bond formation

    High ionic charges

    Similar sizes of the metal ions
  - ➤ Some of the alloys are Steel and Brass.

- **Chemical Reactivity**
  - ➢ Transition metals differ in chemical reactivity.
  - ➢ Many of them are sufficiently electropositive to dissolve in mineral acids while few of them stay unaffected by simple acids.
- **Catalytic Properties**
  - ➢ Many of the transition metals and their compounds acts as catalyst, especially oxides.
  - ➢ Some of the commonly used catalysts are Iron, Nickel, Cobalt, Platinum and their compounds.
- **Interstitial Compound Formation**
  - ➢ These are the compounds formed when small atoms ($H, C,$ and N) get trapped inside the crystal lattices of metals. Example: TiC, Fe_3H, Mn_4N.
  - ➢ They are chemically inert, have a good metallic conductivity and are extremely hard.

Compounds of Transition Elements

- **Potassium dichromate ($K_2Cr_2O_7$)**
  - ➢ It is a crystalline solid orange in color.
  - ➢ It is prepared from the chromate ore using the following reactions:
    $$4FeCr_2O_4 + 8Na_2CO_3 + 7O_2 \rightarrow 8Na_2CrO_4 + 2Fe_2O_3 + 8CO_2$$
    The sodium chromate solution is acidified with sulphuric acid
    $$2Na_2CrO_4 + 2H^+ \rightarrow Na_2Cr_2O_7 + 2Na^+ + H_2O$$
    The solution is treated with potassium chloride.
    $$Na_2Cr_2O_7 + 2KCl \rightarrow K_2Cr_2O_7 + 2NaCl$$
  - ➢ It is used in preparation of azo compounds and in leather industry.
- **Potassium Permanganate ($KMnO_4$)**
  - ➢ It is a crystalline solid dark purple in color.
  - ➢ It is prepared commercially as
    $$MnO_2 + 2e^- \xrightarrow[\text{Oxidised with air}]{\text{Fused with KOH}} MnO_4^{2-}$$
    $$MnO_4^{2-} \xrightarrow[\text{in alkaline solution}]{\text{Electrolytic oxidation}} MnO_4^- + e^-$$
  - ➢ It is used in titration, bleaching of silk and in organic synthesis.
- The f block elements comprises of two series of elements called Lanthanoids and Actinoids.
- The general electronic configuration for f block elements is $(n-2)f^{1-14}(n-1)d^{0-1}ns^2$.
  $$\begin{cases} n=6 & \text{for Lanthanoid} \\ n=7 & \text{for} \quad \text{Actinoid} \end{cases}$$

Lanthanoids

- **General Properties**
  - ➢ They are soft metals silvery white in color.
  - ➢ They are good conductors of electricity.
- **Atomic and ionic sizes**

  There is an overall decrease in atomic and ionic radii from Lanthanium to Lutelium (with increasing atomic number) due to Lanthanoid Contraction.

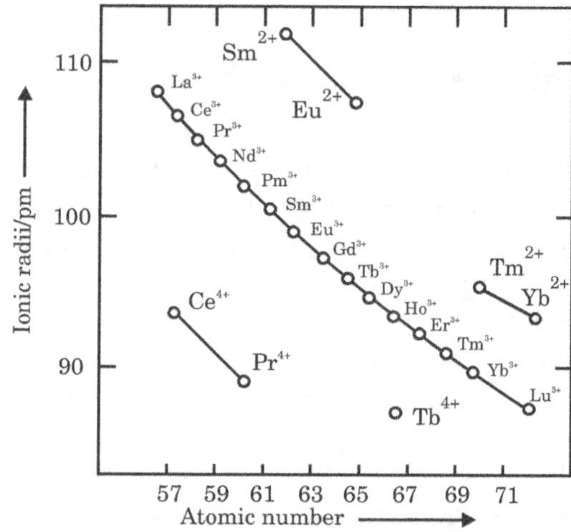

- **Oxidation States**

  Some of the elements exhibit +2 and +4 oxidation states but mainly they show +3 oxidation state.

Actinoids

- **General Properties**
  - ➢ Actinoids are radioactive elements.
  - ➢ They have high melting point and are highly electropositive.
- **Atomic and ionic radii**
  - ➢ With increasing atomic number, the electrons are added to the 5f shell resulting in increase in nuclear charge causing the shell to shrink which is known as actinoid contraction.
  - ➢ Due to actinoid contraction, atomic and ionic radii decrease with increasing atomic number
- **Oxidation States**
  - ➢ They generally exhibit +3 oxidation state but the distribution in oxidation states is uneven.
  - ➢ They exhibit higher oxidation states of +4, +5, +6, +7.

Comparison of Lanthanoids with Actinoids

Lanthanoids	Actinoids
They are less reactive than actinoids.	They are highly reactive metals.
$4f$ orbital is progressively filled.	$5f$ orbital is progressively filled.
They show limited oxidation state +2, +3, +4	A variety of oxidation states is shown. +3, +4, +5, +6, +7
They are non-radioactive except promethium.	They are radioactive elements.

Applications of a and f block elements

- Plutonium is used in atomic reactors and in atomic bombs.
- Oxides of lanthanoids are used as abrasives in cleaning of glass
- Iron is extensively used as a building material.
- d and f block elements are used as catalysts in various reactions.
- MnO_2 is used in dry battery cells.

EXERCISE

1. The number of unpaired electrons in Cr^+ will.
   - (a) 3
   - (b) 4
   - (c) 5
   - (d) 6

2. Which of the following has highest ionic radii
   - (a) Cr^{+3}
   - (b) Mn^{+3}
   - (c) Fe^{+3}
   - (d) Co^{+3}

3. Which forms coloured salts
   - (a) Metals
   - (b) Non-metals
   - (c) P-Block elements
   - (d) Transitional elements

4. The coinage metals are
   - (a) Iron, Cobalt, Nickel
   - (b) Copper and Zinc
   - (c) Copper, Silver and Gold
   - (d) Gold and platinum

5. Which of the following transition metal is present in misch metal
   - (a) La
   - (b) Sc
   - (c) Ni
   - (d) Cr

6. Which of the following has the maximum number of unpaired d-electrons.
   - (a) Zn
   - (b) Fe^{2+}
   - (c) Ni^{3+}
   - (d) Cu^+

7. In the first transition series, the highest B.P. and M.P. is of
   - (a) Cr
   - (b) V
   - (c) Ni
   - (d) Fe

8. Which of the following has second ionisation potential less than expected.
   - (a) Cr
   - (b) Zn
   - (c) V
   - (d) Mo

9. The metal used to recover copper from a solution of $CuSO_4$ is
   - (a) Fe
   - (b) He
   - (c) Na
   - (d) Ag

10. Transition metals are related to which block
    - (a) s-block
    - (b) p-block
    - (c) d-block
    - (d) None of these

11. Which of the following elements is alloyed with copper to form brass.
    - (a) Lead
    - (b) Silver
    - (c) Zinc
    - (d) Antimony

12. Which of the following element has maximum first ionisation potential.
    - (a) V
    - (b) Ti
    - (c) Cr
    - (d) Mn

13. In acidic medium one mole of MnO_4^- accepts how many moles of electrons in a redox process
    - (a) 1
    - (b) 3
    - (c) 5
    - (d) 6

14. A white powder soluble in NH_4OH but insoluble in water in
    - (a) $BaSO_4$
    - (b) $CuSO_4$
    - (c) $PbSO_4$
    - (d) $AgCl$

15. Which oxide of manganese is amphoteric
    - (a) MnO_2
    - (b) Mn_2O_3
    - (c) Mn_2O_7
    - (d) MnO

16. The equivalent weight of potassium permanganate for acid solution is
    - (a) 158
    - (b) 31.6
    - (c) 52.16
    - (d) 79

17. The equivalent weight of $K_2Cr_2O_7$ in acidic medium
(*a*) 294 (*b*) 298
(*c*) 49 (*d*) 50

18. Which of the following will show increase in weight when kept in magnetic field
(*a*) TiO_2 (*b*) $Fe_2(SO_4)_3$
(*c*) $KMnO_4$ (*d*) $SeCl_3$

19. Silver nitrate is supplied in coloured bottles because it is
(*a*) Oxidised in air
(*b*) Decomposes in sunlight
(*c*) Explosive in sunlight
(*d*) Reactive towards air in sunlight

20. Which of the following compounds volatilises on heating
(*a*) $MgCl_2$ (*b*) $HgCl_2$
(*c*) $CaCl_2$ (*d*) $FeCl_3$

Answer Keys

1. (*c*)	2. (*a*)	3. (*d*)	4. (*c*)	5. (*a*)	6. (*b*)	7. (*a*)	8. (*b*)	9. (*a*)	10. (*c*)
11. (*c*)	12. (*d*)	13. (*c*)	14. (*d*)	15. (*a*)	16. (*b*)	17. (*c*)	18. (*b*)	19. (*b*)	20. (*b*)

Solutions

1.

	$3d^5$					$4s'$
Cr	1	1	1	1	1	1
Cr^+	1	1	1	1	1	

Hence, the number of unpaired electron in Cr^+ is 5.

2. Ionic radii $\propto \frac{1}{\text{Atomic no.}}$

$\therefore$ Ionic radius decreases from left to right in a period

3. Transitional elements from coloured salts due to the presence of unpaired electrons in d-orbital.

4. Copper, silver and gold; all the three were used for making coins.

5. Misch metal is an alloy of rare earth metals with composition.

Rare earth metals	– 94.95%
Iron (Fe)	– 5%
S, C, Ca, Al,....	– Traces

6. $Fe^{+2} - 3d^6\,4s^0$ – 4 unpaired e^-

7. Cr has highest M.P and B.P due to maximum no. of unpaired electrons.

8. Zn due to increased shielding effect the attraction of electrons towards nucleus decreases.

9. From a solution of $CuSO_4$, Cu can be recovered by Fe metal. Because Fe is more reactive then Cu, it replace Cu easily.

10. d-block elements are known as transition elements. These show variable valency due to their incomplete d-subshell.

11. 70% Cu and 30% Zn are mixed to form brass which is used in making utensils, artificial jewellary.

12. The first ionization energies of Ti, V, Cr and Mn are 656, 650, 652 and 717 KJ/mole respectively. I.E. increase in a period from L $\rightarrow$ R hence, manganese has maximum first ionisation potential.

13. Oxidation state of Mn Changes from +7 to +2 in acidic medium i.e. one mole of it accepts 5 mole of electrons.

14. AgCl is a covalent compound hence it is insoluble in water also it form complex with NH_4OH. thus is soluble in NH_4OH.

$AgCl + 2NH_4OH \rightarrow [Ag(NH_3)_2]Cl + H_2O$

15. MnO_2 forms amphoteric oxide due to intermediate oxidation state.

16. Equivalent weight of $KMnO_4$ in acidic medium is M/5

$\therefore$ Equivalent weight $= \frac{158}{5} = 31.6$

17. $K_2Cr_2O_7 + 3H_2SO_4 \rightarrow K_2SO_4 + Cr_2(SO_4)_3 + 3(O) + 3H_2$

No. of electrons lossed = 12 – 6 = 6

$\therefore$ Equivalent weight $\frac{M}{6} = \frac{294}{6} = 49$

18. $Fe^{+3} - 3d^5$ – 5 electrons unpaired

Fe will be attracted in magnetic field so will show increase in weight.

19. Decomposes in sunlight

$2AgNO_3 \xrightarrow{\Delta} 2Ag + 2NO_2 + O_2$

20. $HgCl_2$ compound is easily volatile. They are insoluble in water and soluble in acids.

CHAPTER 9

Coordination Compounds

- Coordination compounds are formed when metal atoms bound with anions or neutral molecules to form a compound. For example: $\left[Co(NH_3)_6\right]^{3+}$, $\left[Ni(CO)_4\right]$, $\left[CoCl_2(NH_3)_4\right]^+$, etc.

- **Double Salt:** It differs from coordination compound in such a way that they dissociate into constituent ions when dissolved in water while coordination compounds will not break into its respective ions. Some examples of double salt are Mohr's salt ($FeSO_4$. $(NH_4)_2SO_4.6H_2O$), Potash alum $KAl\ (SO_4)_2.12H_2O$, etc.

- **Coordination entity:** A central metal ion or atom bonded to a fixed number of ions or molecules forms a coordination entity. For example: $[Co(NH_3)_6]^{3+}$ is a coordination entity where a cobalt ion is surrounded by six ammonia molecules.

  - Here cobalt ion is the central ion.
  - The ammonia molecules arranged in a pattern around the central ion are called ligands.
  - When ligand is bound to metal atom/ ion by single donor atom then it is unidentate ligand as in this example ammonia is unidentate.
  - When a ligand is bound to two donor atoms, it is didentate ligand. For example: $C_2O_4^{2-}$ or $H_2NCH_2CH_2NH_2$
  - When several donor atoms are present in a single ligand, it is a polydentate ligand. For example: Ethylenediaminetetraacetate ion which contains several donor atoms.

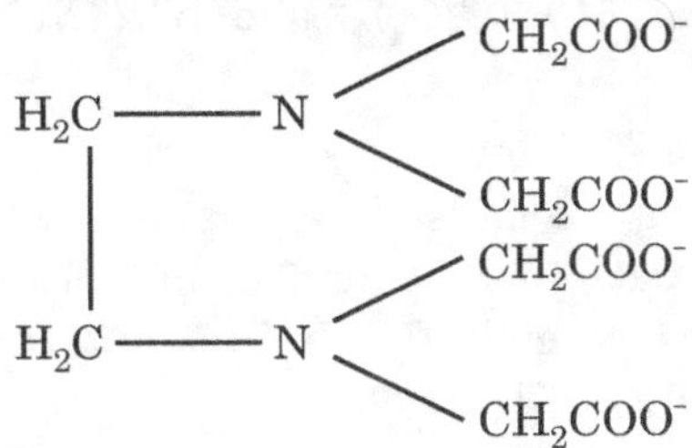

- **Denticity** is the number of ligating groups in a ligand.

- When two or more donor atoms are used by ligands to bind a metal ion, it is called a **chelate ligand**. For example:

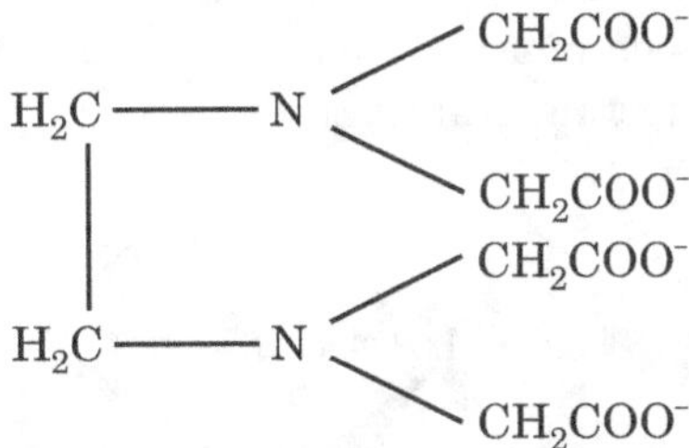

- Ligands which can ligate through two different atoms are called **ambidentate ligands**. Some examples are: SCN^- which can coordinate through sulphur or nitrogen atom. NO_2^- can coordinate through nitrogen or oxygen.

  $\text{M} \longleftarrow \text{SCN}$ $\text{M} \longleftarrow \text{NCS}$

  thiocyanato   isothiocyanato

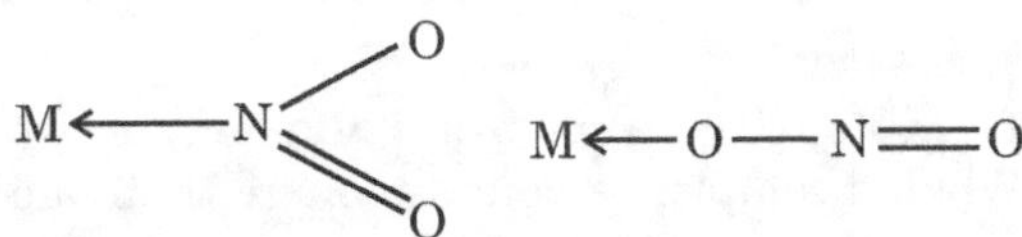

- Ligands can also be classified on the basis of charge. It is of three types:

  Cationic ligands: The ligands which carry positive charge are cationic ligands. For example:

  $N_2H_5^+$, NO_2^+

  Anionic ligands: The ligands which carry negative charge are anionic ligands. For example: OH^-, CN^-, etc.

  Neutral ligands: Ligands which do not carry any charge are neutral ligands. For example: NH_3, N_2, NO, etc.

- **Coordination sphere:** It is a collective term for central atom/ion and ligands written together in square brackets. For example: $[Co\ (NH_3)_6]^{3+}$, $K_4[Fe\ (CN)_6]$ (here $[Fe\ (CN)_6]^{4-}$ is a coordination sphere while K^+ is a counter ion).

- **Coordination number:** Metal atom/ion is bonded to some ligand donor atoms. The number of donor atoms linked to the metal gives the coordination number. For example, in the compound $[Co\ (NH_3)_6]^{3+}$, coordination number of Co is 6 and in the compound $[Co\ (en)_3]^{3+}$, coordination number is 6 because *en* (ethane-1, 2-diamine) is a didentate ligand.

- **Coordination Polyhedron:** The ligand atoms are arranged around the central atom in a definite pattern which forms a coordination polyhedron. Some of the common examples are: square planar, octahedral, tetrahedral, etc.

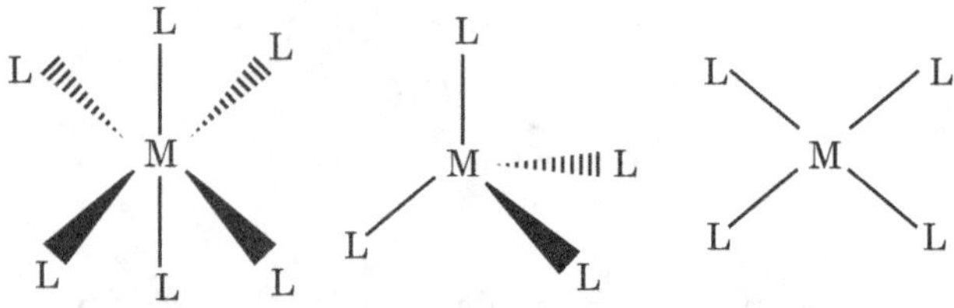

<table>
<tr><td>Octahedral</td><td>Tetrahedral</td><td>Square planar</td></tr>
</table>

- **Oxidation number of central atom:** The charge on the central atom when all the ligands are removed along with the elctron pairs shared with it gives the oxidation number of central atom. For example: oxidation number of copper in $[Cu\ (CN)_4]^{3+}$ is 1 and it is written in Roman numeral as $Cu\ (I)$.

- **Homoleptic and heteroleptic complexes:** When a complex is bound to more than one donor groups, it is a heteroleptic complex. For example: $[Co\ (NH_3)_6]Cl_3$

  When the metal in a complex is bound to just one type of donor atom, it is a homoleptic complex. For example: $[Cu\ (CN)_4]^{3+}$

- **Nomenclature of Coordination Compounds:** It is based on the recommendations of the International Union of Pure and Applied Chemistry (IUPAC). There are some rules for naming coordination compounds which are as follows:

  - Cation is named first while naming any coordination entity.

  - Ligands are written before the central atom/ion in alphabetical order.

  - Anioinc ligands are written with –o at the end. There are some terms for some specific molecules written in (). aqua is used for H_2O, ammine for NH_3, nitrosyl for NO and carbonyl for CO.

  - Number of individual ligands in the coordination entity are represented by some prefixes like mono, di, tri, etc.

  - Oxidation number of the central atom/ion is written in Roman numerals inside parentheses.

  - Cations are named same as the element in complex ion while anions end with –ate.

    For example: Co is written as cobalt if it acts as cation and cobaltate if it is present as anion.

- **Isomerism:** The phenomenon of compounds which have same molecular formula but different structural formulae which are isomers is known as isomerism. For example: C_2H_6O can be written as C_2H_6OH and CH_3OCH_3.

- **Types of isomerism:** Isomerism can either be structural or stereo.

  - **Structural Isomerism:** It can be divided into four types:

    Ionisation isomerism: When isomers have same molecular formula but different ions in solution, it is called ionisation isomerism. For example: $[Co\ (NH_3)_5SO_4]Br$ and $[Co\ (NH_3)_5Br]SO_4$.

    Linkage isomerism: It arises in compounds which contain ambidentate ligand. For example: $[Co\ (NH_3)_5\ (NO_2)]Cl_2$ where nitrile ligand is bound through oxygen to give red color and nitrile ligand is bound through nitrogen to give yellow color.

    Coordination isomerism: Ligands interchange between cationic and anionic entities of different metal ions in a complex. Such isomerism is a type of coordination isomerism. For example: $[Co\ (NH_3)_6][Cr\ (C_2O_4)_3]$ and $[Cr\ (NH_3)_6][Co\ (C_2O_4)_3]$

    Hydration isomerism: In this type of isomerism, isomers have same molecular formula but different number of molecules of water. For example: $[Cr\ (H_2O)_5Cl]\ Cl.\ H_2O$ and $[Cr\ (H_2O)_4Cl_2]Cl.\ 2H_2O$

- ➢ **Stereo Isomerism:** It can be of two types:

  Geometrical isomerism (cis-trans isomerism): For a tetra co-ordinated square planar complex, trans-isomer has same groups on opposite sides while cis-isomer has same group on same sides. For example: cis and trans isomer of $[Co(NH_3)_4Cl_2]^+$

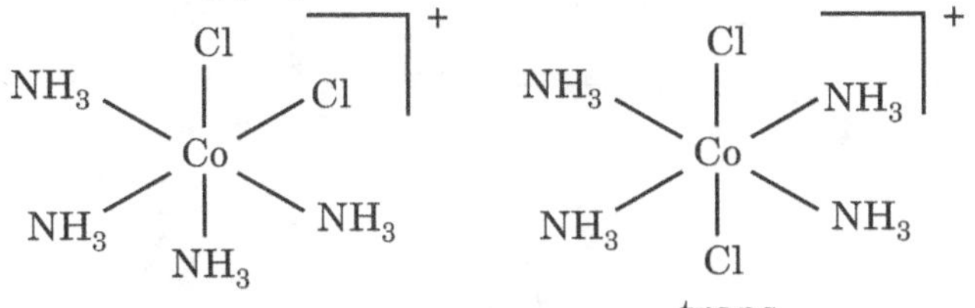

  cis

  trans

  Optical isomerism: Optical isomers also called enantiomers are mirror images which cannot be superimposed on one another. The molecules or ions involved in this isomerism are called chiral. Depending on the direction of rotation of plane polarised light in a polarimeter, there are two forms dextro (d) and laevo (l).

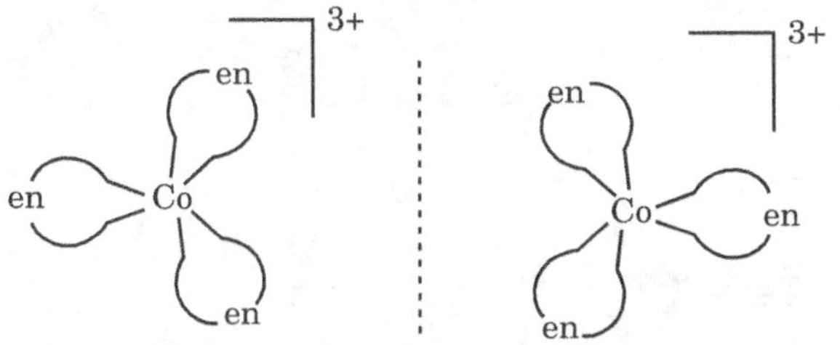

  dextro   mirror   laevo

  Optical isomers of $[Co(en)_3]^{3+}$

- Bonding in coordination compounds can be explained by different theories like Valence Bond Theory (VBT), Werner's Theory, Crystal Field Theory (CFT), Ligand Field Theory (LFT), and Molecular Orbit Theory (MOT).

- **Werner's Theory of Coordination Compounds:**

  This theory explained the nature of bonding in complex compounds. Primary and Secondary valency are the different kinds of valencies shown by metals.

  - ➢ Primary valency is equal to the oxidation state of the metal which is satisfied by anions.

  - ➢ Secondary valencies are similar to coordination number which is satisfied by opposite charged ions, neutral molecules or cations.

- **Limitations of Werner's theory:**

  - ➢ It does not explain the reason of only some elements forming complexes.

  - ➢ It does not explain the magnetic nature of complexes.

  - ➢ It does not explain the directional nature of coordination complexes.

- **Valence Bond Theory:**

  - ➢ A suitable number of vacant orbitals must be present for the formation of coordinate bond in the central metal atom/ion.

  - ➢ s, p or d-orbitals are appropriately used for hybridization by central metal ion depending on the number of ligands.

  - ➢ The ligands which donate electron pair overlap with the hybridized orbitals.

  - ➢ Outer or inner orbital complexes are formed on the basis of outer or inner d-orbitals used.

- **Limitations of Valence Bond Theory:**

  - ➢ Detailed magnetic properties of complex compounds are not explained.

  - ➢ Optical absorption spectra of coordination compounds are not explained by this theory.

  - ➢ It does not differentiate between strong and weak ligands.

  - ➢ Thermodynamic or kinetic stabilities of coordination compounds is not explained by this theory.

  - ➢ Geometry of 4 coordinate complex (square planar or tetrahedral) is not predicted.

- **Crystal Field Theory:**

  - ➢ Ligands are point charges according to this theory.

  - ➢ d-orbitals of metal ion split on approaching ligands.

  - ➢ In tetrahedral complexes, t_{2g} orbitals have high energy.

  - ➢ Splitting of d-orbitals is large when ligands produce strong fields and splitting is small when ligands produce weak fields.

  - ➢ Ligands are arranged according to increasing field strength as follows:

    $$I^- < Br^- < SCN^- < Cl^- < S^{2-} < F^- < OH^- < C_2O_4^{2-} < H_2O < NCS^- < EDTA^{4-} < NH_3 < en < CN^- < CO$$

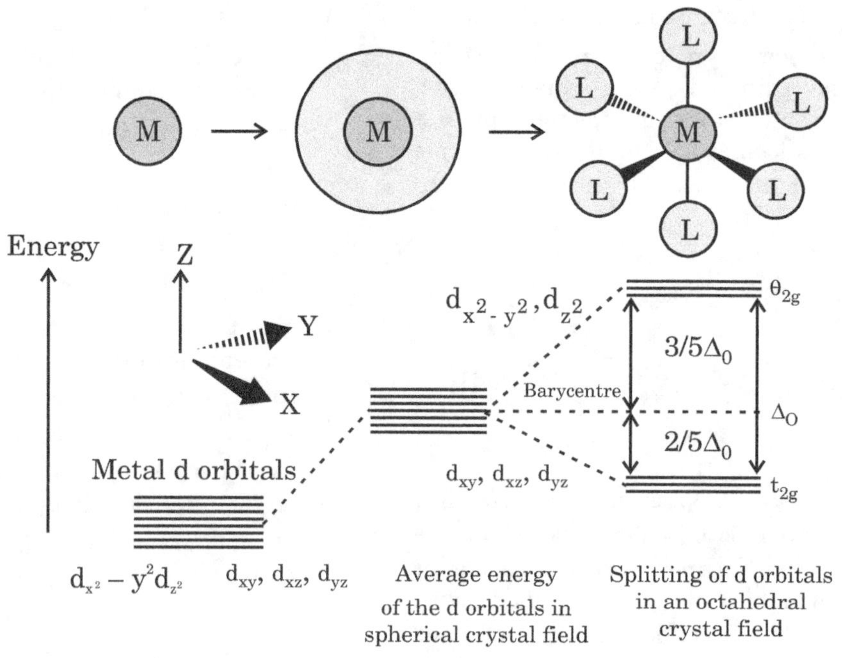

Splitting octahedral crystal field

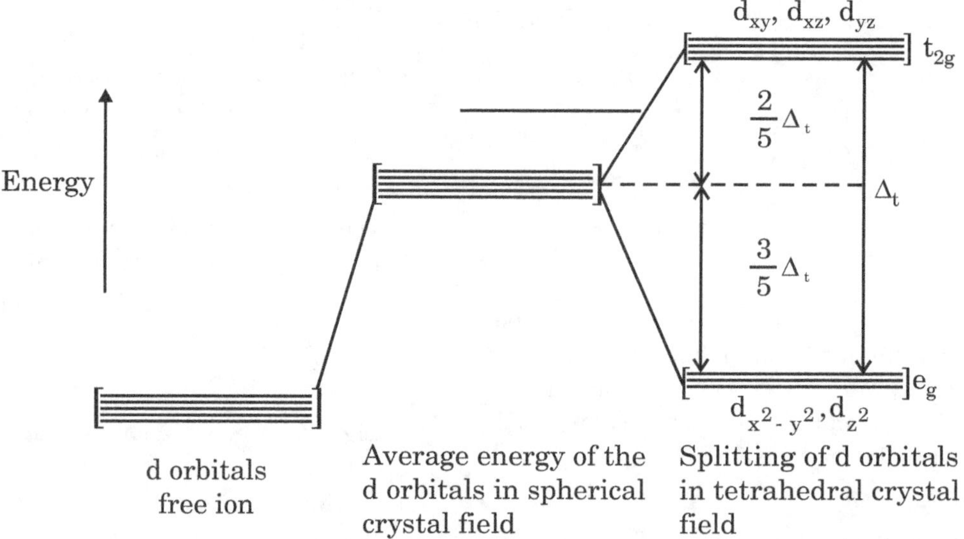

> There is high energy of e_g orbitals in octahedral and lower energy in tetrahedral complexes.

- **Limitations of crystal field theory:**
  - It does not consider the covalent bonding between ligand and central atom.
  - According to this theory anionic ligands exert greatest splitting effect but actually the splitting is small.
- Bonding in metal carbonyls: Homoleptic carbonyls are formed by transition metals. Some examples are pentacarbonyliron (0) is trigonalbipyramidal, tetracarbonylnickel (0) is tetrahedral and hexacarbonyl chromium (0) is octahedral.

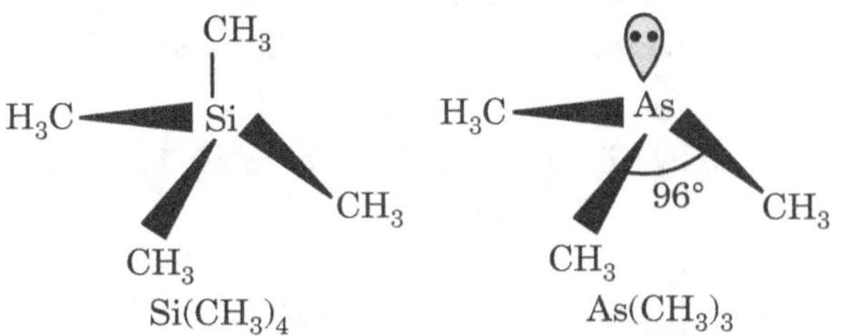

$Ni(CO)_4$
Tetrahedral

$Fe(CO)_5$
Trigonal bipyramidal

$Cr(CO)_6$
Octahedral

- Metal-carbon bond possess both s and p character. There is a synergic effect between the metal and ligand bond which strengthens the bond.

- **Stability of Coordination compounds:** The degree of association between two species gives the stability of complex in solution. Stability is expressed by magnitude of equilibrium constant. Larger the stability constant/ association constant, higher the proportion of the product in solution.

Consider a reaction: $A + 4B \rightleftharpoons AB_4$

Here A is surrounded by solvent molecules, B and the reaction goes in the following order using stability constants:

$$A + B \rightleftharpoons AB \qquad K_1 = \frac{[AB]}{[A][B]}$$

$$AB + B \rightleftharpoons AB_2 \qquad K_2 = \frac{[AB_2]}{[AB][B]}$$

$$AB_2 + B \rightleftharpoons AB_3 \qquad K_3 = \frac{[AB_3]}{[AB_2][B]}$$

$$AB_3 + B \rightleftharpoons AB_4 \qquad K_4 = \frac{[AB_4]}{[AB_3][B]}$$

Here $K_1, K_2, \ldots$ are stepwise stability constants.

$$\beta_4 = \frac{[AB_4]}{[A][B]^4} \text{ , } \beta_4 \text{ is overall stability constant}$$

$$\beta_4 = K_1 \times K_2 \times K_3 \times K_4$$

Dissociation constant or instability constant is the reciprocal of association/ stability constant.

- **Classification of organometallic compounds:** These are divided into two groups as main group organometallics and d- and f- block organometallics.

  - **Main Group organometallics:** These are s- and p- block organometallics. Here are some examples with diagram: Tetramethyl silane, trimethyl arsene, etc.

  - *d*- and *f*- block organometallics: The elements of d- and f- block form these kind of organometallics. Some examples are: Pentamethyl cyclopentadienyl ligand (C_5Me_5) forms f- block compounds, $[PtCl_3 (C_2H_4)^-]$, $(C5H_5)_2Fe$, etc.

- **Applications of complex compounds:**

  - These compounds are used in qualitative and quantitative analysis.

  - Stability constants of calcium and magnesium complexes are different which can be used for selective estimation of calcium and magnesium ions.

  - Purification of metals is carried out by formation and decomposition of coordination compounds.

  - Extraction processes are carried out using complex formation.

  - These compounds are used as catalysts. For example, Wilkinson catalyst (rhodium complex) is used for hydrogenation of alkenes.

  - Medicinal chemistry make use of chelate therapy.

EXERCISE

1. The Coordination number of copper in cuprammonium sulphate is
   - (a) 2
   - (b) 6
   - (c) 4
   - (d) -4

2. Which of the following acts as a bidentate ligand in complex formation
   - (a) Acetate
   - (b) Oxalate
   - (c) Thiocyanate
   - (d) EDTA

3. The coordination number of cobalt in the complex $[Co(en)_2Br_2]Cl_2$ is
   - (a) 2
   - (b) 6
   - (c) 5
   - (d) 4

4. Which of the following ligands forms a chelate
   - (a) Acetate
   - (b) Oxalate
   - (c) Cyanide
   - (d) Ammonia

5. $[Pt(NH_3)_6]Cl_4$ complex gives.
   - (a) 4 ions
   - (b) 3 ions
   - (c) 2 ions
   - (d) 5 ions

6. The coordination number of a metal in coordination compounds is
   - (a) Same as primary valency
   - (b) Sum of primary and secondary valencies
   - (c) Same as secondary valency
   - (d) None of these

7. Which of the following complexes show six coordination number
   - (a) $[Zn(CN)_4]^{2-}$
   - (b) $[Cr(H_2O)_6]^{3+}$
   - (c) $[Cu(CN)_4]^{2-}$
   - (d) $[Ni(NH_3)_4]^{2+}$

8. The number of ions formed when cuprammonium sulphate is dissolved in water is
   - (a) 1
   - (b) 2
   - (c) 4
   - (d) Zero

9. The coordination number of Cu in complex $[Cu(H_2O)_4]^{++}$ is
   - (a) 4
   - (b) 3
   - (c) 2
   - (d) 1

10. The primary valency of metal ion in the coordination compound $K_2[Ni(CN)_4]$ is
    - (a) Four
    - (b) Zero
    - (c) Two
    - (d) Six

11. In $K_4[Fe(CN)_6]$, the E.A.N. of Fe is
    - (a) 33
    - (b) 35
    - (c) 36
    - (d) 26

12. The oxidation number of chromium in sodium tetrafluora oxochromate complex is
    - (a) II
    - (b) IV
    - (c) VI
    - (d) III

13. The oxidation number of Cr in $[Cr(NH_3)_6]Cl_3$ is
    - (a) 8
    - (b) 6
    - (c) 4
    - (d) 3

14. In $[Ni(NH_3)_4]SO_4$, the E.A.N. of Ni is
    - (a) 34
    - (b) 35
    - (c) 36
    - (d) 37

15. The oxidation state of cobalt in the complex compound $[Co(NH_3)_6]Cl_3$ is
    - (a) $+3$
    - (b) $+6$
    - (c) $+5$
    - (d) $+2$

16. The EAN of iron in potassium ferricyanide is
    - (a) 18
    - (b) 54
    - (c) 35
    - (d) 23

17. In the coordination compound, $K_4[Ni(CN)_4]$ oxidation state of nickel is
    - (a) -1
    - (b) 0
    - (c) $+1$
    - (d) $+2$

18. Which one of the following octahedral complexes will not show geometric (A and B are monodentate ligands)
    - (a) $[MA_5B]$
    - (b) $[MA_2B_4]$
    - (c) $[MA_3B_3]$
    - (d) $[MA_4B_2]$

19. The number of unpaired electrons in the complex ion $[CoF_6]^{3-}$ is (Atomic no. of Co = 27)
    - (a) Zero
    - (b) 2
    - (c) 3
    - (d) 4

20. Coordination isomerism is caused by the interchange of ligands between the
    - (a) Cis and Trans structure
    - (b) Complex cation and complex anion
    - (c) Inner sphere and outer sphere
    - (d) Low oxidation and higher oxidation states.

Answer Keys

1. (c)	2. (b)	3. (b)	4. (b)	5. (d)	6. (b)	7. (b)	8. (a)	9. (c)	10. (c)
11. (d)	12. (a)	13. (a)	14. (c)	15. (a)	16. (c)	17. (b)	18. (a)	19. (d)	20. (b)

Solutions

1. In Cuprammonium sulphate $[Cu(NH_3)]_4SO_4$ Coordination number of Cu is 4.

2. As it makes use of its two atoms to form coordinate covalent bonds with the central metal ion.

3. $[CO(en)_2 Br_2]Cl_2$
   C.N. of Co = 2 × number of bidentate ligand + 1 × number of monodentate ligand
   $= 2 \times 2 + 1 \times 2 = 4 + 2 = 6$

4. **Chelating ligand:** When a multidentate ligand simultaneously coordinates to a metal ion by more than one donor site. Then a ring like structure is formed. it is called chelation and in this question only oxalate is bidentate all others are unidentate.

5. $[Pt(NH_3)_6]Cl_4$ complex gives 5 ions in the solution
   $$\left[Pt(NH_3)_6\right]Cl_4 \rightleftharpoons \left[Pt(NH_3)_6\right]^{4+} + 4Cl^-$$

6. According to modern view primary valency of complex compound is its oxidation number while secondary valency is the coordination number.

7. Coordination number is equal to total number of ligands in a complex.

8. Cuprammonium salt $[Cu(NH_3)_4]SO_4$
   $$\left[Cu(NH_3)_4\right]SO_4 \rightleftharpoons \left[Cu(NH_3)_4\right]^{2+} + SO_4^{2-}$$
   So, it will give two ions in water.

9. The coordination no. = no. of ligands attached.

10. Primary valencies are also known as oxidation state.
    $K_2[Ni(CN)_4]$, $2 + x - 4 = 0$
    $\Rightarrow x = +2$

11. EAN = Atomic number-Oxidationstate + 2 × no. of Ligands
    $= 26 - 2 + 2 \times 6 = 24 + 12 = 36$

12. $Na_2[CrF_4O]$
    $\Rightarrow x + 4 \times (-1) + (-2) = -2$
    $\Rightarrow x - 6 = -2 \Rightarrow x = -2 + 6 = +4$

13. $x + 6 \times 0 + 3 \times -1 = 0$
    $x - 3 = 0 \Rightarrow x = +3$
    Hence, Oxidation number of Cr is +3.

14. EAN = (atomic no) – (oxidation state) + 2 × no. of Ligands
    $= 28 - 2 + 2 \times 4 = 26 + 8 = 34$

15. $[Co(NH_3)_6]Cl_3 \rightarrow [Co(NH_3)_6]^{3+} + 3Cl^-$
    $x + 6(0) = +3 \Rightarrow x = +3$

16. EAN of a central metal ion = (atomic no. of central atom) – oxidation state + no. of ligands × 2
    $= 26 - 3 + (6 \times 2) = 23 + 12 = 35$

17. $+1 \times 4 + x - 1 \times 4 = 0$
    $4 + x - 4 = 0 \Rightarrow x = 0$ for Ni

18. Octahedral complexes of the type $[MA_4B_2]$, $[MA_2B_4]$, $[MA_3B_3]$ exhibit geometrical isomerism.

19. The number of unpaired electrons in the complex ion $[CoF_6]^{3-}$ is 4.

20. Coordination isomerism is caused by the interchanged of ligands between cation and anion complexes.

CHAPTER 10

Haloalkanes and Haloarenes

Introduction, Nomenclature and Preparation of Haloalkanes and Haloarenes

Haloalkanes are hydrogen atoms in aliphatic hydrocarbons replaced by halogens, whereas Haloarenes are hydrogen atoms replaced in benzene ring by halogens. In haloalkanes, halogen gets connected with the carbon through $(CO_2 + H_2O)$ hybridisation, while in Haloarenes, it is connected with CO_2 hybridisation.

Classification

- **On the Basis of Number of Halogen Atoms**

  It depends on the number of halogen atoms attached to the structure. It may be mono, di, tri or tetra etc. For example,

$$C_2H_5X$$

Monohaloalkane

$$
\begin{array}{l}
CH_2X \\
| \\
CH_2X
\end{array}
$$

Dihaloalkane

$$
\begin{array}{l}
CHX \\
\| \\
C \\
\| \\
CHX
\end{array}
$$

Trihaloalkane

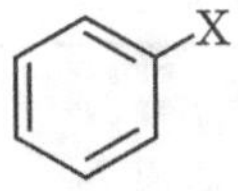

Monohaloarene

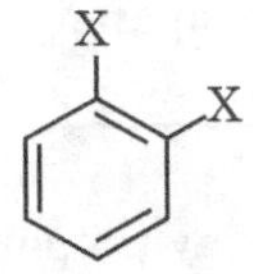

Dihaloarene

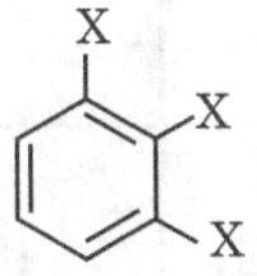

Trihaloarene

- **Compounds Containing** $\text{ppm}\left(\text{mass to mass}\right) = \dfrac{\text{Mass of a component}}{\text{Total mass of solution}} \times 10^6$ **C-X Bond (X= F, Cl , Br, I)**

  ➤ **Alkyl halides or haloalkanes (R-X):** The series is represented as

$$\text{ppm}\left(\text{volume to volume}\right) = \dfrac{\text{Volume of a component}}{\text{Total volume of solution}} \times 10^6.$$

  It has further 3 categories, i.e., primary, secondary or tertiary depending on the nature of carbon to which halogen is attached.

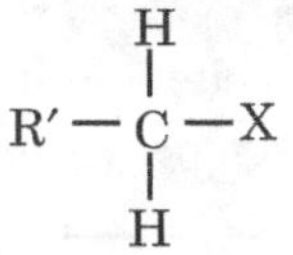

$$
R' - \overset{\displaystyle H}{\underset{\displaystyle H}{\overset{|}{\underset{|}{C}}}} - X
$$

Primary (1°)

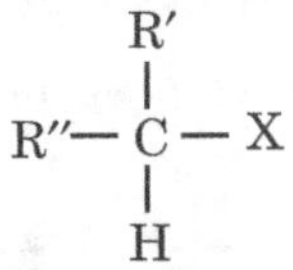

$$
R'' - \overset{\displaystyle R'}{\underset{\displaystyle H}{\overset{|}{\underset{|}{C}}}} - X
$$

Secondary (2°)

$$
R'' - \overset{\displaystyle R'}{\underset{\displaystyle R'''}{\overset{|}{\underset{|}{\quad}}}} -
$$

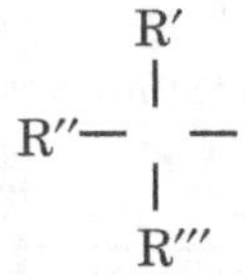

Tertiary (3°)

➤ **Allylic halides:** The halogen atom is attached to the carbon atom just adjacent to carbon-carbon double bond.

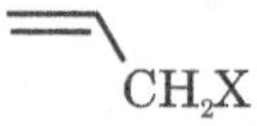

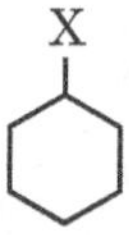

➤ **Benzylic halides:** The halogen atom is attached to the carbon atom right next to an aromatic ring.

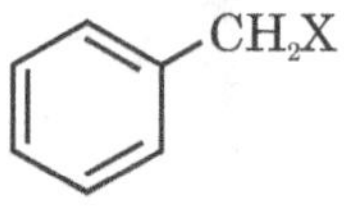

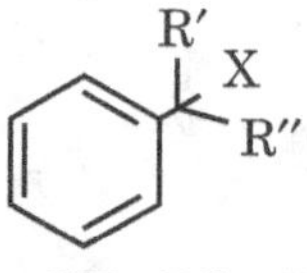

(1°)

$R' = CH_3, R'' = H (2°)$

$R' = R'' = CH3 (3°)$

• **Compounds Containing** $\text{ppm}\left(\text{mass to volume}\right) = \dfrac{\text{Mass of a component}}{\text{Volume of solution}} \times 10^6$ **C-X Bond**

➤ **Vinylic halides:** The halogen atom is attached to the carbon atom just adjacent to carbon-carbon double bond (C=C).

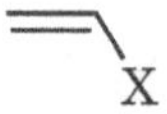

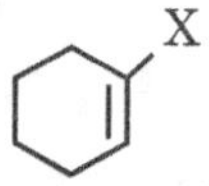

➤ **Aryl halides:** The halogen atom is attached to the carbon atom right next to an aromatic ring.

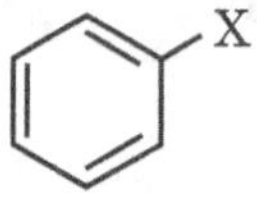

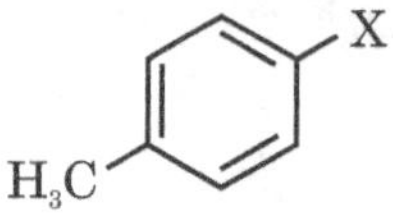

Nomenclature

Alkyl halides are named as halo-substituted hydrocarbons in the IUPAC system of nomenclature. Haloarenes are the common as well as IUPAC names of aryl halides.

Structure	IUPAC Names	Common Names
$CH_3CH_2CH_2Br$	1-Brompropane	n-Propyl bromide
$H_3C - CH - CH_3$ $\quad\quad\ \|$ $\quad\quad Cl$	2-Chloropropane	Isopropyl chloride
CH_3 $\quad\ \|$ $H_3C - CH - CH_2Cl$	1-Chloro-2-methylpropane	Isobutyl chloride
Br (benzene ring)	Bromobenzene	Bromobenzene
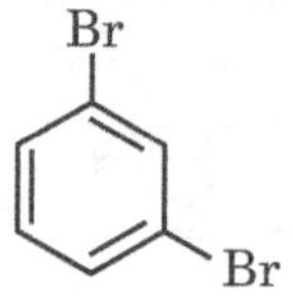 Br, Br (benzene ring)	1,3-Dibromobenzene	m-Dibromobenzene
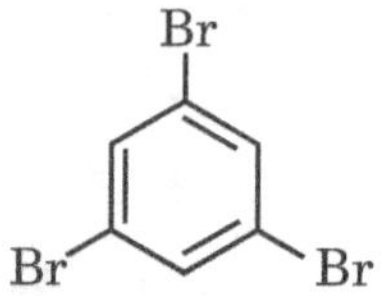 Br, Br, Br (benzene ring)	1,3,5-Tribromobenzene	sym-Tribromobenzene
$H_3C - CHCl_2$	1,1-Dicholoroethane	Ethylidene Chloride

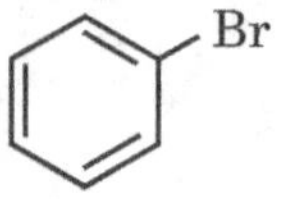

Nature of C-X Bond

They form a polarised bond as the carbon atom bears a partial positive charge whereas the halogen atom bears a partial negative charge.

$$\overset{\delta+}{\underset{}{-C}}-\overset{\delta-}{X}$$

Methods of preparation

- **From Alcohols**

  Alkyl halides are most commonly prepared from alcohols as the hydroxyl group of an alcohol can be easily replaced by any halogen atom.

$$R-OH \ + \ HX \ \xrightarrow{ZnCl_2} \ R-X \ + \ H_2O$$

$$R-OH \ + \ NaBr \ + \ H_2SO_4 \longrightarrow \ R-Br \ + \ NaHSO_4 \ + \ H_2O$$

$$3R-OH \ + \ PX_3 \ \longrightarrow \ 3R-X \ + \ H_3PO_3 \qquad (X = Cl, Br)$$

$$R-OH \ + \ PCl_5 \ \longrightarrow \ R-Cl \ + \ POCl_3 \ + \ HCl$$

$$R-OH \ \xrightarrow[X_2=Br_2,I_2]{red \ P/X_2} \ R-X$$

$$R-OH \ + \ SOCl_2 \ \longrightarrow \ R-Cl \ + \ SO_2 \ + \ HCl$$

From Hydrocarbons

➤ **By free radical halogenation:** Under certain conditions we can obtain mixture of isomeric mono and polyhaloalakanes.

$$CH_3CH_2CH_2CH_3 \xrightarrow[or \ heat]{Cl_2/UV \ light} CH_3CH_2CH_2CH_2Cl + CH_3CH_2CHClCH_3$$

➤ **By electrophilic substitution:** This requires the presence of Lewis acid catalyst like iron or iron(III) chloride. Chloride and bromide compounds can be prepared from this method but not fluoro compounds due to the high reactivity of fluorine.

o-Halotoluene   p-Halotouene

➤ **Sandmeyer's reaction:** This requires suspension of primary aromatic amine in cold aqueous mineral acid in the presence of sodium nitrate. A diazonium salt is formed which on reaction with cuprous chloride or bromide will replace diazonium group by Cl or Br.

Benzene diazonium
halide

Aryl halide
X = Cl, Br

➤ **From alkenes**

   (i) **Addition of hydrogen halides:** This requires a reaction of alkyl halide with hydrogen chloride, bromide or iodide.

$$CH_3CH = CH_2 + \ H-I \ \longrightarrow \ CH_3CH_2CH_2I \ + \ CH_3CHICH_3$$
$$\qquad\qquad\qquad\qquad\qquad minor \qquad\qquad major$$

(*ii*) **Addition of halogens:** The following reaction takes place in presence of

$$M = \frac{\text{Number of moles of solute}}{\text{Volume of solution}} = \frac{W_B \times 1000}{M_B \times V(ml)}.$$

$$H_2C=CH_2 + Br_2 \xrightarrow{CCl_4} BrCH_2 - CH_2Br$$
$$\text{Dibromide}$$

- **Halogen Exchange**

  The reaction in which the alkyl iodides are prepared by the reaction of alkyl chlorides/ bromides with NaI in dry acetone is known as **Finkelstein Reaction**.

  $$R\text{–}X + NaI \longrightarrow R\text{–}I + NaX$$

  $$X = Cl, Br$$

  The reaction in which alkyl fluorides are prepared by the reaction of alkyl chlorides/ bromides with metallic fluoride is known as **Swarts Reaction**.

  $$H_3C\text{–}Br + AgF \longrightarrow H_3C\text{–}F + AgBr$$

Properties of Haloalkanes and Haloarenes Including Polyhalogen Compounds

Physical Properties

- **Melting and boiling points**

  Because of the polarity of halogen compounds, the intermolecular forces of attraction are stronger   due to which the boiling and melting points of chlorides, bromides and iodides are considerably higher than those of the hydrocarbons. The decreasing order of boiling points of some alkyl hydrides is: RI>RBr>RCl>RF. The boiling points of some isomers are high due to the symmetry.

- **Density**

  The density of alkyl hydrides increases with the number of carbon atoms and halogen atoms and their atomic masses.

- **Solubility**

  The solubility of haloalkanes in water is quiet low because of strong hydrogen and carbon bond which is not easy to overcome or break. However, haloalkanes are soluble in solvent molecules because of the new intermolecular interactions between haloalkanes and solvent molecules which do not require much energy.

Chemical Reactions

- **Reactions of Haloalkanes**

  ➢ **Nucleophilic substitution reactions**

  A nucleophile reacts with a partial positive charge on a carbon atom of the haloalkanes, which then gets substituted by the nucleophile and separates out as halide ion.

  $$\overline{Nu} + \overset{\delta+}{\underset{}{C}}-\overset{\delta-}{X} \longrightarrow C-Nu + \overline{X}$$

  ➢ **bimolecular nucleophilic Substitution**

  In this case of nucleophilic substitution, a new carbon-OH bond is formed while simultaneously breaking the carbon-halide bond. Since both the steps take place simultaneously, this process is called **Inversion of configuration**.

➢ **unimolecular nucleophilic Substitution**

These reactions require a presence of polar protic solvents like water or alcohol and follow the first order kinetics in which the reaction rate depends on only one reactant. This happens in two steps. In first step, bromide ion is separated out and then in the next step carbocation formed is attacked upon by the nucleophile.

➢ **Stereochemical aspects of nucleophilic substitution reactions**

(*i*) **Plane polarised light and optical activity:** Those compounds which rotate the plane polarised light when passed through their solutions are called optically active compounds. If the light is rotated to the right by the compound, then it is called dextrorotatory and is represented by placing a positive sign before the degree of rotation. If the light is rotated to the left by the compound, then it is called laevorotatory and is represented by placing a positive sign before the degree of rotation. These isomers are called optical isomers and the phenomenon is called optical isomerism.

(*ii*) **Molecular asymmetry, chirality and enantiomers:** A carbon atom is called asymmetric carbon or stereocentre if the spatial arrangement of four groups around the central carbon is tetrahedral. The molecule so formed is referred to as asymmetric molecule. The super imposable objects when placed in front of the mirror are said to be achiral and the property is called as chirality. Those objects which are non-super imposable are known as chiral. For ex, propanol.

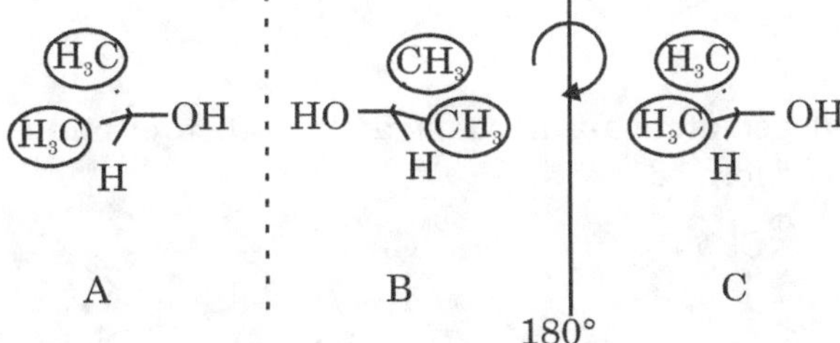

Enantiomers are stereoisomers which are related to each other as non-super imposable mirror images. When the rotation due to one isomer is cancelled by the rotation of other isomer in a mixture containing two equal enantiomers is known as racemic mixture and this process is known as racemisation.

(*iii*) **Retention:** The preservation of integrity of the spatial arrangement of bonds during transformation or a chemical reaction is known as retention.

(−) –2-Methyl butan-1-ol   (+)-1-chloro-2-methyl butane (*iv*) Inversion, retention and racemisation: If in a chemical reaction, compound A is produced, the process is called retention of configuration. If compound B is produced, then it is called inversion of configuration. If a mixture is produced, then the process is called racemisation.

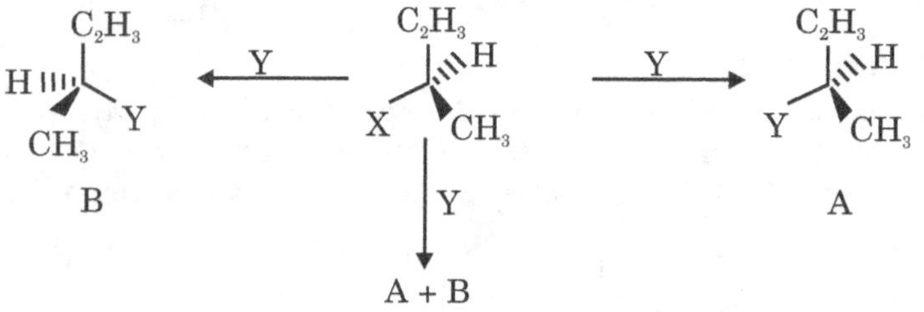

➢ Elimination reactions

This reaction requires the presence of alcoholic potassium hydroxide when a haloalkane with β-hydrogen is heated with it and the process is known as β-elimination.

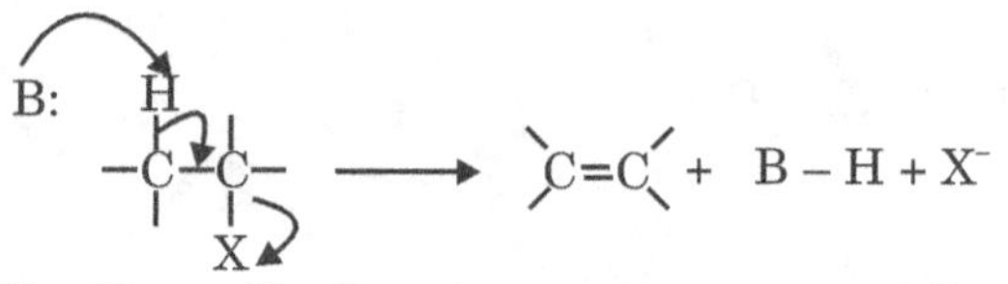

B = Base ; X = Leaving group

➢ Reaction with metals

The compounds obtained when chlorides or bromides react with certain metals are known as organo-metallic compounds. Grignard reagents of the form, RMgX, are obtained in such reactions.

$$CH_3CH_2Br + Mg \xrightarrow{\text{dry ether}} CH_3CH_2MgBr$$
$$\text{Grignard reagent}$$

Wurtz reaction: The reactions in which alkyl halides reacts with sodium in dry ether to produce hydrocarbons with double the number of carbon atoms present in the halide.

$$2RX + Na \longrightarrow RR + NaX$$

- ### Reaction of Haloarenes
  - ### ➢ Nucleophilic substitution

    (*i*) **Resonance effect:** The electron pairs on halogen atom are in conjugation with π- electrons of the ring. The following resonating structures can be formed.

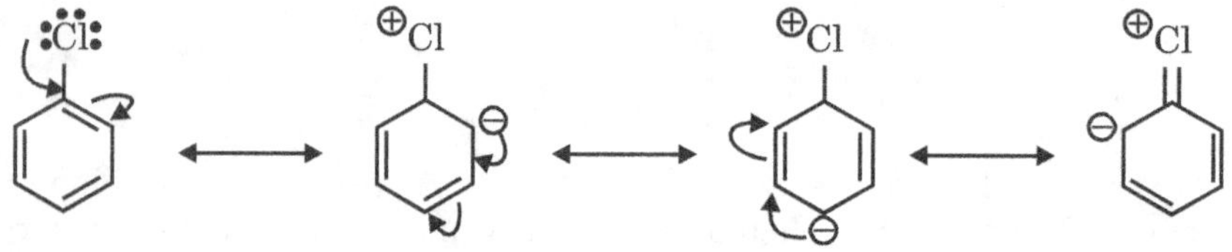

    (*ii*) **Difference in hybridisation of carbon atom in C-X bond:** In haloalkanes, halogen gets connected with the carbon through sp^3 hybridisation, while in Haloarenes, it is connected with sp^2 hybridisation.

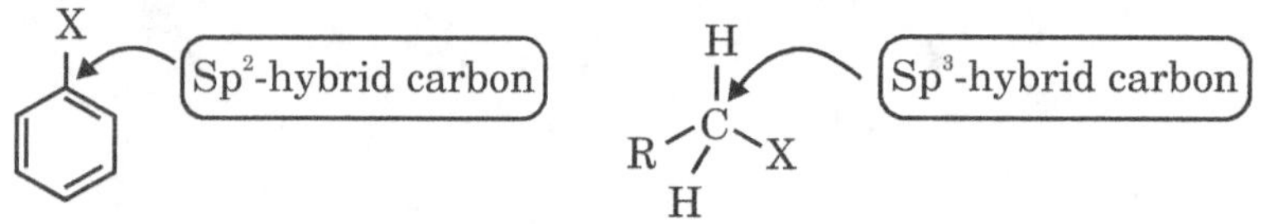

    (*iii*) **Instability of phenyl cation:** In Haloarenes, the phenyl cation formed is not stabilized by resonance due to self-ionisation.

(*iv*) **Replacement by hydroxyl group:** Phenol is formed by heating chlorobenzene in aqueous sodium hydroxide solution.

$$\text{Chlorobenzene} \xrightarrow[\text{(ii) H}]{\text{(i)NaOH, 623K, 300 atm}} \text{Phenol (OH)}$$

$$p\text{-Nitrochlorobenzene} \xrightarrow[\text{(ii) H}]{\text{(i)NaOH 443K}} p\text{-Nitrophenol}$$

$$2,4\text{-Dinitrochlorobenzene} \xrightarrow[\text{(ii) H}]{\text{(i)NaOH, 368K}} 2,4\text{-Dinitrophenol}$$

$$2,4,6\text{-Trinitrochlorobenzene} \xrightarrow[\text{H}_2\text{O}]{\text{Warm}} 2,4,6\text{-Trinitrophenol}$$

➢ **Electrophilic substitution reactions**

(*i*) **Halogenation:**

$$\text{Chlorobenzene} + \text{Cl}_2 \xrightarrow{\text{Anhyd. FeCl}_3} \text{1, 4-Dichlorobenzene (Major)} + \text{1, 2-Dichlorobenzene (Minor)}$$

1, 4-Dichlorobenzene
(Major)

1, 2-Dichlorobenzene
(Minor)

(*ii*) **Nitration:**

$$\text{Chlorobenzene} \xrightarrow[\text{conc. H}_2\text{SO}_4]{\text{HNO}_3} \text{1-Chloro-2-nitrobenzene (Minor)} + \text{1-Chloro-4-nitrobenzene (Major)}$$

1-Chloro-2-nitrobenzene
(Minor)

1-Chloro-4-nitrobenzene
(Major)

(*iii*) **Sulphonation:**

$$\text{Chlorobenzene} \xrightarrow[\Delta]{\text{conc. H}_2\text{SO}_4} \text{2-Chlorobenzene sulfonic acid (Minor)} + \text{4-Chlorobenzene sulfonic acid (Major)}$$

2-Chlorobenzene sulfonic acid
(Minor)

4-Chlorobenzene sulfonic acid
(Major)

(*iv*) **Friedel-Crafts reaction:**

1-Chloro-2-methylbenzene
(Minor)

1-Chloro-4-methylbenzene
(Major)

2-Chloroacetophenone
(Minor)

4-Chloroacetophenone
(Major)

➢ **Reaction with metals**

(*i*) **Wurtz-Fittig reaction**

Alkylarene is obtained on reaction of a mixture of alkyl halide and aryl halide with sodium in dry ether.

(*ii*) **Fittig reaction**

Analogous compounds are also formed in which two aryl groups are joined together.

• **Polyhalogen Compounds**

➢ **Dichloromethane (Methylene chloride):** It is prepared industrially by the direct chlorination of methane.

$$CH_4 + 2Cl_2 \xrightarrow{h\upsilon} CH_2Cl_2 + 2HCl$$

Fractional distillation is used to separate the mixture so obtained. It is used as a solvent, as a paint remover, as a propellant in aerosols and also as a metal cleaning and finishing solvent.

➢ **Trichloromethane (Chloroform):** It is manufactured by chlorination of methane followed by separation by fraction.

$$CH_4 + 3Cl_2 \xrightarrow[\text{Sunlight}]{h\upsilon} CHCl_3 + 3HCl$$

It is extensively used as solvent for waxes, resins, rubber, fats etc. Earlier, chloroform was used as anesthetic but at present this practice has been dropped as it is slowly oxidized by air in the presence of light to form highly poisonous phosgene gas. Therefore, it is stored in closed dark coloured bottles completely filled so that air is kept out.

- **Triiodomethane (Iodoform):** It is prepared by heating ethanol or acetone with sodium hydroxide or Na_2CO_3 and I_2 in water. It is insoluble in water and thus forms yellow precipitate of CHI_3.

$$CH\ CH_2OH + 6NaOH + 4I_2 \xrightarrow{\Delta} CHI_3 + 5NaI + HCOONa + 5H_2O$$

$$CH_3COCH_3 + 4NaOH + 3I_2 \xrightarrow{\Delta} CHI_3 + 3NaI + CH_3COONa + 3H_2O$$

It is used as an antiseptic for dressing wounds.

- **Tetrachloromethane (Carbon tetrachloride):** It is prepared by chlorination of methane and by action of chlorine on CS_2 in the presence of $AlCl_3$ as catalyst.

$$CS_2 + 3Cl_2 \xrightarrow[\Delta]{AlCl_3} CCl_4 + SCl_2$$

$$\left(\text{Sulphur dichloride}\right)$$

$$CH_4 + 4Cl_2 \xrightarrow{h\upsilon} CCl_4 + 4HCl$$

It is used in fire extinguisher. Also, it is used as solvent for fats, resins etc.

- **Freons:** The chlorofluorocarbon compounds of methane and ethane are collectively known as freons. They are extremely stable, unreactive, non-toxic, non-corrosive and easily liquefiable gases.

- **p, p'-Dichlorodiphenyltrichloroethane(DDT):** It is non-biodegradable and extremely stable. It is used as an insecticide. It is manufactured by the condensation of chlorobenzene with chloral in the presence of sulphuric acid. It was earlier used to control malaria and typhoid but due to its highly toxic nature, it was banned in India and USA.

EXERCISE

1. Which of the following halide is 2°
   - (a) Isopropyl chloride
   - (b) Isobutyl chloride
   - (c) n-propyl chloride
   - (d) n-butyl chloride

2. Haloforms are trihalogen derivatives of
   - (a) Ethane
   - (b) Methane
   - (c) Propane
   - (d) Benzene

3. Which of the following is a primary halide
   - (a) Isopropyl iodide
   - (b) Secondary butyl iodide
   - (c) Tertiary butyl bromide
   - (d) Neo hexyl chloride

4. What is the main product of the reaction between 2-methyl propene with HBr
   - (a) 1-bromo butane
   - (b) 1-bromo-2 methyl propane
   - (c) 2-bromo butane
   - (d) 2-bromo-2 methyl propane

5. Silver acetate + $Br_2 \xrightarrow{CS_2}$. The main product of this reaction is
   - (a) $CH_3 - Br$
   - (b) CH_3COI
   - (c) CH_3COOH
   - (d) None of these

6. $C_3H_8 + Cl_2 \xrightarrow{Light} C_3H_7Cl + HCl$ is an example of which of the following types of reactions
   - (a) Substitution
   - (b) Elimination
   - (c) Addition
   - (d) Rearrangement

7. Benzene reacts with chloride to form benzene hexachloride in presence of
   - (a) Nickel
   - (b) $AlCl_3$
   - (c) Bright sunlight
   - (d) Zinc

8. Which of the following is obtained when chloral is boiled with NaOH.

   (*a*) CH_3Cl (*b*) $CHCl_3$
   (*c*) CCl_4 (*d*) None of these

9. Chlorine reacts with ethanol to give

   (*a*) Ethyl chloride   (*b*) Chloroform
   (*c*) Acetaldehyde   (*d*) Chloral

10. Which compound gives yellow ppt. with iodine and alkali

   (*a*) 2-hydroxy propane   (*b*) Acetophenone
   (*c*) Methyl acetone   (*d*) Acetamide

11. Ethanol is converted into ethyl chloride by reacting with

   (*a*) Cl_2 (*b*) $SOCl_2$
   (*c*) HCl   (*d*) NaCl

12. The starting substance for the preparation of CH_3I is

   (*a*) CH_3OH (*b*) C_2H_5OH
   (*c*) CH_3CHO (*d*) $(CH_3)_2CO$

13. Reaction of ethyl chloride with sodium leads to

   (*a*) Ethane   (*b*) Propane
   (*c*) n-butane   (*d*) n-pentane

14. $$2CHCl_3 + O_2 \xrightarrow{\text{X}} 2COCl_2 + 2HCl$$

   In the above reaction, X stands for

   (*a*) An oxidant   (*b*) A reductant
   (*c*) Light and Air   (*d*) None of these

15. Phosgene is the common name for

   (*a*) CO_2 and PH_3
   (*b*) Phosphoryl chloride
   (*c*) Carbonyl Chloride
   (*d*) Carbon tetrachloride

16. When chloroform is treated with amine and KOH, we get

   (*a*) Rose odour smell
   (*b*) Sour almond like smell
   (*c*) Offensive odour
   (*d*) Sour oil of winter green like smell

17. Which of the following compound will make precipitate most readily with $AgNO_3$

   (*a*) CCl_3CHO (*b*) $CHCl_3$
   (*c*) $C_6H_5CH_2Cl$ (*d*) CHI_3

18. Grignard reagent is prepared by the reaction between

   (*a*) Zinc and alkyl halide
   (*b*) Magnesium and alkyl halide
   (*c*) Magnesium and alkane
   (*d*) Magnesium and aromatic hydrocarbon

19. War gas is formed from

   (*a*) PH_3 (*b*) C_2H_2
   (*c*) Zinc phosphate   (*d*) Chloropicrin

20. What happens when CCl_4 is treated with $AgNO_3$

   (*a*) NO_2 will be evolved
   (*b*) A white ppt. of AgCl will be formed
   (*c*) CCl_4 will dissolve in $AgNO_3$
   (*d*) Nothing will happen

21. If we use pyrene (CCl_4) in the Riemer-Tiemann reaction in place of chloroform, the product formed is

   (*a*) Salicylaldehyde   (*b*) phenolphthalein
   (*c*) Salicylic acid   (*d*) Cyclohexanol

22. Ethylidene chloride on treatment with aqueous KOH gives

   (*a*) Ethylene glycol   (*b*) Acetaldehyde
   (*c*) Formaldehyde   (*d*) None

23. Ethylene difluoride on hydrolysis gives

   (*a*) Glycol   (*b*) Fluoroethanol
   (*c*) Oifluoroethanol   (*d*) Freon

24. Benzyl Chloride when oxidised by $Pb(NO_3)_2$ gives

   (*a*) Benzoic acid
   (*b*) Benzaldehyde
   (*c*) Benzene
   (*d*) None

Answer Keys

1. (a)   2. (b)   3. (d)   4. (d)   5. (a)   6. (a)   7. (c)   8. (b)   9. (d)   10. (b)

11. (b)   12. (a)   13. (c)   14. (c)   15. (c)   16. (d)   17. (d)   18. (b)   19. (d)   20. (d)

21. (c)   22. (b)   23. (a)   24. (b)

Solutions

1. Isopropyl chloride $CH_3 - \overset{2°}{\underset{\underset{Cl}{|}}{CH}} - CH_3$ chlorine atom is attached to 2° Carbon atom

2. $CH_4 \xrightarrow[+3X]{-3H} CHX_3$

   Where X = Cl, Br, I

3. Neohexyl chloride is a primary halide as in it Cl-atom is attached to a primary carbon.

$$CH_3 - \underset{\underset{CH_3}{|}}{\overset{\overset{CH_3}{|}}{C}} - CH_2 - CH_2Cl$$

4. $CH_3 - \underset{\underset{CH_3}{|}}{CH} = CH_2 + HBr \longrightarrow CH_3 - \underset{\underset{CH_3}{|}}{\overset{\overset{Br}{|}}{C}} - CH_3$

   2 – bromo, – 2, methyl Propane

   2-bromo,–2, methyl propane

5. $CH_3COOAg + Br_2 \xrightarrow{CS_2} CH_3Br + AgBr + CO_2$

6. $C_3H_8 + Cl_2 \xrightarrow{Light} C_3H_7Cl + HCl$

   This is an example of substitution reaction. Hydrogen atom of alkane is replaced by halogen atom.

7. Benzene $+ 3CL_2 \xrightarrow{Sunlight}$ BHC

8. $CCL_3CHO + NaOH \xrightarrow{Boil} CHCl_3 + HCOONa$
   Chlorol $\qquad\qquad$ Chloroform

9. $CH_3CH_2OH + Cl_2 \longrightarrow CH_3CHO + 2HCl$

   $CH_3CHO + 3Cl_2 \longrightarrow CCl_3CHO + 3HCl$
   $\qquad\qquad\qquad\qquad$ Chloral

10. $CH_3 - \underset{\underset{O}{\|}}{C} C_6H_5 \xrightarrow[I_2]{NaOH} CHI_3 +$ COONa (yellow ppt.)

    A Cetophenone

11. $C_2H_5OH + SOCl_2 \xrightarrow{Pyridine} C_2H_5Cl + SO_2 + HCl$

12. $CH_3OH + HI \xrightarrow{ZnCl_2} CH_3I + H_2O$

13. $C_2H_5Cl + 2Na + ClC_2H_5 \xrightarrow[Ether]{Dry} C_2H_5 - C_2H_5 + 2NaCl$

14. $2CHCl_3O_2 \xrightarrow[air]{Light} 2COCl_2 + 2HCl$
    $\qquad\qquad\qquad\qquad$ Phosgene

15. $COCl_2$ Carbonyl Chloride is Commonly Called as Phosgene

16. $C_2H_5NH_2 + CHCl_3 + 3KOH \longrightarrow C_2H_5 - N = C + 3KCl + 3H_2O$

    (Ethylisocyanide)

17. CHI_3 gives a yellow ppt. of AgI

18. $RX + Mg \xrightarrow[ether]{Dry} R - Mg - X$
    $\qquad\qquad\qquad$ Grignard's reagent

    (Where X = Cl, Br, I)

19. $CHCl_3 + HO - NO_2 \longrightarrow CCl_3NO_2 + H_2O$
    $\qquad\qquad\qquad\qquad$ Chloropicrin (war gas)

20. $CCl_4 + AgNO_3 \longrightarrow$ No reaction

    CCl_4 is a covalent compound. Therefore does not provide Cl⁻ ions.

21.

$\underset{\text{(phenol)}}{C_6H_5OH} + CCl_4 + 4NaOH \longrightarrow$ (salicylic acid) $+ 4NaCl + 2H_2O$

Salicylic acid

22.

$CH_3 - CHCl_2 \xrightarrow[\text{(aqeous)}]{KOH} CH_3 - CH(OH)_2 \xrightarrow{-H_2O} CH_3 - CHO + H_2O$

23.

$\underset{CH_2-F}{\overset{CH_2-F}{|}} \xrightarrow{\text{Hydrolysis}} \underset{CH_2-OH}{\overset{CH_2-OH}{|}}$

24.

$\underset{\text{Benzyl Chloride}}{C_6H_5CH_2Cl} \xrightarrow[Pb(NO_3)_2]{\text{Oxidation}} \underset{\text{Benzaldehyde}}{C_6H_5CHO}$

CHAPTER 11

Alcohols, Phenols and Ethers

Alcohols and Phenols

➢ **Alcohols:** Alcohols have the general formula as $C_nH_{2n+1}OH$ and they are obtained when one hydrogen atom in alkane is replaced by –OH group.

➢ **Classification of alcohols:**

- Alcohols which have one hydroxyl group are called monohydric alcohols.
- Alcohols which have 2 hydroxyl groups are called dihydric alcohols.
- Alcohols which have 3 hydroxyl groups are called trihydric alcohols.
- Alcohols which have many hydroxyl groups are called polyhyric alcohols.
- Monohydric alcohols are further classified according to the hybridization of the carbon atom to which hydroxyl group is attached as shown below:

  (*i*) **Compounds containing $C_{sp^3}-OH$ bond:** In this type of alcohols the –OH group is attached to an sp^3 hybridised carbon atom of an alkyl group.

$$- CH_3-OH \qquad >CH-OH \qquad \gg C-OH$$

Primary (1°)   Secondary (2°)   Tertiary (3°)

  (*ii*) **Allylic alcohols:** In this type of alcohols the –OH group is attached to an sp^3 hybridised carbon next to the C-C double bond, which is an allylic carbon.

$$CH_2 = CH - CH_2 - OH \qquad CH_2 = CH - \overset{H}{\underset{-C-}{C}} - OH \qquad CH_2 = CH - \overset{-C-}{\underset{-C-}{C}} - OH$$

Primary   Secondary   Tertiary

  (*iii*) **Benzylic alcohols:** In this type of alcohols the –OH group is attached to a sp^3-hybridised carbon atom attached to the benzene ring.

Primary   Secondary   Tertiary

(iv) **Vinylic alcohol:** In this type of alcohols –OH group is bonded to the C-C double bond i.e. to a vinylic carbon or to an aryl carbon.

$$CH_2 = CH - OH$$

➢ Common and IUPAC names of some alcohols are given below in the table:

Compound	Common name	IUPAC name
$CH_3 - OH$	Methyl alcohol	Methanol
$CH_3 - CH_2 - CH_2 - OH$	n-Propyl alcohol	Propan-1-ol
$CH_2 - CH - CH_2$ $\|\quad\ \|\quad\ \|$ $OH\ \ OH\ \ OH$	Glycerol	Propane-1, 2, 3-triol
$CH_3 - CH - CH_2 - CH_3$ $\quad\quad\ \|$ $\quad\quad OH$	Sec-Butyl alcohol	Butan-2-ol

➢ **Structure of alcohol:**

In alcohols, the oxygen of the –OH group is attached to sp^3 hybridized carbon by a sigma bond.

142 pm   96 pm

H
$\quad$:O:
$\quad\quad$ C 108.9° H
H $\quad$ |
$\quad\quad$ H

➢ **Preparation of Alcohols:**

 • **From alkenes:** alcohol is prepared when alkenes react with water in presence of acid as catalyst.

$$CH_3CH=CH_2 + H_2O \xrightarrow{H^+} CH_3-CH-CH_3$$
$$\qquad\qquad\qquad\qquad\qquad |$$
$$\qquad\qquad\qquad\qquad\ OH$$

 • **By hydroboration-oxidation:**

$$CH_3-CH=CH_2 + (H-BH_2)_2 \longrightarrow CH_3-CH-CH_2$$
$$\qquad\qquad\qquad\qquad\qquad\qquad\quad |\quad\ |$$
$$\qquad\qquad\qquad\qquad\qquad\qquad\quad H\ \ BH_2$$
$$\qquad\qquad\qquad\qquad\qquad\qquad\quad \downarrow CH_3-CH=CH_2$$
$$(CH_3-CH_2-CH_2)_3B \xleftarrow{CH_3-CH=CH_2} (CH_3-CH_2-CH_2)_2BH$$
$$H_2O \downarrow 3H_2O_2,\ \bar{O}H$$
$$3CH_3-CH_2-CH_2-OH + B(OH)_3$$
$$\text{Propan-1-ol}$$

 • **From carbonyl compounds:**

 (i) **By reduction of aldehydes and ketones:** Corresponding alcohols are produced by the reduction of aldehydes and ketones by addition of hydrogen in the presence of catalysts.

$$RCHO + H_2 \xrightarrow{Pd} RCH_2OH$$

$$RCOR' \xrightarrow{NaBH_4} R-CH-R'$$
$$\qquad\qquad\qquad\qquad |$$
$$\qquad\qquad\qquad\ OH$$

 (ii) **By reduction of carboxylic acids and esters:** In the presence of strong agent, lithium aluminium hydride, carboxylic acids are reduced to primary alcohols.

$$RCOOH \xrightarrow[\text{(ii) } H_2O]{\text{(i) LiAlH}_4} RCH_2OH$$

Commercially, acids are reduced to alcohols by first converting them to esters and then following catalytic hydrogenation.

$$RCOOH \xrightarrow[H^+]{R'OH} RCOOR' \xrightarrow[\text{Catalyst}]{H_2} RCH_2OH + R'OH$$

 • **From Grignard reagents:** The reaction of Grignard reagent with formaldehyde produces a primary alcohol, with other aldehydes it reacts to give secondary alcohols and tertiary alcohols are produced on reaction of Grignard reagent with ketones.

$$HCHO + RMgX \rightarrow RCH_2OMgX \xrightarrow{H_2O} RCH_2OH + Mg(OH)X$$

$$\qquad\qquad\qquad\qquad\qquad\quad R'\qquad\qquad\qquad\qquad R'$$
$$\qquad\qquad\qquad\qquad\qquad\quad |\qquad\qquad\qquad\qquad\ |$$
$$RCHO + R'MgX \xrightarrow{H_2O} R-CH-OMgX \xrightarrow{H_2O} R-CH-OH + Mg(OH)X$$

$$\qquad\qquad\qquad\qquad\qquad\quad R'\qquad\qquad\qquad\qquad R'$$
$$\qquad\qquad\qquad\qquad\qquad\quad |\qquad\qquad\qquad\qquad\ |$$
$$RCOR + R'MgX \longrightarrow R-C-OMgX \xrightarrow{H_2O} R-C-OH + Mg(OH)X$$
$$\qquad\qquad\qquad\qquad\qquad\quad |\qquad\qquad\qquad\qquad\ |$$
$$\qquad\qquad\qquad\qquad\qquad\quad R\qquad\qquad\qquad\qquad\ R$$

➢ **Phenols:**
- It is the simplest hydroxyl derivative of benzene. In its substituted compounds the terms ortho (1, 2- disubstituted), meta (1, 3 –disubstituted) and para (1, 4- disubstituted) are often used in common names.

➢ **Common name and IUPAC name of some phenols are given below in the table:**

Compound	Common name	IUPAC name
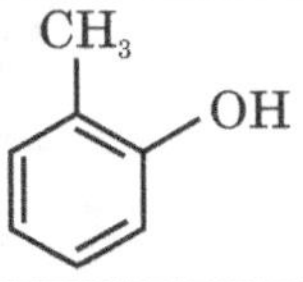 CH₃ —OH (ring)	o-Cresol	2-Methylphenol
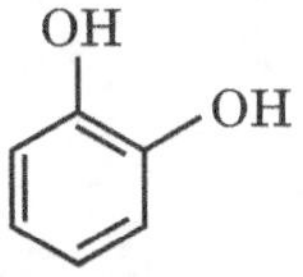 OH —OH (ring)	Catechol	Benzene-1, 2-diol
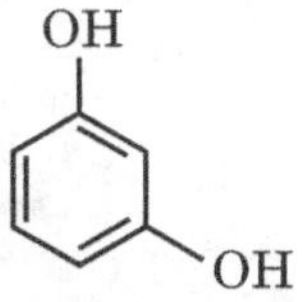 OH —OH (ring)	Resorcinol	Benzene-1, 3-diol
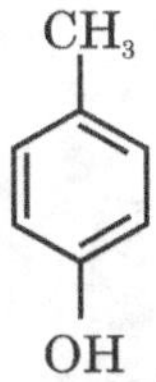 CH₃ OH (ring)	p-Cresol	4-Methyphenol

➢ **Structure of Phenols:**

In phenols, the –OH group is attached to the sp^2 hybridised carbon of an aromatic ring.

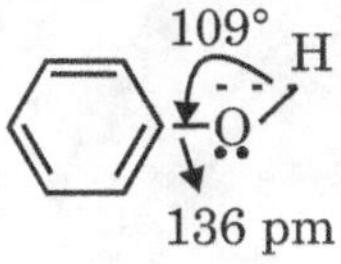

109°

136 pm

➢ Preparation of Phenols:
- **From haloarenes:**

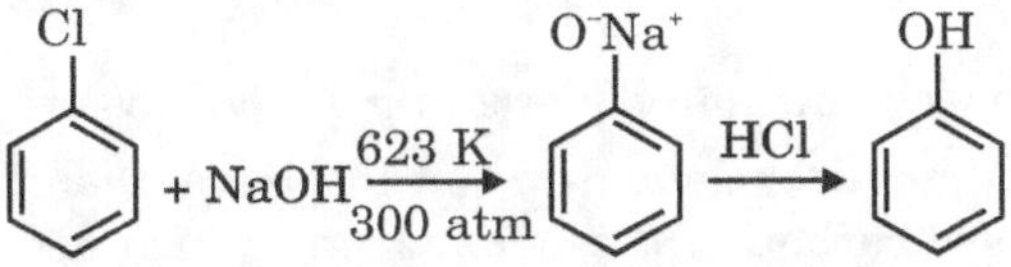

$$\text{Cl-(ring)} + NaOH \xrightarrow[\text{300 atm}]{\text{623 K}} \text{O}^-Na^+\text{(ring)} \xrightarrow{HCl} \text{OH (ring)}$$

- **From benzenesulphonic acid:**

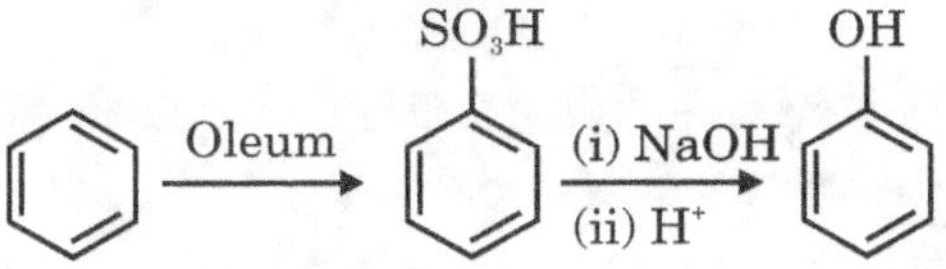

$$\text{SO}_3\text{H (ring)} \xrightarrow{\text{Oleum}} \xrightarrow[\text{(ii) H}^+]{\text{(i) NaOH}} \text{OH (ring)}$$

- **From diazonium salts:**

$$\text{NH}_2\text{ (ring)} \xrightarrow[\text{+HCl}]{\text{NaNO}_2} \text{N}_2\text{Cl (ring)} \xrightarrow[\text{Warm}]{\text{H}_2\text{O}} \text{OH (ring)} + N_2 + HCl$$

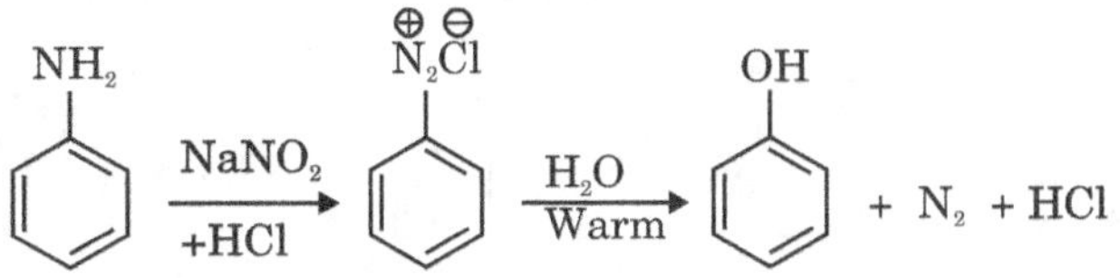

Aniline   Benzene diazonium chloride

- **From cumene:**

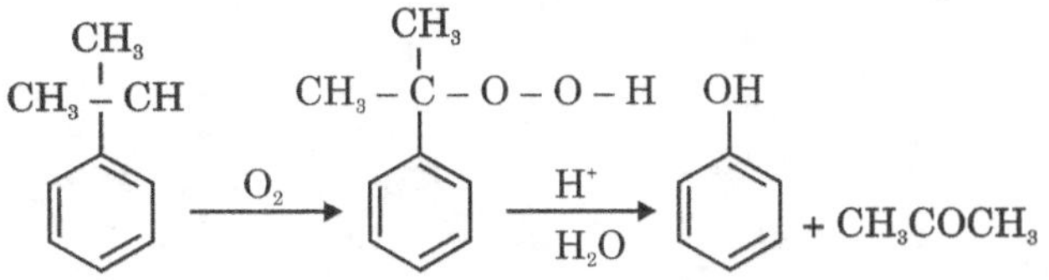

Cumene   Cumene hydroperoxide

$$\xrightarrow{O_2} \xrightarrow[\text{H}_2\text{O}]{\text{H}^+} \text{OH (ring)} + CH_3COCH_3$$

➢ **Physical properties of alcohols and phenols:**
- **Boiling Points:** With increase in the number of carbon atoms van der Waal's forces increase which in turn increases the boiling point of alcohols and phenols. With increase of branching in carbon chain the Van der Waals forces decreases with decrease in surface area which in turn decreases the boiling point of alcohols.

  The high boiling points of alcohols and phenols is mainly because of the presence of intermolecular hydrogen bonding in them which is lacking in ether and hydrocarbons.

  The –OH group in alcohols and phenols is involved in intermolecular hydrogen bonding as shown below:

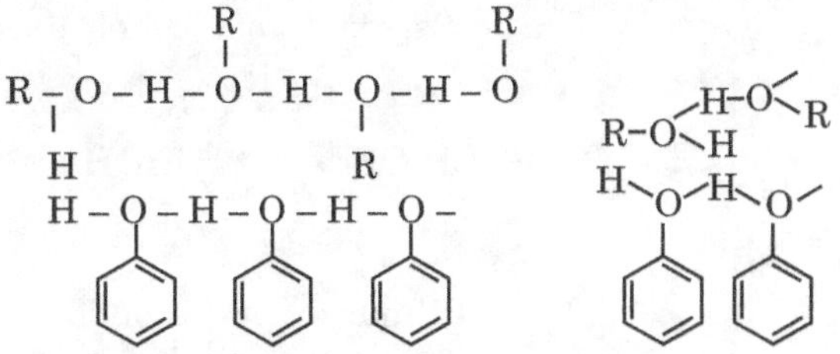

- **Solubility:** Solubility of alcohols and phenols in water is because of their ability to form hydrogen bonds with water molecules.

  With increase in the size of the aryl/alkyl groups the solubility decreases.

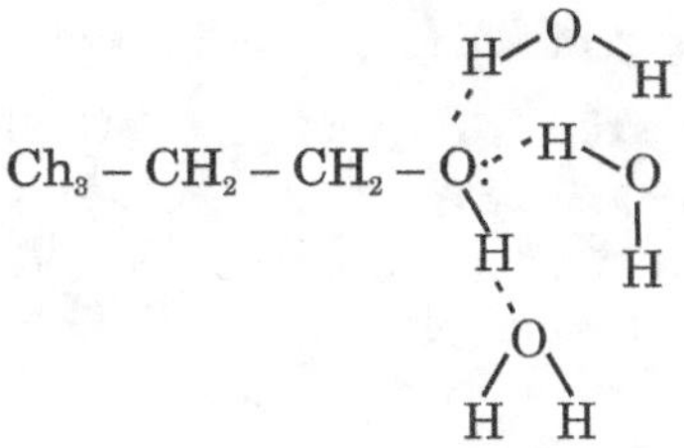

$$Ch_3 - CH_2 - CH_2 - O$$

➢ **Chemical Reactions**

Alcohols react as nucleophiles and electrophiles. When alcohols react as nucleophile the bond between –OH is broken.

$$R - \overset{..}{\underset{..}{O}} - H + \overset{H}{\underset{}{{}^{+}C}} - \;\rightarrow\; R - \overset{..}{\underset{..}{O}} - \overset{|}{\underset{|}{C}} - \;\rightarrow\; R - O - \overset{|}{\underset{|}{C}} - + H^{+}$$

When they react as electrophile the bond between C-O is broken.

$$R - CH_2 - OH + \overset{+}{H} \rightarrow R - CH_2 - \overset{+}{OH_2}$$

$$\underset{\underset{R}{|}}{Br^{-} + CH_2} - OH^{+}_{2} \;\rightarrow\; \underset{\underset{R}{|}}{Br - CH_2} + H_2O$$

- **Reactions of alcohols and phenols involving cleavage of O-H bond:**
  1. **Acidity of alcohols and phenols:**
     (*i*) **Reaction with metals:** They react with active metals like sodium, potassium and aluminium to give corresponding alkoxides/phenoxides and hydrogen.

$$2R\text{-}O\text{-}H + 2Na \longrightarrow \underset{\substack{\text{Sodium} \\ \text{alkoxide}}}{2R\text{-}O\text{-}Na} + H_2$$

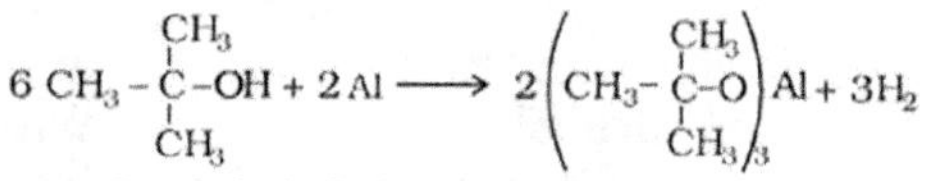

$$6\,CH_3 - \underset{\underset{CH_3}{|}}{\overset{\overset{CH_3}{|}}{C}} - OH + 2\,Al \longrightarrow 2\left(CH_3 - \underset{\underset{CH_3}{|}}{\overset{\overset{CH_3}{|}}{C}} - O \right)Al + 3H_2$$

tert- Butyl alcohol   Aluminium *tert-* butoxide

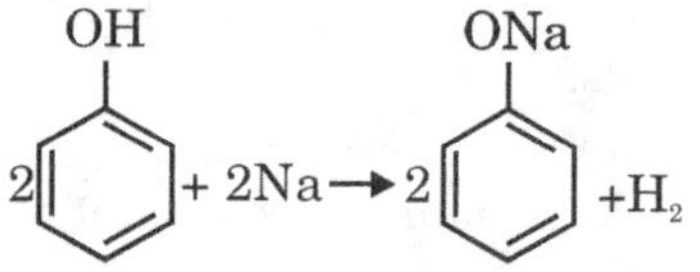

$$2\underset{\text{Phenol}}{\underset{}{\bigcirc}\!\!\overset{OH}{}} + 2Na \longrightarrow 2\underset{\text{Sodium phenoxide}}{\underset{}{\bigcirc}\!\!\overset{ONa}{}} + H_2$$

     (*ii*) **Acidity of alcohols:** The polar nature of O-H brings the acidic character in alcohols. The electron releasing group increase electron density on oxygen which decreases the polarity of O-H bond hence decreases the acid strength.

The acid strength of alcohols decrease in the following order:

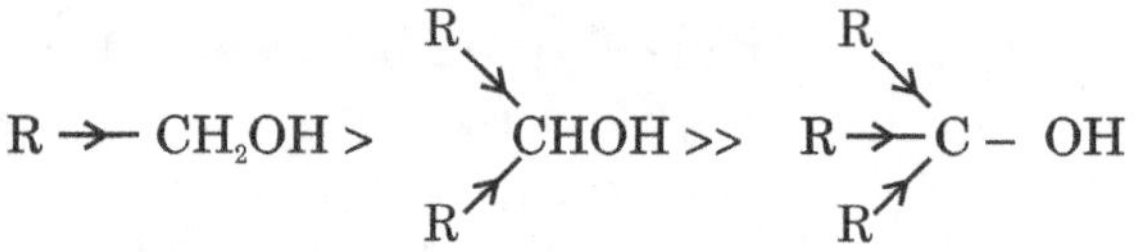

$$R \rightarrow CH_2OH > \underset{R^{\nearrow}}{\overset{R^{\searrow}}{CHOH}} >> R \rightarrow \underset{R^{\nearrow}}{\overset{R^{\searrow}}{C}} - OH$$

Primary   Secondary   Tertiary

Alcohols are weaker acids than water.

Alcohols act as Bronsted bases due to the presence of unshared electron pairs on oxygen.

     (*iii*) **Acidity of phenols:** Phenols are more acidic than alcohols and water. In phenol the hydroxyl group is attached directly to the sp^2 –hybridised carbon of the benzne ring which acts as an electron withdrawing group. Due to this, the charge distribution in phenol molecule, causes the oxygen of –OH group to be positive.

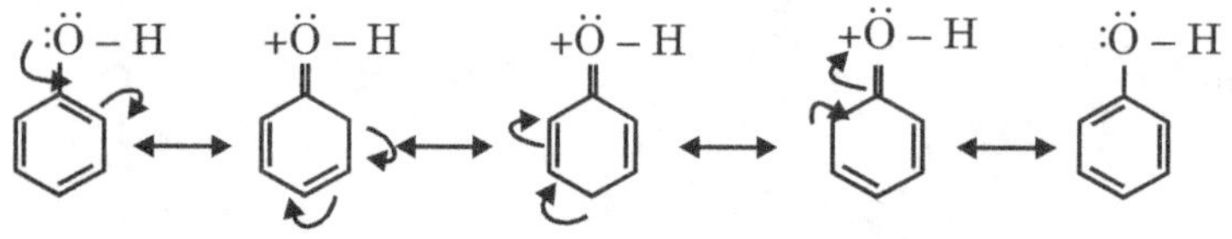

The ionization of an alcohol and a phenol takes place producing alkoxide and phenoxide ions as shown below:

$$R - \ddot{O} - H \rightleftharpoons R - \ddot{O}{:}^- + H^+$$

In alkoxideion, the negative charge is localized on oxygen while in phenoxide ion, the charge is delocalized. The delocalization of negative charge makes phenoxide ion more stable and favours the ionization of phenol.

I	II	III	IV	V

2. **Esterification:** Esters are formed when alcohols and phenols react with carboxylic acids, acid chlorides and acid anhydrides.

The reactions are given below:

$$Ar/RO-H + R'-COOH \underset{}{\overset{H^+}{\rightleftharpoons}} Ar/ROCOR' + H_2O$$

$$Ar/R-OH + (R'CO)_2O \underset{}{\overset{H^+}{\rightleftharpoons}} Ar/ROCOR + R'COOH$$

$$R/ArOH + R'COCl \xrightarrow{Pyridine} R/ArOCOR + HCl$$

- **Reactions involving cleavage of C-O bond in alcohols:**

  Only alcohols undergo this type of reactions which involves cleavage of C-O bond. In phenols this type of reaction takes place only with zinc.

  1. **Reaction with hydrogen halides:**

  $$R-OH + HX \xrightarrow{ZnCl_2} R-X + H_2O$$

  2. **Reaction with phosphorus trihalides:**

  $$3R-OH + PX_3 \longrightarrow 3R-X + H_3PO_3 \qquad (X = Cl, Br)$$

  3. **Dehydration:**

  Dehydration of ethanol is given below:

  $$C_2H_5OH \xrightarrow[443\ K]{H_2SO_4} CH_2 = CH_2 + H_2O$$

  Dehydration of secondary and tertiary alcohols take place under milder condition and reaction is shown below:

  $$CH_3\overset{\overset{OH}{|}}{C}HCH_3 \xrightarrow[440\ K]{85\%\ H_3PO_4} CH_3- CH = CH_2 + H_2O$$

  $$CH_3-\overset{\overset{CH_3}{|}}{\underset{\underset{CH_3}{|}}{C}}- OH \xrightarrow[358\ K]{20\%\ H_3PO_4} CH_3-\overset{\overset{CH_2}{||}}{C}-CH_3 + H_2O$$

  The order of dehydration of alcohols is shown as:

  Tertiary > Secondary > Primary

4. Oxidation:

Primary alcohol can be oxidized to aldehyde which on further oxidizing gives carboxylic acid which depends on the type of oxidizing agent used.

$$RCH_2OH \xrightarrow{\text{Oxidation}} \underset{\text{Aldehyde}}{R-\overset{H}{\underset{}{C}}=O} \longrightarrow \underset{\substack{\text{Carboxylic} \\ \text{acid}}}{R-\overset{OH}{\underset{}{C}}=O}$$

As an oxidizing agent CrO_3 can be used for isolating aldehyde.

$$RCH_2OH \xrightarrow{CrO_3} RCHO$$

Pyridinium chloromate (PCC) can be used an oxidizing reagent to get aldehyde from primary alcohols.

$$CH_3 - CH = CH - CH_2OH \xrightarrow{PCC} CH_3 - CH = CH - CHO$$

On oxidizing secondary alcohols gives ketone using CrO_3 as an oxidizing agent.

$$\underset{\text{Sec- alcohol}}{R-\underset{OH}{\overset{}{CH}}-R'} \xrightarrow{CrO_3} \underset{\text{Ketone}}{R-\underset{O}{\overset{}{C}}-R'}$$

5. Dehydrogenation:

$$RCH_2OH \xrightarrow[573K]{Cu} RCHO$$

$$\underset{OH}{R-\overset{}{CH}-R'} \xrightarrow[573K]{Cu} \underset{O}{R-\overset{}{C}-R'}$$

$$CH_3 - \underset{CH_3}{\overset{CH_3}{\underset{}{C}}} - OH \xrightarrow[573K]{Cu} CH_3 - \overset{CH_3}{\underset{}{C}} = CH_2$$

- **Reactions of phenols:**

Following are the reactions of phenols:

1. Electrophilic aromatic substitution:

(i) Nitration:

o-Nitrophenol

p-Nitrophenol

2.4.6-Trinitrophenol
(Picric acid)

(ii) Halogenation:

Treatment of phenol with bromine water is shown below:

2,4,6-Tribomophenol

2. Kolbe's reaction:

2-Hydroxybenzoic acid
(Salicylic acid)

3. Reimer- Tiemann reaction:

Intermediate

Salicyladehyde

4. Reaction of phenol with zinc dust:

5. Oxidation:

benzoquinone

➤ Some commercially important alcohols are given below:

1. Methanol:

- **Physical properties:**

Methanol is also known by the name 'wood spirit'.

It is a colourless liquid which boils at 337 K.

In paints, varnishes it is used as a solvent.

- **Preparation of Methanol:**By catalytic hydrogenation of carbon monoxide.

$$CO + 2H_2 \xrightarrow[\substack{200\text{-}300\ atm \\ 573\text{-}673\ K}]{ZnO\text{-}Cr_2O_3} CH_3OH$$

2. Ethanol:

- **Physical properties:**

  It is a colourless liquid which boils at 351 K.

  It is made unfit for drinking by mixing it with some copper sulphate which gives it some colour and pyride which gives it a foul smell. This complete process is called denaturation of alcohol.

- **Preparation of Ethanol:**

  Ethanol is prepared by fermentation of glucose and fructose in presence of enzyme, Zymase, which is found in yeast.

  Glucose and fructose are produced from sugar in the presence of enzyme, invertase.

  The reactions are given below:

$$C_{12}H_{22}O_{11} + H_2O \xrightarrow{Invertase} \underset{Glucose}{C_6H_{12}O_6} + \underset{Fructose}{C_6H_{12}O_6}$$

$$C_6H_{12}O_6 \xrightarrow{Zymase} 2C_2H_5OH + 2CO_2$$

Ethers

- They are represented by $R - O - R'$ and have the general formula $C_nH_{2n+2}O$.
- Ethers are classified into 2 categories:
  - **Simple or symmetrical:** When the alkyl or aryl groups attached to the oxygen atom are the same. Example: $C_2H_5OC_2H_5$

  - **Mixed or unsymmetrical:** When the alkyl or aryl groups attached to the oxygen atom are different. Example: $C_2H_5OCH_3$

- Common names and IUPAC names of some ethers are given below:

Compound	Common name	IUPAC name
CH_3OCH_3	Dimethyl ether	Methoxymethane
$C_2H_5OCH_3$	Diethyl ether	Ethoxyethane
$C_6H_5OCH_3$	Methylphenyl ether	Methoxybenzene
$CH_3O-CH-CH_3$ $\quad\quad\;\; \mid$ $\quad\quad CH_3$	Methyl isopropyl ether	2-Methoxypropane

- Structure of ether:

  The four electron pairs in ether, i.e. the two bond pairs and the two lone pairs of electrons are arranged approximately in tetrahedral arrangement as shown below:

141 pm

Methoxymethane

➤ **Preparation of Ethers:**

- **By dehydration of alcohols:** In the presence of protic acid. The product which is formed in the reaction depends on the conditions of the reaction.

$$CH_3CH_2OH \longrightarrow \begin{cases} \xrightarrow[443\ K]{H_2SO_4} CH_2 - CH_2 \\[2mm] \xrightarrow[413\ K]{H_2SO_4} C_2H_5OC_2H_5 \end{cases}$$

- **Williamson synthesis:** In this method alkyl halide reacts with sodium alkoxide.

$$R - X + R - \ddot{O}\ Na \longrightarrow R - \ddot{O} - R + Na\ X$$

$$CH_3 - \underset{\underset{CH_3}{|}}{\overset{\overset{CH_3}{|}}{C}} - \ddot{O}\bar{N}\overset{+}{a} + CH_3 - Br \rightarrow CH_3 - \ddot{O} - \underset{\underset{CH_3}{|}}{\overset{\overset{CH_3}{|}}{C}} - CH_3 + NaBr$$

Phenols can also be converted to ethers using this method of preparation.

$$\underset{}{\overset{:\ddot{O}H}{\bigcirc}} + NaOH \longrightarrow \overset{:\ddot{O}\ \overset{+}{Na}}{\underset{R-X}{\bigcirc}} \longrightarrow \overset{O-R}{\bigcirc}$$

➤ **Physical properties of ethers:**

- The boiling point of ethers is lower than alcohols but is comparable to those of alkanes of the comparable molecular masses. The example is given below:

Formula	$CH_3(CH_2)_3CH_3$	C_2H_5-O-C_2H_5	$CH_3(CH_2)_3$-OH
	n-Pentane	Ethoxyethane	Butan-1-ol
b.p./K	309.1	307.6	390

- The solubility of ethers in water is comparable to those of alcohols of the same molecular masses and this is because of the ability of the oxygen of the ether to form hydrogen bonds with water molecules.

$$\begin{aligned} R\diagdown \\ R\diagup \end{aligned}\ \ddot{O} \cdots H\diagdown \ddot{O}\diagup H \\ \ \ H\diagup\ddot{O}\diagdown H$$

➤ **Chemical reactions of Ethers:**

1. **Cleavage of C-O bond:** This cleavage takes place under severe conditions using excess of hydrogen halides.

$$R-O-R + HX \longrightarrow RX + R-OH$$

$$R-OH + HX \longrightarrow R-X + H_2O$$

$$\overset{O-R}{\bigcirc} + H - X \longrightarrow \overset{OH}{\bigcirc} + R - X$$

$$R-O-R' + HX \longrightarrow R-X + R'-OH$$

If one of the alkyl group is tertiary group then the halide formed will also be a tertiary halide.

Example:

$$CH_3 - \underset{\underset{CH_3}{|}}{\overset{\overset{CH_3}{|}}{C}} - O - CH_3 - HI \rightarrow CH_3OH + CH_3 - \underset{\underset{CH_3}{|}}{\overset{\overset{CH_3}{|}}{C}} - I$$

The order of reactivity of hydrogen halides is given below:

HI > HBr > HCl

2. Electrophilic substitution:

(i) Halogenation:

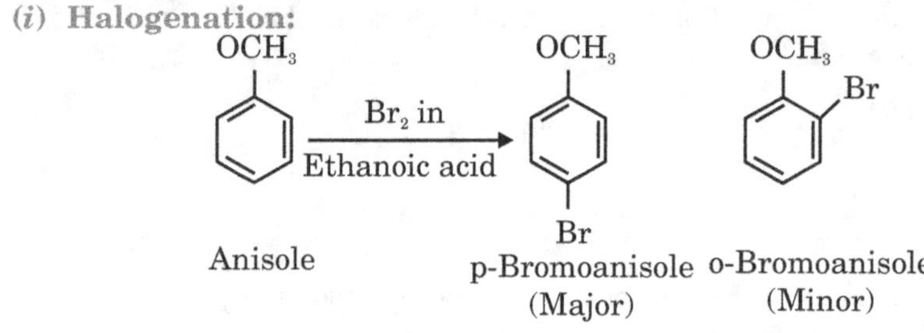

Anisole   p-Bromoanisole   o-Bromoanisole
              (Major)   (Minor)

(ii) Friedel – Crafts reaction:

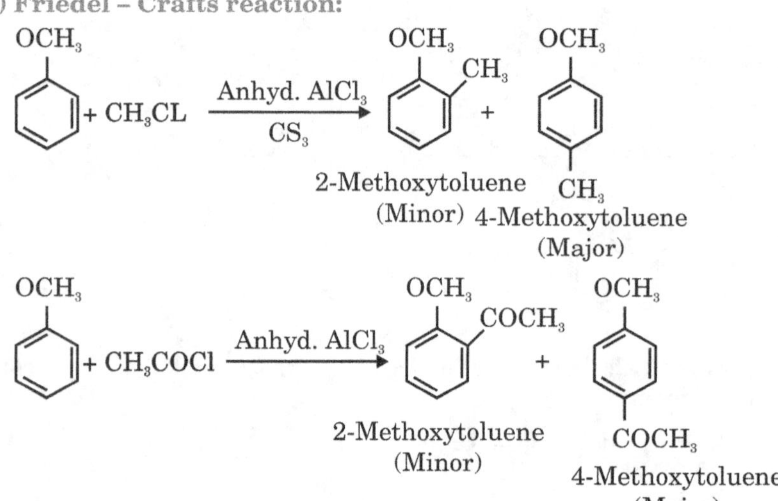

2-Methoxytoluene
(Minor)   4-Methoxytoluene
          (Major)

2-Methoxytoluene
(Minor)

4-Methoxytoluene
(Major)

(iii) Nitration:

2-Nitroanisole
(Minor)

4-Nitroanisole
(Major)

EXERCISE

1. According to Lewis concept of acids and bases, ether is
   - (a) Acidic
   - (b) Basic
   - (c) Neutral
   - (d) Amphoteric

2. In the reaction A is
   - (a) An aldehyde
   - (b) An aryl chloride
   - (c) An ether
   - (d) A ketone

3. When an alkyl halide is allowed to react with a sodium alkoxide the product likely is
   - (a) An aldehyde
   - (b) A Ketone
   - (c) An ether
   - (d) A carboxylic acid

4. Formation of diethyl either from ethanol is based on a
   - (a) Dehydration reaction
   - (b) Dehydrogenation reaction
   - (c) Hydrogenation reaction
   - (d) Heterolytic fission reaction

5. The compound formed when ethyl bromide is heated with dry silver oxide is
   - (a) Dimethyl ether
   - (b) Diethyl ether
   - (c) Methyl alcohol
   - (d) Ethyl alcohol

6. The reagent used for the preparation of higher ether from halogenated ether is
   - (a) Conc. H_2SO_4
   - (b) Sodium alkoxide
   - (c) Dry silver oxide
   - (d) Grignard reagent

7. Methylphenyl ethyl can be obtained by reacting
   - (a) Phenolate ions and methyl iodide
   - (b) Methoxide ions and bromobenzene
   - (c) Methanol and Phenol
   - (d) Bromo benzene and methyl bromide.

8. Which of the following product is formed. When ether is exposed to air
   - (a) Oxide
   - (b) Alkanes
   - (c) Alkenes
   - (d) Peroxide of diethyl ether

9. Ether which is liquid at room temperature is
   - (a) $C_2H_5OCH_3$
   - (b) $CH_3O\,CH_3$
   - (c) $C_2H_5OC_2H_5$
   - (d) None of these

10. Methyl-tert-butyl ether on heating with HI of one molar concentration gives
    - (a) $CH_3I + (CH_3)_3\,COH$
    - (b) $CH_3\,OH + (CH_3)_3\,Cl$
    - (c) $CH_3I + (CH_3)_3\,Cl$
    - (d) None of these

11. Picric acid is
    - (a) Trinitroaniline
    - (b) Trinitratoluene
    - (c) A volatile liquid
    - (d) $2,4,6$ trinitrophenol

12. Glycerol is a
    - (a) Primary alcohol
    - (b) Secondary alcohol
    - (c) Tertiary alcohol
    - (d) None of these

13. Glycerine is
    - (a) One primary and two secondary –OH groups.
    - (b) One secondary and two primary –OH groups.
    - (c) Three Primary –OH groups.
    - (d) Three secondary –OH groups.

14. Cyclohexanol is a
    - (a) Primary alcohol
    - (b) Secondary alcohol
    - (c) Tertiary alcohol
    - (d) Phenol

15. Methylated spirit is
    - (a) Methanol
    - (b) Methanol + ethanol
    - (c) Methanoic acid
    - (d) Methanamide

16. Which one of the following will produce a primary alcohol by reacting with CH_3MgI
    - (a) Acetone
    - (b) Methyl Cyanide
    - (c) Ethylene oxide
    - (d) Ethyl acetate

17. Coconut oil upon alkaline hydrolysis gives
    - (a) Glycol
    - (b) Alcohol
    - (c) Glycerol
    - (d) Ethylene oxide

18. Which enzyme converts glucose and fructose both into ethanol
    - (a) Diastase
    - (b) Invertase
    - (c) Zymase
    - (d) Maltase

19. Which of the following explains the viscous nature of glycerol
    - (a) Covalent bonds
    - (b) Hydrogen bonds
    - (c) Vander Waal's Forces
    - (d) Ionic Forces

20. Phenol is treated with bromine water and shaken well. The white precipitate formed during the process is
    - (a) m - bromophenol
    - (b) 2, 4 - dibromophenol
    - (c) 2, 4, 6 - tribromophenol
    - (d) A mixture of o- and p-bromophenols.

21. The reaction of conc. HNO_3 and Phenol forms
    (a) Benzoic acid   (b) Salicylic acid
    (c) o- and p-nitro phenol   (d) Picric acid

22. Which compound has hydrogen bonding
    (a) Toluene   (b) Phenol
    (c) Chlorobenzene   (d) Nitrobenzene

Answer Keys

1. (b)   2. (c)   3. (c)   4. (a)   5. (b)   6. (d)   7. (a)   8. (d)   9. (c)   10. (a)

11. (d)   12. (d)   13. (b)   14. (b)   15. (b)   16. (c)   17. (c)   18. (c)   19. (b)   20. (c)

21. (d)   22. (b)

Solutions

1. Ether is basic because lone pairs of electrons are present on oxygen atom, $R-\overset{\cdot\cdot}{\underset{\cdot\cdot}{O}}-R$

2.
$$\underset{}{\overset{OH}{C_6H_5}} + RX \xrightarrow{\text{Alkali}} \overset{O-R}{C_6H_5} + HX$$

3. $RX + RONa \longrightarrow R-O-R + NaX$
                               Ether

   It is a Williamson's synthesis reaction.

4. Dehydration of alcohols gives ethers.

5. $2C_2H_5Br + Ag_2O \longrightarrow C_2H_5-O-C_2H_5 + 2AgBr$

   If we take moist Ag_2O then alcohol is formed

   $Ag_2O + H_2O \longrightarrow 2AgOH$

   $C_2H_5Br + AgOH \longrightarrow C_2H_5OH + AgBr$

6. $CH_3OCH_3 \xrightarrow{Cl_2/h\nu} CH_3OCH_2Cl \xrightarrow[-Mg\,Br(Cl)]{CH_3MgBr} CH_3OCH_2CH_3$

   Methoxy methane α – Chlorodimethyl   Methoxyethane
   (Lower ether)   ether   (Higher ether)

7. $C_6H_6O^- + CH_3I \longrightarrow C_6H_5OCH_3 + I^-$

8. $C_2H_5-O-C_2H_5 + O_2 \xrightarrow[25°C]{h\nu} CH_3-CH(OOH)-O-C_2H_5$.

9. CH_3OCH_3 and $C_2H_4OCH_3$ are gases while $C_2H_5OC_2H_5$ is low boiling liquid (B.P $\to$ 308K)

10. $CH_3-\overset{CH_3}{\underset{CH_3}{\overset{|}{\underset{|}{C}}}}-O-CH_3 + HI \longrightarrow CH_3I + (CH_3)_3COH$

11.

$$O_2N \overset{\displaystyle OH}{\underset{\displaystyle NO_2}{\bigcirc}} NO_2$$

2, 4, 6-trinitrophenol or picric acid.

12.
$$\underset{OH}{CH_2} - \underset{OH}{CH} - \underset{OH}{CH_2}$$

Glycerol is trihydric alcohols.

13.
$$\begin{array}{l} CH_2 - OH \\ | \\ CH - OH \\ | \\ CH_2 - OH \end{array}$$

One secondary and two primary alcoholic groups.

14.

$$\overset{\displaystyle OH}{\bigcirc}$$

Cyclohexanol is a secondary alcohol because –OH group is linked to 2° carbon.

15. 5-10% methyl alcohol and remaining ethanol is called methylated spirit. It is also known as denatured alcohol because it is unfit for drinking.

16.
$$\underset{O}{\overset{CH_2 - CH_2}{\diagdown \diagup}} + CH_3MgI \longrightarrow \underset{CH_3 \quad OMgI}{CH_2 - CH_2} \longrightarrow$$

$$CH_3 - CH_2 - CH_2 - OH + Mg\underset{OH}{\overset{I}{\diagup}}$$

Propyl alcohol

17. Coconut oil + Alkali $\longrightarrow$ Soap + Glycerol

It is a saponification reaction.

18. $C_6H_{12}O_6 \xrightarrow{\text{Zymase}} 2C_2H_5OH + 2CO_2$

Glucose or Fructose　　Ethyl alcohol

19. Glycerol undergoes extensive hydrogen bonding due to the presence of 3–OH groups. As a result the glycerol molecules are highly associated and thus it has high viscosity.

20.

$$\overset{\displaystyle OH}{\bigcirc} \xrightarrow{Br_2 \text{ Water}} Br\overset{\displaystyle OH}{\underset{\displaystyle Br}{\bigcirc}}Br$$

Phenol

21.

$$\overset{\displaystyle OH}{\bigcirc} + \text{Conc. HNO}_3 \xrightarrow[\text{(Conc.)}]{H_2SO_4} O_2N\overset{\displaystyle OH}{\underset{\displaystyle NO_2}{\bigcirc}}NO_2$$

Picric acid

22.

$$\overset{\delta- \ \ \delta+}{O-H} - - - - - \overset{\delta- \ \ \delta+}{O-H} - - - - - \overset{\delta- \ \ \delta+}{O-H}$$

CHAPTER 12

Aldehydes, Ketones & Carboxylic Acids

Aldehydes and ketones

They are the organic compounds containing carbon-oxygen double bond. ($> C = O$)

- The carbonyl group is bonded with a carbon and hydrogen in aldehydes and it is bonded to two carbon atoms in ketones.

$$\underset{\text{Aldehyde}}{\underset{R \qquad\qquad H}{\overset{O}{\overset{\|}{C}}}} \qquad \underset{\text{Ketone}}{\underset{R \qquad\qquad R}{\overset{O}{\overset{\|}{C}}}}$$

Nomenclature

- **Common Names**
  - ➤ Instead of IUPAC names, common names are used for aldehydes and ketones.
  - ➤ The location of the substituent in the carbon chain is indicated by Greek letters α, β, γ etc, α-carbon being the one directly linked to the aldehyde group, carbon the next, and so on.

$$\underset{\beta\text{-Bromobutyraldehyde}}{H_3C - \underset{\underset{\gamma}{\overset{\overset{Br}{|}}{CH}}}{} - \underset{\alpha}{\overset{}{CH_2}} - \overset{\overset{O}{\|}}{C} - H}$$

- **IUPAC Names**
  - ➤ They are derived from IUPAC names of corresponding alkanes, by replacing ending e with –al in aldehydes and –one in ketones.
  - ➤ Longest carbon chain is numbered starting from the carbon of the aldehyde group while in case of ketones the numbering begins from the end nearer to the carbonyl group.

$$\underset{\text{4-Bromo-3-methylheptanal}}{CH_3 - CH_2 - CH_2\,\underset{}{\overset{\overset{Br}{|}}{CH}} - \underset{}{\overset{\overset{CH_3}{|}}{CH}} - CH_2 - \overset{\overset{O}{\|}}{C} - H}$$

Structure of the Carbonyl Group

- The carbonyl carbon atom forms three sigma bonds and a π bond with oxygen and is sp^3 hybridized.
- The angles between the bonds is 120° as shown below

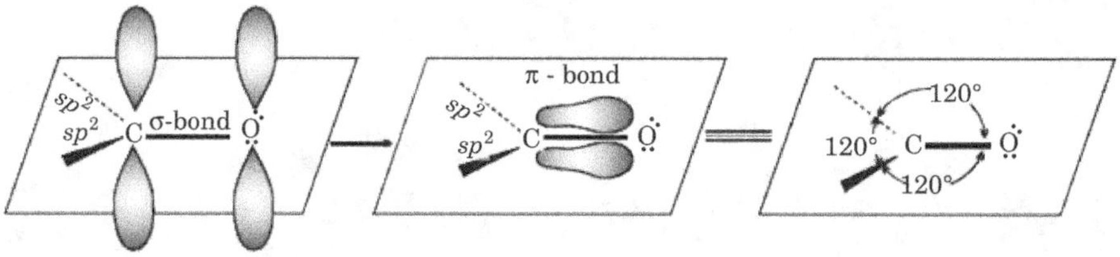

- As oxygen is more electronegative than oxygen, the carbon-oxygen double bond is polarized.

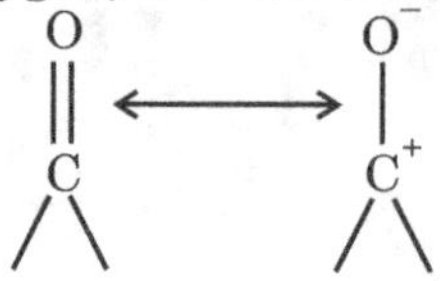

Preparation of Aldehydes and Ketones

- **Oxidation of alcohols**
- By oxidation of primary and secondary alcohols, aldehydes and ketones are prepared.

$$RCH_2OH \xrightarrow{[O]} \underset{\text{Aldehyde}}{R-\overset{\overset{H}{|}}{C}=O} \longrightarrow \underset{\text{Carboxylic acid}}{R-\overset{\overset{OH}{|}}{C}=O}$$

- Secondary alcohols are oxidized in presence of CrO_3 to ketones.
- **Dehydrogenation of alcohols**

$$\underset{1^\circ\text{ Alcohol}}{R-CH_2-OH} \xrightarrow[573K]{Cu} \underset{\text{Aldehyde}}{RCHO + H_2}$$

- **Using hydrocarbons**
  - **Using ozonolysis of alkenes**

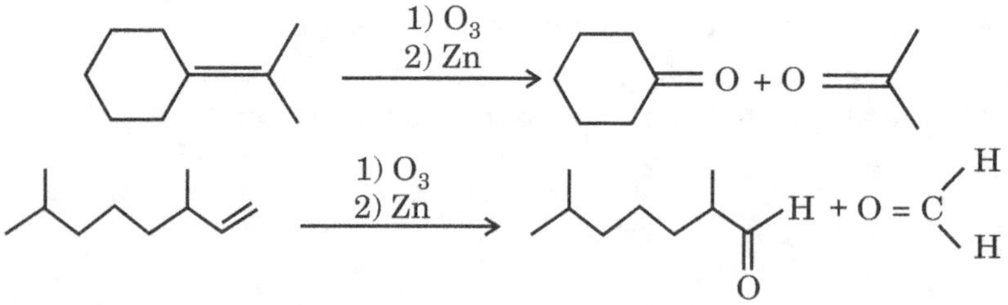

  - **By hydration of alkynes**

    Addition of water to ethyne in the presence of H_2SO_4 and $HgSO_4$ gives acetaldehyde

Preparation of Alhehydes

- **Rosenmund Reaction:**

  Acid chloride is hydrogenated in presence of a catalyst (Palladium on Barium Sulphate)

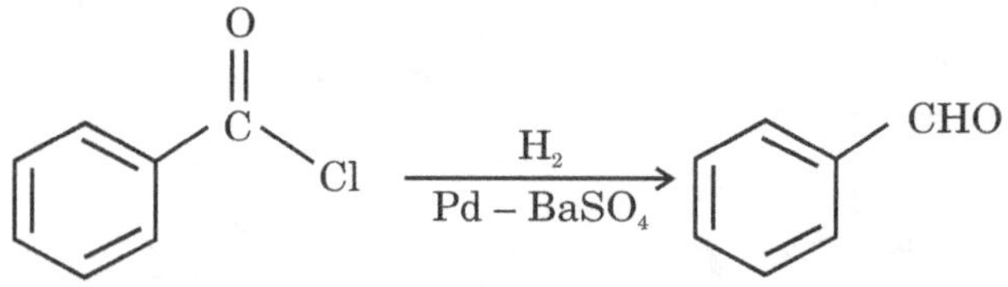

Benzoyl chloride Benzaldehyde

- **Stephen Reaction:**
  Nitrites are reduced to imine which on hydrolysis gives aldehyde.

$$RCN + SnCl_2 + HCl \longrightarrow RCH = NH \xrightarrow{H_3\overset{+}{O}} RCHO$$

- **From hydrocarbons**
  - **By oxidation of methylbenzene**
    Etard Reaction:

Toluene $+ CrO_2Cl_2 \xrightarrow{CS_2}$ Chromium complex $CH(OCrOHCl_2)_2$ $\xrightarrow{H_3O^+}$ Benzaldehyde CHO

By side chain chlorination followed by hydrolysis

Toluene CH_3 $\xrightarrow{Cl_2/hv}$ Benzal chloride $CHCl_2$ $\xrightarrow[373\ K]{H_2O}$ Benzaldehyde CHO

Gatterman-Koch Reaction:

Benzal chloride $\xrightarrow[\text{Anhyd. AlCl}_3/\text{CuCl}]{\text{CO, HCl}}$ Benzaldehyde CHO

Preparation of Ketones

- **Using acyl chlorides**

$$2R - Mg - X \ + \ CdCl_2 \longrightarrow R_2Cd + 2Mg(X)Cl$$

$$2R' - \underset{\underset{O}{||}}{C} - Cl \ + \ R_2Cd \longrightarrow 2R' - \underset{\underset{O}{||}}{C} - R + CdCl_2$$

- **Using nitriles**
  When nitriles are treated with Grignard reagent followed by hydrolysis, it gives ketones.

$$CH_3 - CH_2 - C \equiv N + C_6H_5MgBr \xrightarrow{ether}$$

$$CH_3CH_2 - C \overset{NMgBr}{\underset{C_6H_5}{\diagdown}} \xrightarrow{H_3O^+} C_2H_5 - C \overset{O}{\underset{C_6H_5}{\diagdown}}$$

Propiophenone
(1-Phenylpropanone)

- **Acylation Reaction**

$$+ \ Ar/R - \underset{\underset{O}{||}}{C} - Cl \xrightarrow{\text{Anhyd. AlCl}_3} \underset{\underset{Ar/R}{}}{C} \overset{O}{||}$$

Physical Properties

- A large amount of aldehydes are liquids at room temperature.
- As aldehydes and ketones have hydrogen bonding capacity, they are soluble in water (upto 4 carbon atoms)
- Most of them have high boiling point when compared to hydrocarbons and higher than those of alcohols.

Chemical Properties

Nucleophilic Addition Reactions

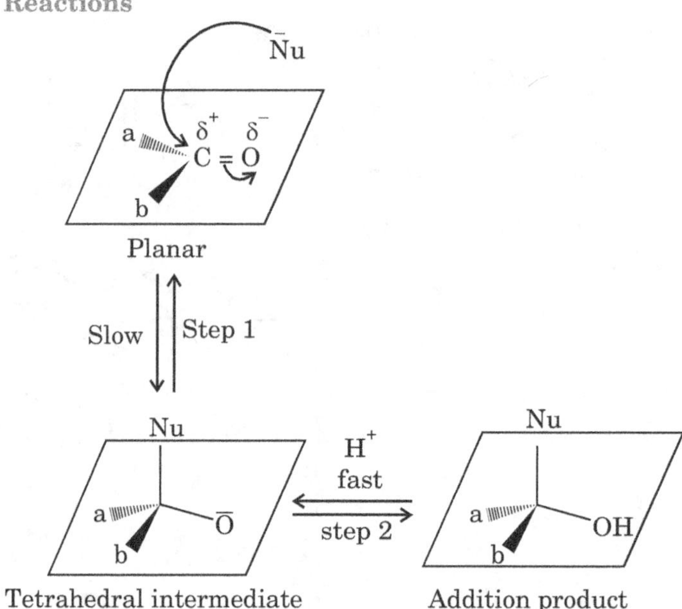

- **Addition of hydrogen cyanide:**

  Cyanohydrins are obtained when aldehydes and ketones are treated with

$$HCN + OH^- \rightleftharpoons : \bar{C}N + H_2O$$

- **Addition of sodium hydrogensulphite**

- **Addition of Grignard Reagent**

- **Addition of alcohols**

$$R-CHO \xrightleftharpoons[]{\substack{R'OH \\ HCl\ gas}} \left[R-CH \begin{array}{c} OR' \\ \diagdown \\ OH \end{array} \right] \xrightleftharpoons[H^+]{R'OH} R-CH \begin{array}{c} OR' \\ \diagdown \\ OR' \end{array} + H_2O$$

Hemiacetal   Acetal

Ketones don't react with monohydric alcohols but react with dihydric alcohols to give ketals.

$$\begin{array}{c} R \\ \diagdown \\ \diagup \\ R \end{array} C = O + \begin{array}{c} CH_2OH \\ | \\ CH_2OH \end{array} \xrightleftharpoons[dil.\ HCl]{HCl\ gas} \begin{array}{c} R \\ \diagdown \\ \diagup \\ R \end{array} C \begin{array}{c} O - CH_2 \\ | \\ O - CH_2 \end{array} + H_2O$$

Ethylene glycol ketal

- **Addition of ammonia**

$$\begin{array}{c} \diagdown \\ \diagup \end{array} C = O + H_2N-Z \rightleftharpoons \left[C \begin{array}{c} OH \\ \diagdown \\ NHZ \end{array} \right] \longrightarrow \begin{array}{c} \diagdown \\ \diagup \end{array} C = N\text{-}Z + H_2O$$

Reduction Reactions

- **Clemmensen Reduction or Wolf Kishner Reduction:**

  The carbonyl group is reduced to CH_2 group as shown below

$$\begin{array}{c} \diagdown \\ \diagup \end{array} C = O \xrightarrow[HCl]{Zn\text{-}Hg} \begin{array}{c} \diagdown \\ \diagup \end{array} CH_2 + H_2O \quad \text{(Clemmensen reduction)}$$

$$\begin{array}{c} \diagdown \\ \diagup \end{array} C = O \xrightarrow[-H_2O]{NH_2NH_2} \begin{array}{c} \diagdown \\ \diagup \end{array} C = NNH_2 \xrightarrow[heat]{KOH/ethylene\ glycol} \begin{array}{c} \diagdown \\ \diagup \end{array} CH_2 + N_2$$

(wolff-Kishner reduction)

- **Reduction to alcohols**

  In presence of $NaBH_4$, a primary alcohol is obtained while in presence of $LiAlH_4$, a secondary alcohol is obtained.

$$R-CHO + 2[H] \xrightarrow{LiAlH_4} R-CH_2-OH$$

Oxidation

- On oxidation, aldehydes result in carboxylic acids on treatment with nitric acid, and mild oxidizing agents like Tollen's reagent and Fehling's reagent.

$$R-CHO \xrightarrow{[O]} R-COOH$$

- Ketones are oxidized by strong oxidizing agents at high temperatures which involves the cleavage of carbon-carbon bond.

$$\overset{1}{R}-CH_2-\overset{2}{C}-\overset{3}{CH_2}\text{-}R' \xrightarrow{[O]} R-COOH + R'-CH_2COOH$$
$$\underset{O}{\overset{||}{}}$$

(By cleavage of $C_1 - C_2$ bond)

+

$$R-CH_2COOH + R'-COOH$$
(By cleavage of $C_2 - C_3$ bond)

Reactions due to α hydrogen.

- **Aldol Condensation**

  β hydroxyl aldehydes or β hydroxyl ketones are obtained when Aldehydes and ketones having at least one α-hydrogen undergo a reaction in the presence of dilute alkali as catalyst.

$$2CH_3 - CHO \underset{}{\overset{\text{dil. NaOH}}{\rightleftharpoons}} CH_3 - \underset{\underset{OH}{|}}{CH} - CH_2 - CHO \xrightarrow[-H_2O]{\Delta} CH_3 - CH = CH - CHO$$

   Ethanal   3-Hydroxybutanal   But-2-enal
                                                    (Aldol)   (Aldol condensation product)

- **Cross Aldol Condensation**

  When two different aldehydes or/and ketones undergo aldol condensation, it is known as cross aldol condensation.

$$\begin{matrix} CH_3CHO \\ + \\ CH_3CH_2CHO \end{matrix} \xrightarrow[2. \ \Delta]{1. \ NaOH} \begin{matrix} CH_3-CH=CH-CHO \\ \text{But-2-enal} \end{matrix} + CH_3CH_2 - CH = \underset{\underset{CH_3}{|}}{C} - CHO$$

         from two molecules of ethanal   2-Methylpent-2-enal
                                          from two molecules of propanal

simple or self aldol products

+

$$CH_3 - CH = \underset{\underset{CH_3}{|}}{C} - CHO + CH_3CH_2 - CH = CHCHO$$

      2-Methylbut-2-enal   Pent-2-enal

from one molecule of ethanal and one molecule of propanal

cross aldol products

Other Reactions

- **Cannizzaro Reaction:**

  In this reaction, one molecule of the aldehyde is reduced to alcohol while another is oxidised to carboxylic acid salt.

$$\underset{H}{\overset{H}{>}}C = O + \underset{H}{\overset{H}{>}}C = O + Conc.KOH \longrightarrow H - \underset{\underset{H}{|}}{\overset{\overset{H}{|}}{C}} - OH + H - C\overset{\overset{O}{\diagup}}{\underset{OK}{\diagdown}}$$

                                            Methanol   Potassium formate

- **Electrophilic Substitution**

  Aromatic aldehydes and ketones undergo this reaction.

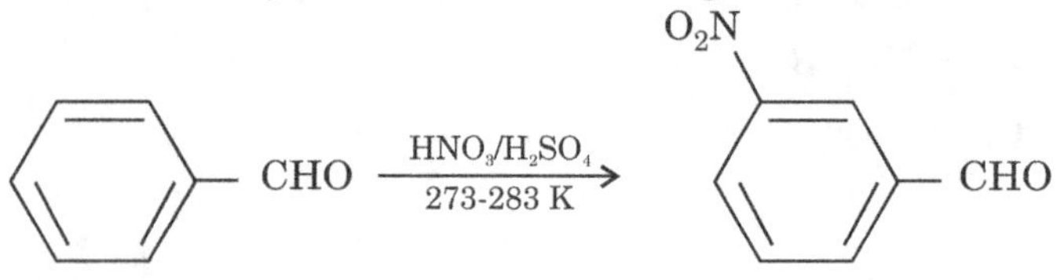

$$C_6H_5-CHO \xrightarrow[273\text{-}283 \ K]{HNO_3/H_2SO_4} \ O_2N-C_6H_4-CHO$$

   Benzaldehyde   m-Nitrobenzaldehyde

Uses of Aldehydes and Ketones

- Formalin solution (Formaldehyde) is used in preserving biological specimens and to prepare polymer products.
- Many aldehydes and ketones have a pleasant smell and flavor.
- Acetaldehyde is used as a starting material to manufacture acetic acid, polymers and drugs.

Carboxylic Acids

- These are the carbon compounds containing $-COOH$ functional group.
- Carboxylic acids may be aliphatic ($RCOOH$)or aromatic ($ArCOOH$) depending on the group, alkyl or aryl, attached to carboxylic carbon.

Nomenclature

- Many of the carboxylic acids are known by their common names. Example: Ethanoic Acid is called as Acetic acid.
- In the IUPAC system, aliphatic carboxylic acids are named by replacing the ending –e in the name of the corresponding alkane with – oic acid.
- In numbering the carbon chain, the carboxylic carbon is numbered one. Example: The IUPAC name of is

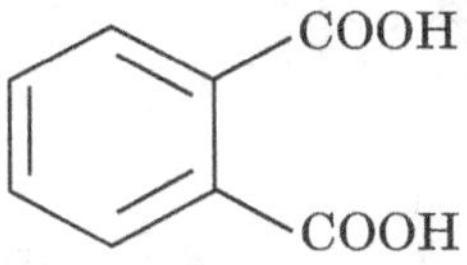

is Benzene-1, 2-dicarboxylic acid.

Structure of Carboxyl Group

- The bonds are in one plane and the angle between the bonds is 120°.
- Due to difference in electrophilic nature, resonance is present as shown below:

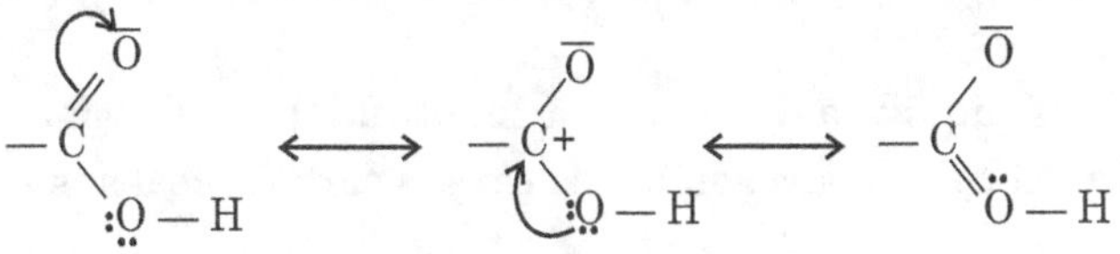

Preparation of Carboxylic Acids

- **From primary alcohols and aldehydes**

  In the presence of oxidizing agents like potassium permanganate and potassium dichromate, primary alcohols are oxidized to carboxylic acids.

$$RCH_2OH \xrightarrow[\text{2. } H_3O^{\oplus}]{\text{1. alkaline } KMnO_4} RCOOH$$

$$CH_3(CH_2)_8CH_2OH \xrightarrow{CrO_3-H_2SO_4} CH_2(CH_2)_8COOH$$
$$\text{1–Decanol} \qquad\qquad\qquad \text{Decanoic acid}$$

- **From alkylbenzenes:**

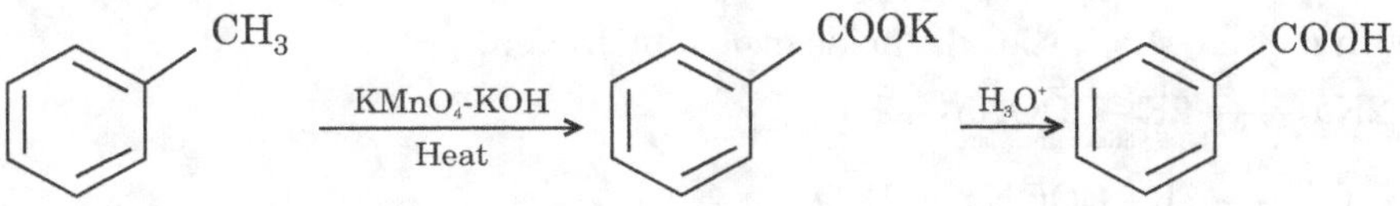

Benzoic acid

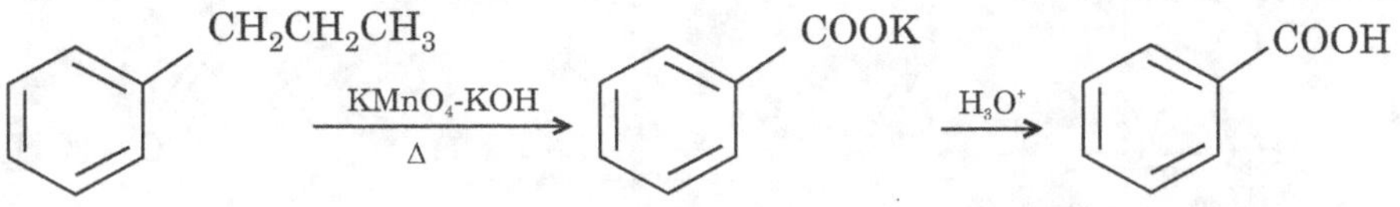

Benzoic acid

- **Using nitriles and amides**

  To stop the reaction at the amide stage, mild reaction conditions are used.

  $$R\text{-}CN \xrightarrow[H_2O]{\overset{+}{H} \text{ or } \overset{-}{O}H} R - \overset{\overset{\displaystyle O}{\|}}{C} - NH_2 \xrightarrow[\Delta]{\overset{+}{H} \text{ or } \overset{-}{O}H} RCOOH$$

- **Using Grignard Reagent**

  Salts of carboxylic acids are formed when Grignard's reagent react with carbon dioxide(dry ice) which on acidification with mineral acid give carboxylic acids.

  $$R - Mg - X \ + \ O = C = O \xrightarrow{Dry\ ether} R - C \overset{\displaystyle O}{\underset{\displaystyle O^-MgX^+}{<}} \xrightarrow{H_3O^+} RCOOH$$

- **Using acyl halides and anhydrides**

  $$RCOCl \begin{cases} \xrightarrow{H_2O} RCOOH \ + \ \overset{-}{C}l \\ \xrightarrow{\overset{-}{O}H/H_2O} RCOO^- \ + \ \overset{-}{C}l \xrightarrow{H_3O^+} RCOOH \end{cases}$$

  $$\underset{\text{Benzoic anhydride}}{(C_6H_5CO)_2O} \xrightarrow{H_3O} \underset{\text{Benzoic acid}}{2C_6H_5COOH}$$

- **Using esters**

  Esters when subjected to acidic hydrolysis give carboxylic acids.

  Ethyl benzoate $\xrightleftharpoons{H_3O^+}$ Benzoic acid $+ \ C_2H_5OH$

Physical Properties

- Lower members are colorless liquid having pungent smell and the higher members are odourless waxy solid.
- The ability to form intermolecular hydrogen bonds causes carboxylic acids to have higher boiling point.

Hydrogen bonding of
RCOOH with H_2O

Chemical Reactions

- **Reactions with metals and alkalies**

  On reacting with metals, the carboxylic acids evolve hydrogen.

  $$2R - COOH + 2Na \longrightarrow \underset{\text{Sodium carboxylate}}{2R - C\overline{O}ONa^+} + H_2$$

  $$R - COOH + NaOH \longrightarrow R - C\overline{O}ONa^+ + H_2O$$

- **Formation of anhydride**

  $$H_3C - \overset{\displaystyle O}{\underset{\displaystyle OH}{\overset{\|}{C}}} \ + \ \overset{\displaystyle O}{\underset{\displaystyle HO}{\overset{\|}{C}}} - CH_3 \xrightarrow[\text{or } P_2O_5,\ \Delta]{H^+,\ \Delta} CH_3C - \overset{\displaystyle O}{\overset{\|}{C}} \overset{\displaystyle O}{\underset{\displaystyle O}{\overset{\|}{C}}} - CH_3$$

  Ethanoic acid   Ethanoic anhydride

- Esterification:

$$RCOOH + PCl_5 \longrightarrow RCOCl + PCl_3 + HCl$$

$$3RCOOH + PCl_3 \longrightarrow 3RCOCl + H_3PO_3$$

$$RCOOH + SOCl_2 \longrightarrow RCOCl + SO_2 + HCl$$

- Reactions with $PCl_5, PCl_3, SOCl_2$

  The hydroxyl group gets replaced by chlorine atom.

$$RCOOH + R'OH \underset{}{\overset{H^+, \Delta}{\rightleftharpoons}} RCOOR' + H_2O$$

- Reaction with ammonia

  Reaction of carboxylic acids with ammonia gives ammonium salts which when heated further gives amides.

$$CH_3COOH + NH_3 \rightleftharpoons \underset{\text{Ammonium acetate}}{CH_3CO\overset{-}{O}\overset{+}{N}H_4} \xrightarrow[-H_2O]{\Delta} \underset{\text{Acetamide}}{CH_3CONH_2}$$

Reactions involving –COOH group

- Reduction

  Carboxylic acids, when reduced by diborane give primary alcohols.

$$R-COOH \xrightarrow[\text{(ii) } H_3O^+]{\text{(i) LiAlH}_4 \text{ /ether or } B_2H_6} R-CH_2OH$$

- Decarboxylation: The loss of carbon dioxide from carboxylic acids to form hydrocarbons when their sodium salts are heated with sodalime (NaOH and CaO in the ratio 3 :1) is called decarboxylation.

$$R-COONa \xrightarrow[\text{Heat}]{\text{NaOH \& CaO}} R-H + Na_2CO_3$$

Substitution Reactions

- Halogenation (Hell Volhard-Zelinsky Reaction)

  Carboxylic acids which have an -hydrogen are halogenated at the α-position on treatment with chlorine or bromine in the presence of small amount of red phosphorus which results in α halocarboxylic acids.

$$R-CH_2-COOH \xrightarrow[\text{(ii) } H_2O]{\text{(i) } X_2 \text{ Red phosphorus}} R\text{-}CH\text{-}COOH$$

$$|$$
$$X$$

X = Cl, Br

α - Halocarboxylic acid

- Ring Substitution

  In aromatic carboxylic acids, carboxyl group acts as a deactivating and meta-directing group.

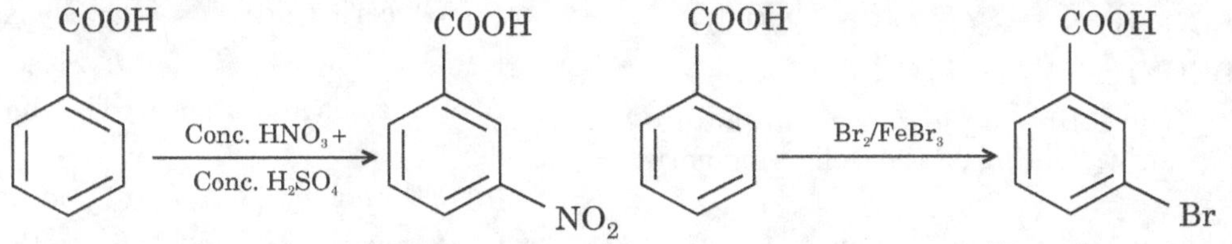

$$\text{COOH} \xrightarrow[\text{Conc. } H_2SO_4]{\text{Conc. } HNO_3 +} \text{COOH (}m\text{-Nitrobenzoic acid, } NO_2\text{)}$$

m-Nitrobenzoic acid

$$\text{COOH} \xrightarrow{Br_2/FeBr_3} \text{COOH (}m\text{-Bromobenzoic acid, } Br\text{)}$$

m-Bromobenzoic acid

Applications of Carboxylic Acids

- Ethanoic acid is used as vinegar and as solvent.
- Methanoic acid is used in rubber, dyeing, leather,textile, and electroplating industries.
- Esters of benzoic acid are often used in perfume industry.
- For the manufacturing of soaps and detergents, higher fatty acids are used.

EXERCISE

1. Which of the aldehyde is most reactive?
   (a) $C_6H_5 - CHO$
   (b) CH_3 CHO
   (c) HCHO
   (d) All equally reactive

2. Which of the following is general formula of aldehyde and ketone
   (a) $C_nH_{2n+2}O$
   (b) $C_nH_{2n}O_2$
   (c) $C_nH_{2n}O$
   (d) $C_nH_{2n+1}O$

3. The end product in the following sequence of reaction is

   $$HC \equiv CH \xrightarrow[20\%,\ H_2SO_4]{1\%\ Hg\ SO_4} A \xrightarrow{CH_3MgX} B \xrightarrow{[O]}$$

   (a) Acetic acid
   (b) Isopropyl alcohol
   (c) Acetone
   (d) Ethanol

4. Which one of the following compounds is prepared in the laboratory from benzene by a substitution reaction
   (a) Glyoxal
   (b) Cyclohexane
   (c) Acetophenone
   (d) Hexabromo Cyclohexane

5. From which of the following tertiary butyl alcohol is obtained by the action of methyl magnesium iodide.
   (a) HCHO
   (b) CH_3 CHO
   (c) CH_3COCH_3
   (d) CO_2

6. Dry heating of calcium acetate gives
   (a) Acetaldehyde
   (b) Ethane
   (c) Acetic acid
   (d) Acetone

7. Identify the product C in the series.

   $$CH_3CN \xrightarrow{Na/C_2H_5OH} A \xrightarrow{HNO_2} B \xrightarrow{Cu/573K} C$$

   (a) CH_3COOH
   (b) CH_3CH_2NHOH
   (c) CH_3CONH_2
   (d) CH_3CHO

8. Which of the following organic compounds exhibits positive Fehling test as well as iodoform test
   (a) Methanal
   (b) Ethanol
   (c) Propanone
   (d) Ethanal

9. C_2H_5CHO and $(CH_3)_2CO$ can be distinguished by testing with
   (a) Phenyl hydrazine
   (b) Hydroxylamine
   (c) Fehling solution
   (d) Sodium bisulphite

10. Which of the following will not give iodoform test
    (a) Ethanal
    (b) Ethanol
    (c) 2-Propanone
    (d) 3-Pentanone

11. Formaldehyde when treated with KOH gives methanol and Potassium formate. The reaction is known as
    (a) Parkin reaction
    (b) Claisen reaction
    (c) Cannizzaro reaction
    (d) Knoevenagel reaction

12. The addition of HCN to carbonyl compounds is an example of
    (a) Nucleophilic substitution
    (b) Electrophilic addition
    (c) Nuclophilic additon
    (d) Electrophilic substitution

13. Palmitic acid is
    (a) $C_{16}H_{31}$ COOH
    (b) $CO_{17}H_{35}$ COOH
    (c) $C_{15}H_{31}$ COOH
    (d) $C_{17}H_{31}$ COOH

14. $(RCO)_2$ NH is
    (a) Primary amine
    (b) Secondary amine
    (c) Secondary amide
    (d) Tertiary amide

15. Wax are long chain compounds belonging to the class.
    (a) Acids
    (b) Alcohols
    (c) Esters
    (d) Ethers

16. Urea
    (a) is an amide of carbonic acid
    (b) It is diamide of carbonic acid
    (c) Gives carbonic acid on hydrolysis
    (d) Resembles Carbonic acid.

17. Glycerol on oxidation with bismuth nitrate produce
    (a) Glyceric acid
    (b) Glyoxalic acid
    (c) Oxalic acid
    (d) Meso oxalic acid

18. Acetic acid is manufactured by the fermentation of
    (a) Ethanol
    (b) Methanol
    (c) Ethanal
    (d) Methanal

19. Which of the following acids has the smallest dissociation constant.
    (a) $CH_3CHFCOOH$
    (b) FCH_2CH_2COOH
    (c) $Br\ CH_2\ CH_2\ COOH$
    (d) $CH_3\ CH\ Br\ COOH$

20. The reaction of acetamide with water is an example of
    (a) Alcoholysis
    (b) Hydrolysis
    (c) Ammonolysis
    (d) Saponification

21. The acid which reduces Fehling solution is
    (a) Methanoic acid (b) Ethanoic acid
    (c) Butanoic acid   (d) Propanoic acid

22. In CH_3COOH and $HCOOH$ will be
    (a) Less acidic   (b) Equally acidic
    (c) More acidic   (d) None

Answer Keys

1. (c) 2. (c) 3. (c) 4. (c) 5. (c) 6. (d) 7. (d) 8. (d) 9. (c) 10. (d)

11. (c) 12. (c) 13. (c) 14. (c) 15. (c) 16. (b) 17. (d) 18. (a) 19. (c) 20. (b)

21. (a) 22. (c)

Solutions

1. Among Carbonyl Compounds, reactivity decrease with increase with alkyl groups and alkyl groups (+I effect) decrease positive character on C-atom. Thus the correct order of reactivity is, $HCHO > CH_3CHO > C_6H_5CHO$

2. Both aldehydes and ketones have the same general formula $CnH_{2n}O$.

3. $HC \equiv CH \xrightarrow[20\% \ H_2SO_4]{1\% \ Hg \ SO_4} CH_3CHO \xrightarrow[H_2O]{CH_3MgX}$
   (A)

   $CH_3CHOHCH_3 \xrightarrow{[O]} CH_3COCH_3$
   $[B]$ $\qquad$ Acetone

4. ⬡ + CH_3COCl (Conc.) $\xrightarrow{AlCH_3}$ ⬡–$COCH_3$ + HCl

   Acetophenone

   It is Friedel – crafts reaction.

5. $CH_3CO \ CH_3 \xrightarrow{CH_3MgI} (CH_3)_3 COH$
   Acetone $\qquad$ tert – Butyl alcohol

6. $CH_3 – \overset{\overset{O}{||}}{C} – O$ ⟍ $Ca \xrightarrow{Dry \ heating}$
   $CH_3 – \underset{\underset{O}{||}}{C} – O$ ⟋

   $CH_3 – CO – CH_3 + CaCO_3$

   Acetone

7. $CH_3CN \xrightarrow{Na/C_2H_5OH} CH_3CH_2NH_2$
   $\xrightarrow{HNO_2} CH_3CH_3OH \xrightarrow{Cu/573 \ K} CH_3CHO$
   $\qquad\qquad$ [C]

8. Ethanal among the given compounds gives positive iodoform test.

9. $C_2H_5CHO + 2Cu^{2+} + 5OH^- \longrightarrow Cu_2O + 3H_2O +$
   $C_2H_5COO^- \ CH_3COCH_3 + 2Cu^{+2} + 5OH^- \longrightarrow$
   No reaction

10. $CH_3 – CH_2 – \overset{\overset{O}{||}}{C} – CH_2 – CH_3$ do not have

    $CH_3 – \overset{\overset{O}{||}}{C}$ – group

11. In cannizzaro's reaction the substance is oxidized and other is reduced.

    $HCHO + HCHO \xrightarrow{KOH} CH_3OH + HCOOK$

12. Addition of HCN to carbonyl compounds is an example of nucleophilic addition.

13. Fromula of Palmitic acid is $C_{15}H_{31} \ COOH$

14. $R – CONH_2$ $\quad$ and $\quad$ $(RCO)_2 \ NH$
    Primary amide $\quad$ Secondary amide

15. Wax are long chain ester

16. Urea is diamide of carbonic acid.

$$HO-\overset{\overset{O}{\|}}{C}-OH + 2NH_3 \xrightarrow{-H_2O} H_2N-\overset{\overset{O}{\|}}{C}-NH_2$$

    Carbonic acid   Urea

So, two mole of NH_3 are required that is why it is called the diamide of carbonic acid.

17.

$$\begin{array}{c} CH_2OH \\ | \\ CHOH \\ | \\ CH_2OH \end{array} \xrightarrow[\text{nitrate}]{\overset{[O]}{\text{Bismuth}}} \begin{array}{c} COOH \\ | \\ COOH \end{array}$$

  Glycerol   Meso oxalic acid

Thus, glycerol produce meso-oxalic acid.

18. $C_2H_5OH \xrightarrow{\text{Acetobacter}} CH_3COOH$

19. $Br\,CH_2\,CH_2\,COOH$ is least acidic or has less k_a i.e., dissociation constant. It is (a) due to lesser -1 effect of Br than F and (b) Br atom further away form $-COOH$ group.

20. The reaction of acetamide with water is an example of hydrolysis

21. Methanoic acid resemble with aldehyde due to its structure. So it reduces Fehlings reagent.

$$\overset{\overset{O}{\|}}{H-C}-OH$$

  Aldehydic group

22. Presence of methyl group decrease the acidic character of acetic acid due to positive inductive effect $(+I)$.

CHAPTER 13

Organic Compounds Containing Nitrogen

Introduction, Methods of Preparation and Physical Properties

- **Amines:** Amines can be considered as the amino derivatives of hydrocarbons or alkyl derivatives of ammonia. Amines are obtained by replacing one, two or three hydrogen atoms by alkyl and/or aryl groups.

  For example, $CH_3NH_2, C_2H_5NH_2, C_6H_5NH_2$ *etc.*

- **Classification of amines:**

  $$-NH_2 \qquad -\overset{|}{N}H \qquad -\overset{|}{N}-$$

  $$Pr\,imary \qquad Secondary \qquad Tertiary$$

  $$\left(1^o\right) \qquad \left(2^o\right) \qquad \left(3^o\right)$$

- **Structure of amines:**

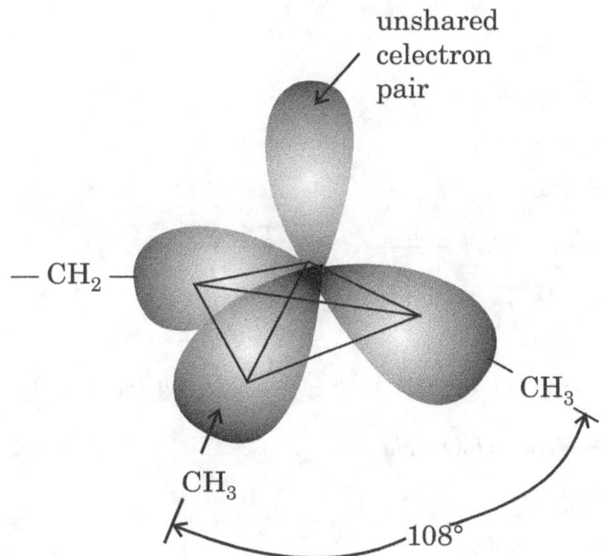

Pyramidal shape of trimethylamine

Nitrogen orbitals in amines are sp^3 hybridised and the geometry of amines is pyramidal. The fourth orbital of nitrogen in all amines contains an unshared pair of electrons. Due to the presence of unshared pair of electrons, the angle $C - N - E$ is less than $109.5°$.

- **Nomenclature of some alkylamines and arylamines:**

Amines	Common Names	IUPAC name
$CH_3 - CH_2 - NH_2$	Ethylamine	Ethanamine
$CH_3 - CH_2 - CH_2 - NH_2$	n-Propylamine	Propan-1-amine
$CH_3 - \underset{\underset{NH_2}{\mid}}{C}H - CH_3$	Isopropylamine	Propane-2-amine
$CH_3 - \underset{\underset{H}{\mid}}{N} - CH_2 - CH_3$	Ethylmethylamine	N-Methylethanamine
$CH_3 - \underset{\underset{CH_3}{\mid}}{N} - CH_3$	Trimethylamine	N,N-Dimethylmethaneamane
NH_2 (benzene ring)	Aniline	Aniline or benzenamine
NH_2 (benzene ring, Br)	p-Bromoanaline	4-Bromobenzylamine Or 4-Bromoaniline

- **Preparation of Amines:**
  - By reduction of nitro compounds:

$$R - NO_2 + 3H_2 \xrightarrow{\ Ni\ } R - NH_2 + 2H_2O$$
$$1^0 \text{ amine}$$

  - By ammonolysis of alkyl halides:

$$R - X + NH_3 \rightarrow RNH_2 \xrightarrow{\ RX\ } R_2NH \xrightarrow{\ RX\ } R_3N \xrightarrow{\ RX\ } R_4 \overset{+}{N} \overset{-}{X}$$
$$\left(1^o\right) \qquad \left(2^o\right) \qquad \left(3^o\right) \qquad Quaternary$$
$$ammonium\,salt$$

The free amine can be obtained from the ammonium salt by treatment with a strong base:

$$R - \overset{+}{N} H_3 \overset{-}{X} + NaOH \rightarrow R - NH_2 + H_2O + \overset{+}{Na} \overset{-}{X}$$

  - By reduction of nitriles:

$$2H_2 + R - C \equiv N \xrightarrow{\ Ni\ } R - CH_2 - NH_2$$

$$R - C \equiv N + 4[H] \xrightarrow[\text{or LiAlH}_4]{\text{Na(Hg)}/\text{C}_2\text{H}_5\text{OH}} R - CH_2 - NH_2$$

$$1^0 \text{ amine}$$

➤ Gabriel phthalmide synthesis:

➤ By reduction of amides:

$$R-\overset{\overset{O}{\|}}{C}-NH_2 \xrightarrow[(ii)\,H_2O]{(i)\,LiAlH_4} R-CH_2-NH_2$$

➤ By Hoffmann Bromamide degradation reaction:

$$R-\overset{\overset{O}{\|}}{C}-NH_2 + Br_2 + 4NaOH \longrightarrow R-NH_2 + Na_2CO_3 + 2NaBr + 2H_2O$$

• **Physical properties:**

➤ Lower members are combustible gases, members from C_3 to C_1 are volatile liquids and C_{12} onwards are gaseous. Lower aromatic amines are liquids.

➤ Pure amines are colourless, although they develop colour on keeping in air for a long time.

➤ With increase in molecular weight, the boiling point also increases. The order of boiling points of isomeric amines is, Primary > Secondary > Tertiary.

➤ Lower members of amine are readily soluble in water. They decrease in water and increase in organic solvents with an increase in molecular weight.

Chemical Reaction of Amines and Diazonium Salts

• **Chemical properties:**

➤ **Reactions due to alkyl group:**

$$R-\overset{\bullet\bullet}{N}H_2 + HX \rightleftharpoons R-\overset{+}{N}H_3\,\overset{-}{X}\,(Salt)$$

Aniline　　　　　　　Anilinium chloride

Amines, being basic in nature, react with acids to form salts. When these amine salts are treated with a base such as $NaOH$, they regenerate the parent amine.

$$R\overset{+}{N}H_3\,\overset{-}{X} + \overset{-}{O}H \longrightarrow R\overset{\bullet\bullet}{N}H_2 + H_2O + \overset{-}{X}$$

Amine　　base　　parent
Salts　　　　　　amine

Amine salts are soluble in water but insoluble in organic compounds like ether. This reaction helps in separating the amines from the non basic organic compounds insoluble in water.

The reaction of amines with mineral acids to form ammonium salts shows that these are basic in nature. The order of basic strength in case of methyl Substituted amines and ethyl substituted amines in aqueous solution is as follows:

$$(C_2H_5)_2\,NH > (C_2H_5)_3\,N > C_2H_5NH_2 > NH_3$$

$$(CH_3)_2\,NH > CH_3NH_2 > (CH_3)_3\,N > NH_3$$

The $-NH_2$ group is attached directly to the benzene ring in aryl amines, which results in the unshared electron pair on nitrogen atom to be in conjugation with the benzene ring and thus making it less available for protonation.

In case of substituted aniline, it is observed that electron releasing groups increase basic strength whereas electron withdrawing groups decrease it.

Alkylation:

$$CH_3 - CH_2 - NH_2 \xrightarrow[-HBr]{+CH_3-CH_2-Br} (CH_3 - CH_2)_2\,NH \xrightarrow[-HBr]{+CH_3-CH_2-Br} (CH_3 - CH_2)_3N$$
$$\textit{Triethylamine}$$

$$(CH_3 - CH_2)_3\,N \xrightarrow[-HBr]{+CH_3-CH_2-Br} (CH_3 - CH_2)_4\,\overset{+}{N}\,\overset{-}{Br}$$
$$\textit{Tetraethyl}$$
$$\textit{ammonium bromide}$$

Acylation:

Aliphatic and aromatic primary and secondary amines react with acid chlorides, anhydrides and esters by nucleophillic substitution reaction. This reaction is known acylation.

$$C_6H_5 - \overset{..}{N} - H \;+\; CH_3 - \underset{O}{\overset{O}{C}} - O - \underset{O}{\overset{O}{C}} - CH_3 \longrightarrow C_6H_5 - \overset{..}{\underset{H}{N}} - \underset{O}{\overset{O}{C}} - CH_3 + CH_3COOH$$

Benzenamine   Ethanoic anhydride   N-Phenylethanamide
                                                     or Acetanilide

Benzoylation:

$$CH_3NH_2 \;+\; C_6H_5COCl \longrightarrow CH_3NHCOC_6H_5 \;+\; HCl$$
$$\textit{Methyl amine}\quad \textit{Benzoyl}\qquad N-Methylbenzamide$$
$$\textit{Chloride}$$

Carbylamine reaction: Secondary and tertiary amines do not give this reaction. This reaction is used as a test for primary amines.

$$R - NH_2 + CHCl_3 + 3KOH \xrightarrow{Heat} R - NC + 3KCl + 3H_2O$$

$$\text{Aniline} \xrightarrow[KOH]{CHCl_3} \text{Phenyl isocyanide}$$

Reaction with nitrous acid:

$$R - NH_2 + HNO_2 \xrightarrow{NaNO_2+HCl} \left[R - \overset{+}{N_2}\,\overset{-}{Cl} \right] \xrightarrow{H_2O} ROH + N_2 + HCl$$

1° amine

$$R_2NH + HNO_2 \longrightarrow R_2N - N = O + H_2O$$

2° amine   N-Nitrosamine

$$R_3N + HNO_2 \longrightarrow \text{No Reaction}$$

3° amine

$$C_6H_5 - NH_2 \xrightarrow[273-278k]{NaNO_2+2HCl} C_6H_5 - \overset{+}{N_2}\,\overset{-}{Cl} + NaCl + 2H_2O$$

Aromatic   Benzenediazonium

amine   chloride

Secondary and tertiary amines react with nitrous acid in a different manner.

Reaction with arylsulphonyl chloride:

N-Ethylbenzenesulphonamide
(soluble in alkali)

N, N-Diethylbenzenesulphonamide

Tertiary amines do not react with benzenesulphonyl chloride and therefore, benzenesulphonyl chloride is used to differentiate between primary, secondary and tertiary amines.

Bromination:

Aniline reacts with bromine water at room temperature to give a white precipitate of 2, 4, 6-tribromoanaline.

Aniline $+ 3Br_2 \xrightarrow{Br_2/H_2O}$ $+ 3\,HBr$

2, 4, 6- Tribromoaniline

Nitration:

Direct nitration of aniline yields nitro derivatives.

$\xrightarrow{HNO_3, H_2SO_4, 288K}$

(51%)   (47%)   (2%)

Preparation of monosubstituted aniline derivative by acetylation of group:

$NH_2 \xrightarrow[\text{Pyridine}]{(CH_3CO)_2O} NHCOCH_3 \xrightarrow{HNO_3,\ H_2SO_4,\ 288K} NHCOCH_3 \xrightarrow{\bar{O}H\ or\ H^+} NH_2$

Acetanilide

p-Nitroacetanilide (NO_2)

p-Nitroaniline (NO_2)

Sulphonation:

$\overset{..}{N}H_2 \xrightarrow{H_2SO_4} \overset{+}{N}H_2H\bar{S}O_4 \xrightarrow{453\text{–}473\ K} NH_2 \rightleftharpoons \overset{+}{N}H_2$

Anilinium
hydrogensulphate

Sulphanilic acid (SO_3H)

Zwitter ion ($\bar{S}O_3$)

Aniline does not undergo Friedel-Crafts reaction (alkylation and acetylation) due to salt formation with aluminium chloride.

Ammonolysis:

Alkyl halide reacts with ammonia to form primary amine. The reaction of ammonia with alkyl halide is known as ammonolysis.

$$C_2H_5I \xrightarrow{NH_3/343K} C_2H_5NH_2 \xrightarrow[-HI]{C_2H_5I} (C_2H_5)_2NH$$

$$(C_2H_5)_2NH \xrightarrow[-HI]{C_2H_5I} (C_2H_5)_3N \xrightarrow[-HI]{C_2H_5I} \left[(C_2H_5)_4\overset{+}{N}\right]\bar{I}$$

Gabriel Phthalimide Synthesis: In Gabriel phthalimide synthesis, phthalimide reacts with alcoholic KOH to get potassium phthalimide which reacts with alkyl halide to form N-alkyl phthalimide which on basic hydrolysis gives primary amine and phthalic acid.

Phthalimide $\xrightarrow{KOH}$ $\xrightarrow{R-X}$ N-Alkyphthalimide

Friedel-Crafts reaction: Aniline does not undergo Friedel-Crafts reaction as it forms a salt with $AlCl_3$ which is a Lewis acid.

- **Diazonium salts:**

  - **General formula:** $R\overset{+}{N}_2\bar{X}$, where R stands for an aryl group and $\bar{X}$ ion may be for halides

  - **Stability of diazonium salts:** Primary aliphatic amines are highly unstable alkyldiazonium salts. Arenediazonium salts, made up of primary aromatic amines are more stable than alkyl diazonium salts due to the dispersal of the positive charge over the benzene ring.

➢ **Preparation of diazonium salts:**

$$NH_2 \quad + NaNO_2 + 2HCl \xrightarrow{0°-5°C} \quad N_2^+Cl^- \quad + NaCl + 2H_2O$$

Benzene diazonium

➢ **Chemical properties:**

Reactions involving displacement of nitrogen:

Replacement by halide or cyanide ion-

$$ArN_2^+X^- \begin{cases} \xrightarrow{CuCl/HCl} ArCl + N_2 \\ \xrightarrow{CuBr/HBr} ArBr + N_2 \\ \xrightarrow{CuCN/KCN} ArCN + N_2 \end{cases}$$

Sandmeyer reaction

$$ArN_2^+X^- \begin{cases} \xrightarrow{Cu/HCl} ArCl + N_2 + CuX \\ \xrightarrow{Cu/HBr} ArBr + N_2 + CuX \end{cases}$$

Gatterman's reaction

Replacement by iodide ion-

$$Ar\overset{+}{N_2}\overset{-}{Cl} + KI \longrightarrow ArI + KCl + N_2$$

Benzene diazonium chloride   *Iodobenzene*

Replacement by fluoride ion-

$$Ar\overset{+}{N_2}\overset{-}{Cl} + HBF_4 \longrightarrow Ar\overset{+}{N_2}\overset{-}{BF_4}$$

$$Ar\overset{+}{N_2}\overset{-}{BF_4} \xrightarrow{\Delta} Ar-F + BF_3 + N_2$$

Replacement by H-

$$Ar\overset{+}{N_2}\overset{-}{Cl} + H_3PO_2 + H_2O \longrightarrow ArH + N_2 + H_3PO_3 + HCl$$

$$Ar\overset{+}{N_2}\overset{-}{Cl} + CH_3CH_2OH \longrightarrow ArH + N_2 + CH_3CHO + HCl$$

Replacement by hydroxyl group-

$$Ar\overset{+}{N_2}\overset{-}{Cl} + H_2O \xrightarrow{\Delta} ArOH + N_2 + HCl$$

Phenol

Replacement by $-NO_2$ group-

$$\overset{+}{N_2}\overset{-}{Cl} \quad + HBF_4 \longrightarrow \overset{+}{N_2}\overset{-}{BF_4} \xrightarrow[Cu, \Delta]{NaNO_2} \overset{}{NO_2} + N_2 + NaBF_4$$

Fluroboric acid

Reactions involving retention of diazo group:

> **Coupling reaction:** The reaction of diazonium salts with phenols and aromatic amines to form azo compounds with the general formula, $Ar - N = N\, Ar$ is known as coupling reaction.

$$C_6H_5\overset{+}{N}\equiv N\overset{-}{Cl} + H\text{—}C_6H_4\text{—OH} \xrightarrow{\overset{-}{OH}} C_6H_5\text{—}N=N\text{—}C_6H_4\text{—OH} + \overset{-}{Cl} + H_2O$$

p-Hydroxyazobenzene (orange dye)

$$C_6H_5\overset{+}{N}\equiv N\overset{-}{Cl} + H\text{—}C_6H_4\text{—}NH_2 \xrightarrow{\overset{-}{OH}} C_6H_5\text{—}N=N\text{—}C_6H_4\text{—}NH_2 + \overset{-}{Cl} + H_2O$$

p-Aminoazobenzene (yellow dye)

> Importance of Diazonium salts: They are very good intermediates for the introduction of $-F$, $-Cl$, Br, $-I$, $-CN$, $-OH$, $-NO_2$ groups into aromatic ring. Cyanobenzene can be prepared from diazonium salts.

- **Synthesis of organic compounds from diazonium salts:**

$$C_6H_5\overset{+}{N_2}\overset{-}{Cl}\xrightarrow{\ CH_3CH_2OH\ }C_6H_6$$

$$C_6H_5\overset{+}{N_2}\overset{-}{Cl}\xrightarrow{\ H_2O\ }C_6H_5OH$$

$$C_6H_5\overset{+}{N_2}\overset{-}{Cl}\xrightarrow{\ HBF_4\ }C_6H_5F$$

$$C_6H_5\overset{+}{N_2}\overset{-}{Cl}\xrightarrow{\ C_6H_6/NaOH\ }C_6H_5C_6H_5$$

$$C_6H_5\overset{+}{N_2}\overset{-}{Cl}\xrightarrow{\ C_6H_5NH_2/acid\ }C_6H_5\text{—}N=N\text{—}C_6H_4\text{—}NH_2$$

- **Identification of primary, secondary and tertiary amines:**

Test	Primary amine	Secondary amine	Tertiary amine
Reaction with nitrous acid.	Gives alcohol with effervescence of N_2 gas.	Gives only nitrosoamine which gives Liebermann's nitrosoamine test.	Forms nitrite in cold soluble in water and on heating gives nitrosoamine.
Recation with benzene sulphonyl chloride (Hiesenberg's reagent).	Gives N-alkyl benzene-sulphonamide which is soluble in alkali.	Gives N, N-dialkyl benzene sulphonamide which is insoluble in alkali.	No reaction.
Carbylamine test: Reaction with chloroform and alcoholic KOH.	Forms carbylamines or isocyanide (RNC) with characteristic unpleasant odour.	No reaction.	No reaction.
Hoffman's Mustard oil reaction: Recation with CS_2 and $HgCl_2$.	Forms N-substituted isotiocyanate with characteristic unpleasant smell of mustard oil.	No reaction.	No reaction.

EXERCISE

1. C_3H_9N represents
   (a) Primary amine   (b) Secondary amine
   (c) Tertiary amine   (d) All of these

2. Triaminobenzene is a
   (a) $2°$ amine   (b) $3°$ amine
   (c) $1°$ amine   (d) Quarternary salt

3. Which of the following is not a nitro-derivative.
   (a) $C_6H_5NO_2$ (b) CH_3CH_2ONO

   (c) 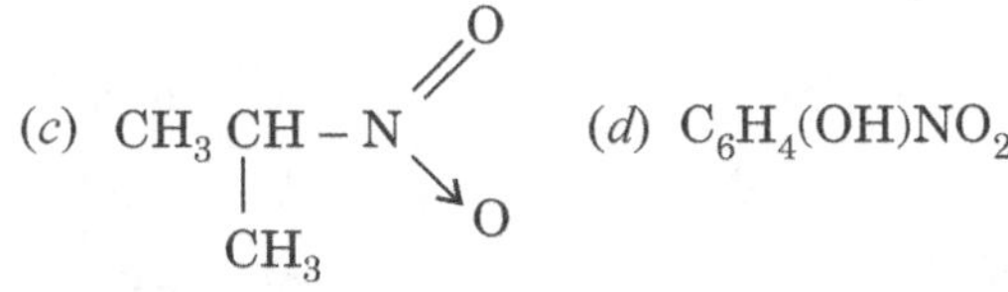   (d) $C_6H_4(OH)NO_2$

4. Number of isomeric primary amines obtained from $C_4H_{11}N$ are
   (a) 3   (b) 4
   (c) 5   (d) 6

5. The molecular formula of benzonitrile is
   (a) C_6H_5CN (b) C_6H_5NC
   (c) C_6H_5CNO (d) C_6H_5NCO

6. Amides may be converted into amines by reaction named after
   (a) Parkin   (b) Claisen
   (c) Hoffmann   (d) Kolbe

7. $CH_3C \equiv N + 4[H] \xrightarrow[\text{Reduction}]{\text{Na+C}_2\text{H}_5\text{OH}} CH_3CH_2NH_2$

   The compound 'X' is
   (a) CH_3CONH_2 (b) $CH_3CH_2NH_2$
   (c) C_2H_6 (d) CH_3NHCH_3

8. Reduction of nitroalkanes yields
   (a) Acid   (b) Alcohol
   (c) Amine   (d) Diozo compounds

9. When methyl iodide is heated with ammonia, the product obtained is
   (a) Methylamine
   (b) Dimethylamine
   (c) Trimethylamine
   (d) A mixture of the above three amines

10. Identify 'B' in the reaction

    Acetamide $\xrightarrow[\Delta]{P_2O_5} A \xrightarrow{4H} B$

    (a) CH_3NH_2
    (b) $CH_3CH_2NH_2$
    (c) CH_3CN
    (d) CH_3COONH_4

11. When aniline reacts with $NaNO_2$ and dil. HCl at $0° – 5°$ C, the product formed is
    (a) Nitroaniline
    (b) Benzene diazonium chloride
    (c) Benzene
    (d) Trinitroaniline

12. $CH_3Br + KCN$ (alc) $\longrightarrow X \xrightarrow[\text{Na+C}_2\text{H}_5\text{OH}]{\text{Reduction}} Y$
    What is Y in the series?
    (a) CH_3CN (b) C_2H_5CN
    (c) $C_2H_5NH_2$ (d) CH_3NH_2

13. Which of the following compound is expected to be most basic
    (a) Aniline   (b) Methylamine
    (c) Hydroxylamine   (d) Ethylamine

14. Aniline when treated with HNO_2 and HCl at $0°C$ gives.
    (a) Phenol   (b) Nitrobenzene
    (c) A diazo compound (d) None of these

15. Ethyl amine undergoes oxidation in the presence of $KMnO_4$ to form
    (a) An acid   (b) An alcohol
    (c) An aldehyde   (d) A nitrogen oxide

16. Reaction of primary amines with aldehyde yields.
    (a) Amides   (b) Aldimines
    (c) Nitriles   (d) Nitro compounds

17. Nitrobenzene on nitration gives
    (a) o-dinitrobenzene
    (b) p-dinitrobenzene
    (c) m-dinitrobenzene
    (d) o-and p-nitrobenzene

18. When primary amines are treated with HCl. the Product obtained is
    (a) An Alcohol   (b) A cyanide
    (c) An amide   (d) Ammonium salt

19. Which of the following do not react with HNO_2
    (a) Primary nitroalkanes
    (b) Secondary nitroalkanes
    (c) Tertiary nitroalkanes
    (d) All of these

20. The product of mustard oil reaction is
    (a) Alkyl isothiocyanate
    (b) Dithio carbonamide
    (c) Dithio ethylacetate
    (d) Thioether

21. The maximum number of $-NO_2$ groups that can be introduced by nitration in benzene is usually

(*a*) 4   (*b*) 2

(*c*) 3   (*d*) 6

22. Primary nitro compounds when reacts with HNO_2 forms crystalline solids which on treatment with NaOH gives

(*a*) Red solution   (*b*) Blue solution

(*c*) White precipitate   (*d*) Yellow colouration

23. When methyl cyanide is hydrolysed in presence of alkali, the product is

(*a*) Acetamide   (*b*) Methane

(*c*) $CO_2 + H_2O$ (*d*) Acetic acid

24. Methyl amine reacts with HNO_2 giving

(*a*) $CH_3O - N = O$ (*b*) $CH_3–O–CH_3$

(*c*) CH_3OH (*d*) (*a*) and (*b*) both

Answer Keys

1. (*d*)	**2.** (*c*)	**3.** (*b*)	**4.** (*b*)	**5.** (*a*)	**6.** (*c*)	**7.** (*b*)	**8.** (*c*)	**9.** (*d*)	**10.** (*b*)
11. (*b*)	**12.** (*c*)	**13.** (*d*)	**14.** (*c*)	**15.** (*c*)	**16.** (*b*)	**17.** (*c*)	**18.** (*d*)	**19.** (*c*)	**20.** (*a*)
21. (*c*)	**22.** (*a*)	**23.** (*d*)	**24.** (*d*)						

Solutions

1. C_3H_9N can form all the 3 amines.

$CH_3CH_2CH_2–NH_2$,

1° amine

$CH_3–CH_2–NH–CH_3$,

2° amine

$$CH_3 - N - CH_3$$
$$|$$
$$CH_3$$

3° amine

2.

NH₂ — (benzene ring) — NH₂, NH₂

1° amine

3. $CH_3CH_2–O–N = O$ is a nitrite derivative, hence it is not a nitro derivative.

4. Four 1° amines are possible

$CH_3CH_2CH_2CH_2NH_2$, $(CH_3)_2 CHCH_2NH_2$, $CH_3CH(NH_2) CH_2CH_3$, $(CH_3)_3 CNH_2$

5. The molecular formula of benzonitrile of phenyl cyanide is C_6H_5CN.

6. Hofmann's bromamide reaction

$$\underset{\text{Acetamide}}{CH_3 - CO - NH_2} + Br_2 + 4KOH \xrightarrow{H_2O}$$

$$\underset{\text{Methyl amine}}{CN_3NH_2} + K_2CO_3 + 2KBr + 2H_2O$$

7. $CH_3C \equiv N + 4[H] \xrightarrow[\text{Reduction}]{Na+C_2H_5OH} CH_3CH_2NH_2$

8. $\underset{\text{Nitro ethane}}{CH_3 - CH_2 - NO_2} + 6[H] \xrightarrow{Sn/HCl}$

$$\underset{\text{Ethyl amine}}{CH_3 - CH_2 - NH_2} + 2H_2O$$

9. $CH_3 \xrightarrow[\Delta]{NH_3} \underset{\text{Methyl amine}}{CH_3NH_2} \xrightarrow{CH_3I}$

$$\underset{\text{Dimethyl amine}}{(CH_3)_2 NH} \xrightarrow{CH_3I} \underset{\text{Trimethyl amine}}{(CH_3)_3 N}$$

10. $CH_3CONH_2 \xrightarrow{P_2O_5} CH_3CN \xrightarrow{4H} CH_3CH_2NH_2$

11.

$$\underset{\text{Aniline}}{\text{NH}_2-C_6H_5} \xrightarrow[0° - 5°C]{Na\,NO_2/HCl} \underset{\text{Benzene diazonium Chloride}}{\overset{+}{N}_2\bar{Cl}-C_6H_5} + 2H_2O$$

12. $CH_3Br \xrightarrow{\text{alc. KCN}} \underset{[x]}{CH_3CN} \xrightarrow[\text{reduction}]{Na/C_2H_5OH} \underset{\text{Ethyl amine}}{CH_3CH_2NH_2}$

13. Due to +ve I.E. of alkyl group, N-atom of amines acquires partial –ve charge thus electron pair is easily donated.

14.

$$\underset{\text{Aniline}}{\text{NH}_2-C_6H_5} + HNO_2 + HCl \xrightarrow[\text{Diazotization}]{0°C} \underset{\substack{\text{Benzene diazonium} \\ \text{Chloride}}}{\text{N}=NCl-C_6H_5} + 2H_2O$$

15. $CH_3CH_2 - NH_2 \xrightarrow[[O]]{KMnO_4} CH_3CH = NH \xrightarrow{H_3O^+} CH_3 - CHO$

    Ethylamine   Aldimine   Acetaldehyde

16. $R - CH_2 - NH_2 + O = CH - R \rightarrow R - CH_2 - N = CH - R + H_2O$

       $1°$ amine   aldehyde   Aldimine

17.

$$\text{Nitrobenzene} + HNO_3 \text{ (Conc.)} \xrightarrow{\text{Conc. } H_2SO_4} \text{m-dinitrobenzene}$$

    $-NO_2$ group is meta directed group.

18. $CH_3 - CH_2 - NH_2 + HCl \rightarrow CH_3CH_2 - NH_3{}^+Cl^-$

                           Ethyl ammonium chloride

    Amines are basic in nature they reacts with acid to form salt.

19. Tertiary nitroalkanes do not react with HNO_2 because in tertiary nitroalkanes $\alpha - H$ atom is absent.

20. Mustard oil reaction

$$CH_3 - CH_2 - NH_2 + CS_2 \xrightarrow{HgCl_2} CH_3 - CH_2 - N = C = S + H_2S$$

    Ethyl amine   Ethyl isothiocyanate

21.

$$\text{Benzene} \xrightarrow{\text{Nitration}} \text{1, 3, 5-trinitrobenzene}$$

    3-nitro group can be introduced.

22. $R - CH_2 - NO_2 \xrightarrow{HNO_2} \underset{\underset{\text{Nitrolic acid}}{N - OH}}{R - \overset{\|}{C} - NO_2} \xrightarrow{NaOH} \underset{\underset{\text{(Blood red)}}{N - O^-Na^+}}{R - \overset{\|}{C} - NO_2}$

    $1°$ nitro

23. $CH_3 - C \equiv N + 2H_2O \rightarrow CH_3COOH + NH_3$

       Methyl cyanide   Acetic acid

24. $CH_3NH_2 + 2HNO_2 \rightarrow CH_3 - O - N = O + N_2 + 2H_2O$

    $2CH_3NH_2 + 2HNO_2 \rightarrow CH_3 - O - CH_3 + 2N_2 + 3H_2O$

CHAPTER 14

Biomolecules

Carbohydrates

- There are various complex biomolecules of which living systems are made up of. These biomolecules include carbohydrates, proteins, nucleic acids, lipids etc.
- Carbohydrates are primarily produced by plants and most of them have general formula, $C_x(H_2O)_y$. Example: the molecular formula of glucose is $(C_6H_{12}O_6)$. Carbohydrates are classified into three groups on the basis of their behaviour on hydrolysis:
    - ➤ **Monosaccharides:** A carbohydrate that cannot be hydrolysed further to give simpler unit of polyhydroxy aldehyde or ketone. Example: glucose, fructose etc.
    - ➤ **Oligosaccharides:** A carbohydrate that yields two to ten units of monosaccharide units on hydrolysis. The most common oligosaccharides are disaccharides. The two monosaccharides units obtained on hydrolysis of a disaccharide may be same or different. Example: Sucrose of hydrolysis gives one molecule of glucose and one molecule of fructose whereas maltose of hydrolysis gives two molecules of glucose only.
    - ➤ **Polysaccharides:** These are the carbohydrates which yield a large number of monosaccharide units on hydrolysis. Example: Starch, cellulose etc. They are also called non-sugars.
- The carbohydrates which reduce Fehling's solution and Tollen's reagent are called **reducing sugars**. Example: Maltose.
- If the reducing group of monosaccharides i.e. aldehydic or ketonic groups are bonded they are called **non-reducing sugars**. Example: Sucrose.
- **Glucose:**

Preparation of glucose:

- **From Sucrose:** When Sucrose is boiled with dilute HCl or H_2SO_4 in alcoholic solution, glucose and fructose are obtained in equal amounts.

$$C_2H_{22}O_{11} + H_2O \xrightarrow{H^+} C_6H_2O_6 + C_6H_2O_6$$

Sucrose   Glucose   Fructose

- **From starch:** Hydrolysis of starch by boiling it with dilute H_2SO_4 at 393 K under pressure.

$$\left(C_6H_{10}O_5\right)_n + nH_2O \xrightarrow[393K;\ 2-3\ atm]{H^+} nC_6H_{12}O_6$$

Starch or cellulose   Glucose

Structure of Glucose:

- Glucose is also called dextrose. It is a monomer of many larger carbohydrates. The structure of glucose was assigned on the basis of the following facts:
    - ➤ The molecular formula was found to be $C_6H_{12}O_6$.
    - ➤ Prolonged heating of glucose with HI forms n-Hexane.

$$\underset{CH_2OH}{\overset{\displaystyle CHO}{\mid \ \ (CHOH)_4 \ \ \mid}} \xrightarrow{HI,\ \Delta} CH_3-CH_2-CH_2-CH_2-CH_2-CH_3$$

$$(n-Hexane)$$

   - ➤ Glucose on reacting with hydroxylamine forms an oxime and adds molecule of hydrogen cyanide to give cyanohydrin. This confirms the presence of carbonyl group in glucose.

$$\underset{CH_2OH}{\overset{CHO}{\mid \ (CHOH)_4 \ \mid}} \xrightarrow{NH_2OH} \underset{CH_2OH}{\overset{CH=N-OH}{\mid \ (CHOH)_4 \ \mid}} \qquad \underset{CH_2OH}{\overset{CHO}{\mid \ (CHOH)_4 \ \mid}} \xrightarrow{HCN} \underset{CH_2OH}{\overset{CH{\small\begin{smallmatrix}CN\\ OH\end{smallmatrix}}}{\mid \ (CHOH)_4 \ \mid}}$$

> On reacting with mild oxidizing agent like bromine water it oxidise to six carbon carboxylic acid. This indicates the presence of carbonyl group as an aldehydic group.

$$
\underset{\text{Gluconic acid}}{\begin{array}{c} CHO \\ | \\ (CHOH)_4 \\ | \\ CH_2OH \end{array}} \xrightarrow{\text{Br}_2 \text{ water}} \begin{array}{c} COOH \\ | \\ (CHOH)_4 \\ | \\ CH_2OH \end{array}
$$

> To confirm the presence of five –OH groups glucose is acetylated with acetic anhydride to give glucose pentaacetate.

$$
\begin{array}{c} CHO \\ | \\ (CHOH)_4 \\ | \\ CH_2OH \end{array} \xrightarrow{\text{Acetic Anhydride}} \begin{array}{c} CHO \\ | \\ (CH-O-\overset{O}{\overset{||}{C}}-CH_3)_4 \\ | \\ CH_2-O-\overset{O}{\overset{||}{C}}-CH_3 \end{array}
$$

> To indicate the presence of a primary alcoholic (-OH) group in glucose, glucose as well as gluconic acid are both oxidized with nitric acid to yield dicarboxylic acid, saccharic acid.

$$
\begin{array}{c} CHO \\ | \\ (CHOH)_4 \\ | \\ CH_2OH \end{array} \xrightarrow{\text{Oxidation}} \underset{\substack{\text{Saccharic} \\ \text{acid}}}{\begin{array}{c} COOH \\ | \\ (CHOH)_4 \\ | \\ COOH \end{array}} \xleftarrow{\text{Oxidation}} \underset{\substack{\text{Gluconic} \\ \text{acid}}}{\begin{array}{c} COOH \\ | \\ (CHOH)_4 \\ | \\ CH_2OH \end{array}}
$$

Cyclic Structure of Glucose:

> Glucose does not give 2, 4-DNP test, Schiff's test and does not form the hydrogensulphite addition product with $NaHSO_3$.

> The absence of free-CHO group is indicated as the pentaacetate of glucose does not react with hydroxylamine.

> Glucose exist in two different crystalline forms which are named as α and β. It was found that glucose forms a six-membered ring in which –OH at C5 in involved in ring formation.

> The cyclic structure is given below:

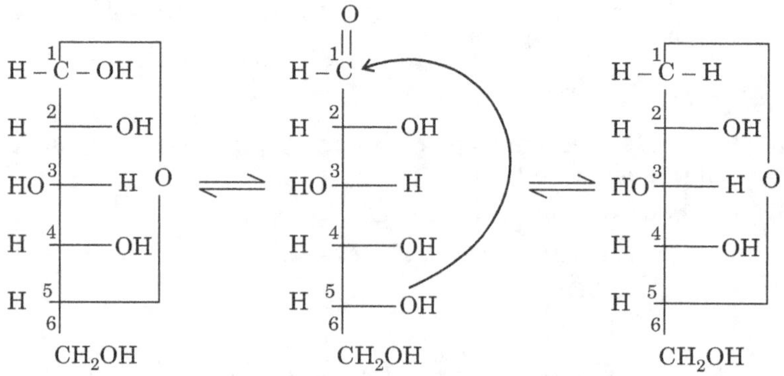

$$
\alpha - D - (+) - \text{Glucose} \rightleftharpoons \quad \rightleftharpoons \quad \beta - D - (+) - \text{Glucose}
$$

> Haworth structure of glucose is given below:

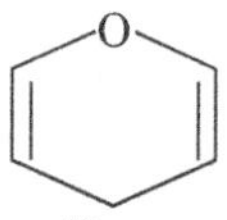

Pyran

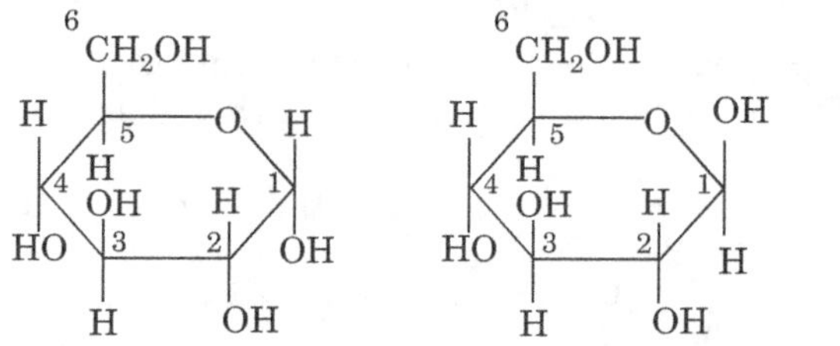

α – D – (+) – Glucose   β – D – (+) – Glucose

- **Fructose**

    It is obtained along with glucose by the hydrolysis of sucrose.

    ➢ **Structure of Fructose:**

    Fructose has the molecular formula $C_6H_{12}O_6$. It is found to have a ketonic functional group at carbon 2 and six carbons which are in straight chain.

    ➢ The open chain structure of fructose is:

    $$
    \begin{array}{c}
    CH_2OH \\
    | \\
    C = O \\
    H \longrightarrow H \\
    HO \longrightarrow OH \\
    H \longrightarrow OH \\
    CH_2OH
    \end{array}
    $$

    D – (–) – Fructose

    ➢ **Cyclic structure of fructose:**

    Fructose exists in two cyclic forms and they are obtained by adding –OH at C5 to the ketonic group. The ring is a five membered ring.

    ➢ **The structures are given below**

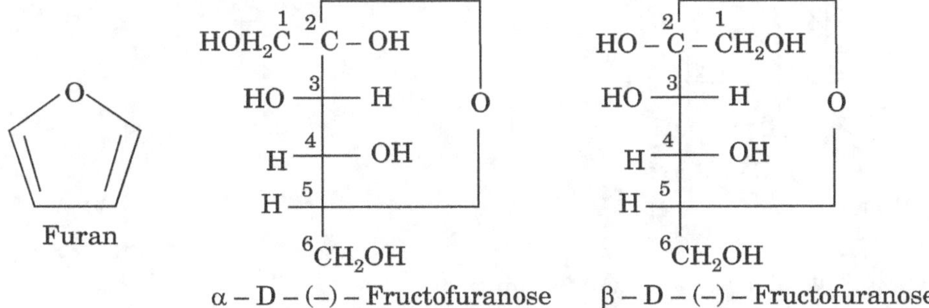

α – D – (–) – Fructofuranose β – D – (–) – Fructofuranose

    ➢ **The Haworth structures of fructose are given below:**

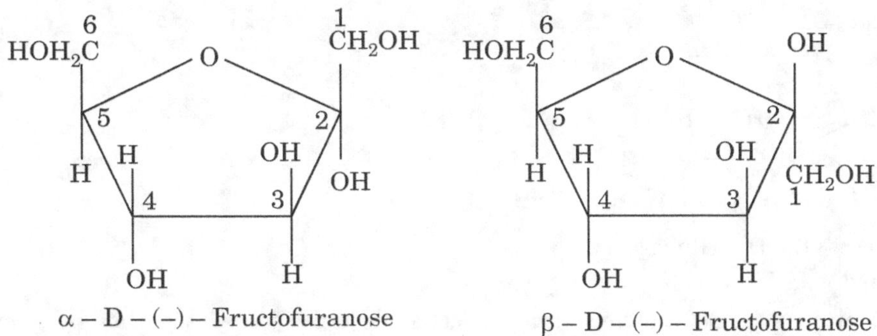

α – D – (–) – Fructofuranose β – D – (–) – Fructofuranose

- **Sucrose**

    ➢ Sucrose on hydrolysis gives equimolar mixture of D-(+)-glucose and D-(-) fructose.

    $$C_{12}H_{22}O_{11} + H_2O \xrightarrow{\ H^+\ } C_6H_{12}O_6 + C_6H_{12}O_6$$

    Sucrose   D-(+)-Glucose D-(–)-Fructose

> The structure of sucrose is given below:

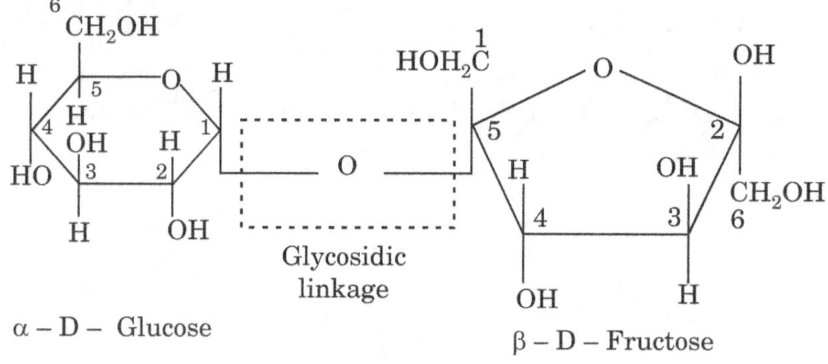

Sucrose

> The two monosaccharides in sucrose are held together by a glycosidic linkage. The product obtained on hydrolysis of sucrose is called invert sugar as the hydrolysis brings about a change in the sign of rotation from dextro (+) to laevo (-).

- **Maltose:**
  > Maltose has two α-*D*-glucose units. In maltose the C 1 of one glucose (I) is linked to C4 of another glucose unit (II).
  > Structure of Maltose:

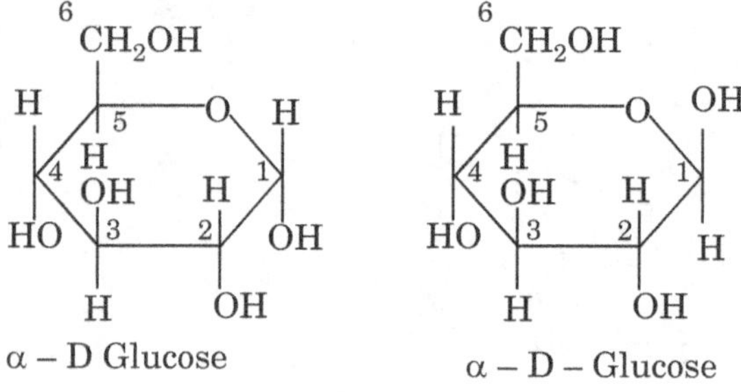

Maltose

- **Lactose:**
  > It is commonly known as milk sugar as it is found in milk.
  > Structure of lactose:

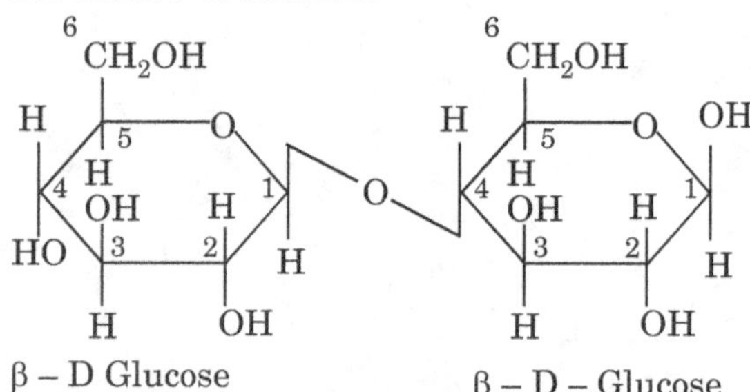

Lactose

- **Polysaccharides:** They contain a large number of monosaccharide units joined together by glycosidic linkage.

- **Starch**
  > It is the main storage polysaccharide of plants and important dietary source for human beings. It consists of two components namely Amylose and Amylopectin.
  > Amylose: It is water soluble component and constitutes 15-20% of starch. It is a long unbranched chain with 200-1000 α-*D*-(+)-glucose units held by C1-C4 glycosidic linkage.

➢ **Structure of Amylose is given below:**

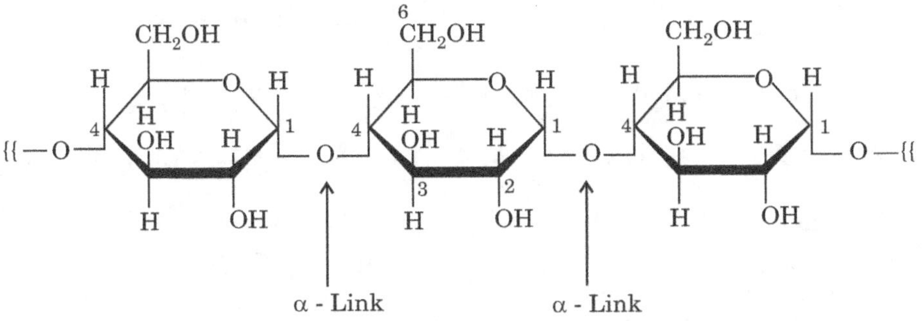

α - Link   α - Link

Amylose

➢ Amylopectin: It is insoluble in water and constitutes 80-85% of starch. It is a branched chain polymer of   units in which chain is formed by C1-C4 glycosidic linkage whereas branching occurs by C1-C6 glycosidic linkage.

➢ **Structure of Amylopectin is given below:**

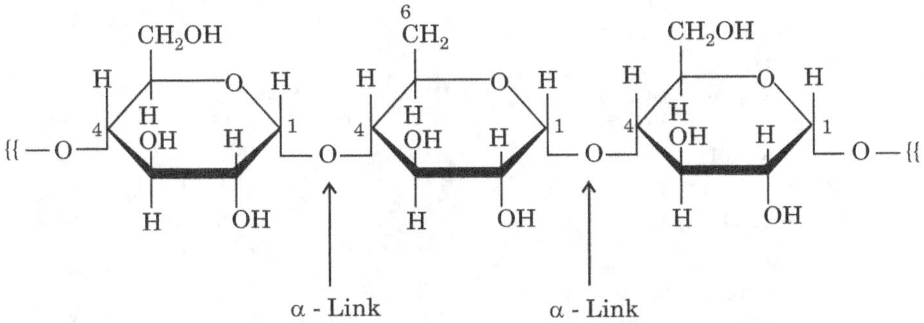

α - Link   α - Link

- **Cellulose:**
  - ➢ It occurs exclusively in plants. It is an important constituent of cell wall of plant cells. Its fundamental unit is β-*D*-glucose which are joined by glycosidic linkage between C1 of one glucose unit and C4 of the next glucose unit.
  - ➢ **Structure of cellulose is:**

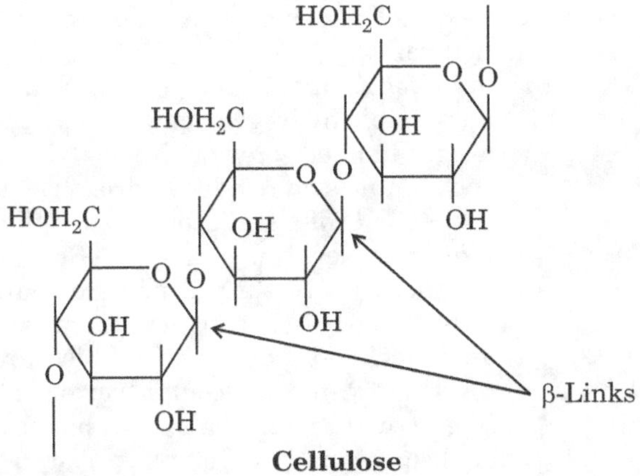

β-Links

Cellulose

- **Glycogen:**
  - ➢ Carbohydrates are stored in animals as glycogen. Its structure is similar to amylopectin and is rather more branched therefore it is also known as animal starch. It is present in liver, muscles and brain.
- **Importance of carbohydrates:**
  - ➢ They are essential for both plants and animals as they are the source of energy.
  - ➢ They are used as storage molecules.
  - ➢ Cell wall of plants and bacteria is made of cellulose.
  - ➢ They also act as raw materials for many important industries like textiles, paper etc.

Protein, Vitamins and Nucleic Acids

- **Proteins:** They are the most abundant biomolecules of the living system. They form the fundamental basis of structure and functions of life.
- **Amino acids:** Amino acids contain amino $(-NH_2)$ and carboxyl $(-COOH)$ function groups.
- α-Amino acids: These are formed by the hydrolysis of proteins. In this the amino and the carboxyl function groups are attached to the same carbon.
- **Classification of amino acids:**

  Acidic, Basic and Neutral Amino Acids: Amino acids are classified as acidic, basic and neutral depending upon the relative number of amino and carboxyl groups in their molecules. If there are equal number of amino and carboxyl groups it makes it neutral; if there are more number of amino groups than carboxyl groups it makes it basic and if there are more number of carboxyl groups than amino groups it makes it acidic.
- **Non-Essential amino acids:** Those which can be generated in the body. Example: Glycine.
- **Essential amino acids:** Those which cannot be generated in the body and must be obtained through diet. Example: Valine
- **Some amino acids are given below in the table:**

Name of amino acids	Characteristic feature of side chain, R	Three letter symbol	One letter code
1. Glycine	H	Gly	G
2. Alanine	$-CH_3$	Ala	A
3. Valine	$(H_3C)_2\, CH-$	Val	V
4. Leucine	$(H_3C)_2\, CH{-}CH_2-$	Leu	L
5. Glutamine	$H_2N-\overset{\overset{\textstyle O}{\|}}{C}-CH_2-CH_2-$	Gln	Q
6. Phenyla-lanine	$C_6H_5{-}CH_2{-}$	Phe	F

- **Properties of amino acids:**
  - They are colourless, crystalline solids.
  - They are water soluble, have high melting point and behave like salts.
- **Structure of proteins:**

  They are the polymers of α-amino acids and are connected to each other by peptide bond or peptide linkage.

Example: Formation of Glyclalanine

$$H_2N - CH_2 - COOH + H_2N - CH - COOH$$

$$-H_2O \downarrow \qquad CH_3$$

$$H_2N - CH_2 - \boxed{CO - NH} - CH - COOH$$

$$CH_3$$

Peptide linkage

Glycylalanine (Gly-Ala)

- **Classification of proteins on the basis of molecular shape:**
  - **Fibrous proteins:** They are fibre like structure which is formed when the polypeptide chains run parallel and are held together by hydrogen disulphide bonds. They are insoluble in water. Example: Keratin
  - **Globular proteins:** This shape of protein is formed when the chains of polypeptides coil around to give a spherical shape. Such proteins are soluble in water. Example: Insulin.
- **Classification of proteins on the basis of structure and shape:**
  - **Primary structure of proteins:** Each polypeptide in a protein has amino acids linked with each other in a specific sequence and this sequence of amino acids is called primary structure of proteins.
  - **Secondary structure of proteins:** It is the shape in which a long polypeptide chain can exist. They exist in two different types of structure:
  - (*i*) *a – Helix*: In this polypeptide chain forms all possible hydrogen bonds by twisting into a right handed screw with the –NH group of each amino acid residue hydrogen bonded to the > C = O of an adjacent turn of the helix. Example: Keratin.
  - (*ii*) β-structure : In this all peptide chains are stretched out to nearly maximum extension and then laid side by side which are held together by intermolecular hydrogen bonds. The structure resembles the pleated folds of drapery and therefore is known as β–pleated sheet .
  - **Tertiary structure of proteins:** It shows the overall folding of the polypeptide chains. The forces which stabilize the 2 and 3 structures of proteins are hydrogen bonds, disulphide linkages, van der Walls and electrostatic forces of attraction.

- ➤ **Quaternary structure of proteins:** The spatial arrangement of the two or more polypeptide chains with respect to each other is known as quaternary structure.
- **Denaturation of Proteins:**

  When protein in its native form is given any physical change like change in temperature or chemical changes like change in pH, the hydrogen bonds are disturbed. Due to this, globules gets unfolded and helix gets uncoiled and protein loses its biological activity. The complete process is called denaturation of proteins.

  Example: coagulation of egg white on boiling.
- **Enzymes:** They are essential biocatalysts which are needed to catalyse biochemical reactions. Example: The enzyme that cataylses hydrolysis of maltose into glucose is maltase.

- **Vitamins:** These are the organic compounds that are required in the diet in small amounts to perform specific biological functions for normal maintenance of optimum growth and health of the organism.
  - ➤ **Classification of vitamins:**
    - (*i*) **Fat soluble vitamins:** Vitamins which are soluble in fat and oils but insoluble in water. They are stored in liver and adipose tissues. Vitamin A, D, E and K are fat soluble.
    - (*ii*) **Water soluble vitamins:** Vitamins such as B group vitamins and vitamin C are soluble in water. These vitamins are readily excreted in urine and cannot be stored (except vitamin B12) in our body so they must be supplied regularly in diet.

- **Some important Vitamins, their sources and their deficiency diseases are shown below in the table:**

Name of Vitamins	Sources	Deficiency diseases
Vitamin A	Fish liver oil, butter and milk	Xerophthalmia, night blindness
Vitamin B_1 (Thiamine)	Yeast, milk, green vegetables and cereals	beriberi
Vitamin B_2 (Riboflavin)	Milk, egg white, liver, kidney	Cheilosis, digestive disorders
Vitamin B_6 (Pyridoxine)	Yeast, milk, egg york	Convulsions
Vitamin B_{12}	Meat, fish, egg and curd	Pernicious anaemia
Vitamin C	Citrus fruits, amla and green leafy vegetables	Scurvy
Vitamin D	Exposure to sunlight, fish and egg yolk	Rickets and osteomalacia
Vitamin E	Vegetable oils like wheat germ oil, sunflower oil etc.	Increased fragility of RBCs and muscular weakness
Vitamin K	Green leafy vegetables	Increased blood clotting time

- **Nucleic Acids:**
  - ➤ These are the long chain polymers of nucleotides which help in synthesis of protein and transfer of genetic traits.
  - ➤ There are two types of nucleic acids:
    - (*i*) Deoxyribonucleic acid (DNA)
    - (*ii*) Ribonucleic acid (RNA)
- **Chemical composition of Nucleic Acids:**
  - ➤ Complete hydrolysis of DNA (or RNA) gives a pentose sugar, phosphoric acid and nitrogenous bases.
  - ➤ DNA contains four bases, which are adenine, guanine, cytosine and thymine.
  - ➤ In RNA also there are four bases. The first three bases (adenine, guanine and cytosine) are same as in DNA, but the fourth one is uracil.

- **Structure of Nucleic Acids:**
  - ➤ **Nucleoside:** The unit which is formed by the attachment of a base to   position of sugar is known as nucleoside.

    Structure of nucleoside is given below:

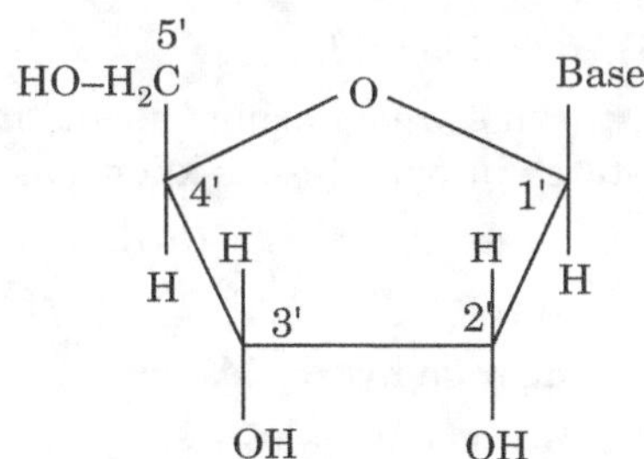

  - ➤ **Nucleotide:** When nucleoside is linked to phosphoric acid at -position of sugar moiety.

    Structure of nucleotide is given below:

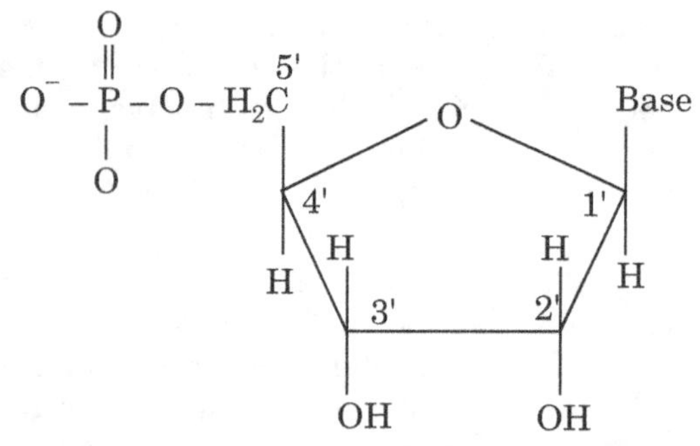

- The simplified version of nucleic acid chain is given below:

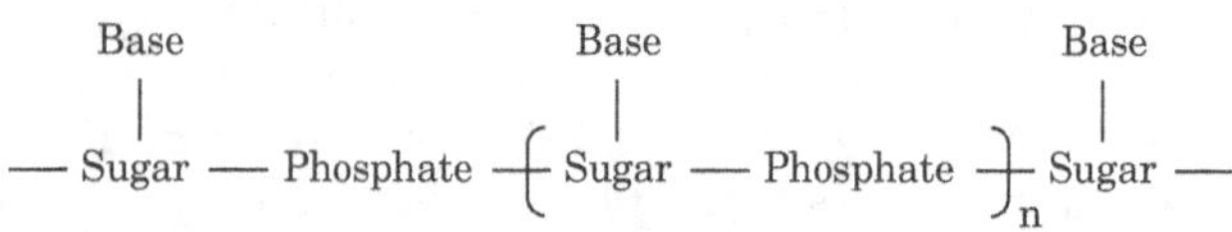

- **DNA:**

  - James Watson and Francis Crick gave a double strand helix structure for DNA.

  - There are two nucleic acid chains which are turned around each other and are held together by hydrogen bonds between pairs of bases.

  - The two strands in the DNA structure are complementary to each other due to the hydrogen bonding between specific pairs of bases.

- **RNA:**

  - In RNA helices are only single stranded which sometimes fold on themselves to form a double helix structure.

  - The three types of RNA molecules are given which perform different function.
    (*i*) Messenger RNA (m-RNA)
    (*ii*) Ribosomal RNA (r-RNA)
    (*iii*) Transfer RNA (t-RNA)

- **Biological functions of Nucleic Acids:**

  - DNA is responsible for maintaining the identity of different species of organisms.

  - Nucleic Acid helps in protein synthesis.

  - DNA is chemical basis for heredity.

  - DNA is regarded as reserve of genetic information.

EXERCISE

1. Which of the following is a carbohydrate.
   - (*a*) Leucine
   - (*b*) Albumin
   - (*c*) Inulin
   - (*d*) Maltose

2. General formula for carbohydrates is
   - (*a*) $C_nH_{2n}O_{2n+2}$
   - (*b*) $C_x(H_2O)_{2x}$
   - (*c*) $C_x(H_2O)y$
   - (*d*) None of these

3. A certain compound gives negative test with Cyanohydrin and positive test with Benedict's solution. The compound is
   - (*a*) A protein
   - (*b*) A monosaccharide
   - (*c*) A lipid
   - (*d*) An amino acid.

4. An enzyme which brings about the conversion of starch into maltose is known as
   - (*a*) Maltase
   - (*b*) Zymase
   - (*c*) Invertase
   - (*d*) Diastase

5. Canesugar on hydrolysis gives.
   - (*a*) Glucose and maltose
   - (*b*) Glucose and lactose
   - (*c*) Glucose and fructose
   - (*d*) Only glucose

6. A carbohydrate that cannot be hydrolysed to simpler forms is called
   - (*a*) Disaccharide
   - (*b*) Monosaccharide
   - (*c*) Polysaccharide
   - (*d*) Trisaccharide

7. Starch is converted into maltose by the
   - (*a*) Maltase
   - (*b*) Invertase
   - (*c*) Zymase
   - (*d*) Diastase

8. The charring of sugar, when treated with conc. H_2SO_4 is due to.
   - (*a*) Oxidation
   - (*b*) Reduction
   - (*c*) Dehydration
   - (*d*) Hydrolysis

9. Which among the following is the simplest sugar.
   - (*a*) Glucose
   - (*b*) Cellulose
   - (*c*) Starch
   - (*d*) Glycogen

10. In fructose, the possible optical isomers are
    - (*a*) 12
    - (*b*) 8
    - (*c*) 16
    - (*d*) 4

11. Which is false
    - (*a*) Glucose is a disaccharide
    - (*b*) Starch is a polysaccharide
    - (*c*) Glucose and fructose are not anomers
    - (*d*) Invert sugar consists of glucose and fructose

12. Cellulose is soluble in
    (*a*) Ammoniacal cupic hydroxide solution
    (*b*) Organic solvents
    (c) Water
    (*d*) None of these
13. Insulin is
    (*a*) An amino acid　　(*b*) Protein
    (c) A carbohydrate　　(*d*) A lipid
14. The proteins which are insoluble in water are
    (*a*) Fibrous proteins　　(*b*) Globular proteins
    (c) Both (*a*) and (*b*)　　(*d*) None of these
15. The proteins with a prosthetic group are called
    (*a*) Pseudo proteins
    (*b*) Complex proteins
    (c) Conjugated proteins
    (*d*) Polypeptides
16. Proteins when heated with Conc. HNO_3 give a yellow colour. This is
    (*a*) Oxidising test　　(*b*) Xanthoprotic test
    (c) Hoppe's test　　(*d*) Acid-base test

17. Proteins are built up of
    (*a*) Dicarboxylic acids　　(*b*) Amino acids
    (c) Alcohols　　(*d*) Hydroxy acids
18. The chemical name of vitamin C is
    (*a*) Ascorbic acid　　(*b*) Folic acid
    (c) Nicotinic acid　　(*d*) Tartaric acid
19. Vitamin B_6 is known as
    (*a*) Pyridoxin　　(*b*) Thiamine
    (c) Tocopherol　　(*d*) Riboflavin
20. The best source of vitamin A is
    (*a*) Beans　　(*b*) Pulses
    (c) Orange　　(*d*) Carrot.
21. Deficiency of vitamin H causes
    (*a*) Skin diseases　　(*b*) Scurvy
    (c) Burning of eyes　　(*d*) Anaemia
22. Which one of the following vitamins is water-soluble
    (*a*) Vitamin B　　(*b*) Vitamin E
    (c) Vitamin K　　(*d*) Vitamin A

Answer Keys

1. (c)　　2. (c)　　3. (*b*)　　4. (*d*)　　5. (c)　　6. (*b*)　　7. (*d*)　　8. (c)　　9. (*a*)　　10. (*b*)

11. (*a*)　　12. (*a*)　　13. (*b*)　　14. (*a*)　　15. (c)　　16. (*b*)　　17. (*b*)　　18. (*a*)　　19. (*a*)　　20. (*d*)

21. (*a*)　　22. (*a*)

Solutions

1. Inulin is a carbohydrate which is stored in "Roots of Dahliya".

2. Carbohydrates are hydrates of carbon. Their general formula is $C_x(H_2O)_y$.

3. A monosaccharide gives negative test with Cyanohydrin and positive test with Benedicts solution.

4. $\text{Starch} \xrightarrow{\text{Diastase}} \text{Maltose}$

5. $C_{12}H_{22}O_{11} + H_2O \rightarrow C_6H_{12}O_6 + C_6H_{12}O_6$
   Cane sugar   Glucose   Fructose

6. Monosaccharide cannot be hydrolysed to simple forms.

7. Diastase enzyme converts starch into maltose.

8. Charring of sugar, when it is treated with sulphuric acid (H_2SO_4) is due to dehydration. In this reaction water is removed from the sugar.

9. Glucose is a monosaccharide while others are polysaccharide. So glucose is the simplest sugar.

10. Fructose has three chiral centres and hence 2^3 = 8. Optical isomers are possible.

11. Glucose is a monosaccharide having chemical composition $C_6H_{12}O_6$.

12. Cellulose dissolves in ammoniacal copper hydroxide solution (Schwitzer's reagent), it also dissolves in a solution of zinc chloride in HCl. When treated with conc. H_2SO_4 in cold, it slowly passes into solution.

13. Insulin is a protein consisting of 51 amino acids in two chains α and β

    α – 21 amino acids, β – 30 amino acids

    It is secreted by pancreas for controlling the sugar level in blood.

14. Fibrous proteins are insoluble in water.

15. Simple protein + non-protein material $\rightarrow$ Conjugated protein (Prosthetic group or co-factor)

16. Protein + Conc. $HNO_3 \rightarrow$ Yellow colour.

    This test is given by a protein which consists of α-amino acids containing a benzene ring such as tyrosine, phenylalanine etc. The yellow colour is due to nitration of benzene ring.

17. Proteins are polymers of amino acids

    Amino acid $\rightarrow$ Dipeptide $\rightarrow$ Polypeptide $\rightarrow$ Protein

18. The chemical name of vitamin C is Ascorbic acid.

19. Vitamin B_6 is called pyridoxin. It is found in fruits, green-vegetables, milk, etc. Due to its deficiency anaemia disease is caused.

20. The best source of vitamin A is carrot. Other sources are butter, milk, spinach, cheese, etc. Its deficiency causes night blindness.

21. Deficiency of vitamin H causes skin lesions, loss of appetite, weakness, hairfall and paralysis.

22. Vitamin B and C are water soluble vitamin.

CHAPTER 15

Polymers

The word polymer means having many parts. It is built of very large molecules having high molecular masses which can be called as Macromolecules. This means that they are formed by joining same structural units on a large scale. This process which requires joining these molecules by covalent bonds is called **Polymerisation.** The structural unit derived from simple molecules is called a **monomer.**

Classification of polymers

- **Classification based on Sources**
  - **Natural polymers:** They are found in animals and plants. For example, starch, cellulose, proteins and rubber.
  - **Semi-synthetic polymers:** These are derived from cellulose. For example, cellulose nitrate.
  - **Synthetic polymers:** These are produced from chemical reactions. For example, Buna-S which is a synthetic rubber.
- **Classification Based on Structure of Polymers**
  - **Linear polymers:** They comprise of straight and long chains. For example, high density polythene, polyvinyl chloride, etc.
  - **Branched chain polymers:** They also comprise of long chains but with some branches. For example, low density polythene.
  - **Cross linked or Network polymers:** They are formed by cross-linking monomers and consist of strong covalent bonds between the chains. For example, Bakelite, melamine etc.
- **Classification Based on Mode of Polymerisation**
  - **Addition polymers:** They are formed by repeatedly adding monomer molecules that have double or triple bonds. The polymers formed are known as homopolymers. For example, polyethene.

$$nCH_2 = CH_2 \longrightarrow (CH_2 - CH_2)_n \text{ Homopolymer}$$
$$\text{Ethene} \qquad \text{Polythene}$$

The polymers formed by adding two different monomers are called copolymers. For example, Buna-S and Buna-N etc.

$$nCH_2 = CH - CH = CH_2 + nC_6H_5CH = CH_2 \longrightarrow (CH_2 - CH = CH - CH_2 - CH_2 - \overset{\overset{\displaystyle C_6H_6}{|}}{CH})_n$$

$$\text{1,3–Butadiene} \qquad \text{Styrene} \qquad \text{Butadiene–styrene copolymer} \atop \text{(Buna–S)}$$

  - **Condensation polymers:** These are formed as a result of condensation reaction between two distinct bi-functional or tri-functional monomeric units. For example, nylon 6, 6. It is made from the condensation of hexamethylene diamine with adipic acid.

$$nH_2N(CH_2)_6 NH_2 + nHOOC(CH_2)_4 COOH \longrightarrow (NH(CH_2)_6 NHCO(CH_2)_4 CO)_n + nH_2O$$
$$\text{Nylon 6, 6}$$

- **Classification Based on Molecular Forces**
  - **Elastomers:** The polymer chains are held together by the weakest intermolecular forces due to which these polymers are stretchable. For example, buna-S, buna-N etc.

> **Fibers:** These polymers are held together by strong intermolecular forces like hydrogen bonding due to which they have high tensile strength. For example, polyamides (nylon 6, 6), polyesters (terylene), etc.

> **Thermoplastic polymers:** These polymer chains are moderately branched and are held together by intermolecular forces of attraction due to which they soften on heating and then harden on cooling. For example, polythene, polystyrene, polyvinyls, etc.

> **Thermosetting polymers:** These polymer chains are heavily branched and if heated can create extensive cross-linking and become infusible. For example, bakelite, urea-formaldelyde resins, etc.

- **Classification Based on Growth Polymerisation**

  The addition and condensation polymers are nowadays also known as chain growth polymers and step growth polymers.

Types of Polymerisation Reactions

- **Addition Polymerisation or Chain Growth**

  > **Free radical mechanism:** Different alkenes or dienes and their derivatives can be polymerized in the presence of a free radical generating initiator (catalyst) like benzoyl peroxide, acetyl peroxide, tert-butyl peroxide, etc. There are 3 steps involved.

  (*i*) Chain initiation step

$$C_6H_5 - \overset{O}{\overset{\|}{C}} - O - O - \overset{O}{\overset{\|}{C}} - C_6H_5 \longrightarrow 2C_6H_5 - \overset{O}{\overset{\|}{C}} - \overset{.}{O} \longrightarrow 2\overset{.}{C_6}H_5$$

  Benzoyl peroxide   Phenyl radical

$$\overset{.}{C_6}H_5 + CH_2 = CH_2 \longrightarrow C_6H_5 - CH_2 - \overset{.}{C}H_2$$

  (*ii*) Chain propagating step

$$C_6H_5 - CH_2 - \overset{.}{C}H_2 + CH_2 = CH_2 \longrightarrow C_6H_5 - CH_2 - CH_2 - CH_2 - \overset{.}{C}H_2$$

$$C_6H_5(CH_2 - CH_2)_n CH_2 - \overset{.}{C}H_2$$

  (*iii*) Chain terminating step

$$C_6H_5(CH_2 - CH_2)_n CH_2 - \overset{.}{C}H_2$$
$$+$$
$$C_6H_5(CH_2 - \overset{.}{C}H_2)_n CH_2 - \overset{.}{C}H_2 \longrightarrow C_6H_5(CH_2 - CH_2)_n CH_2 - CH_2 - CH_2(CH_2 - CH_2)_n C_6H_5$$

  Polythene

> **Preparation of some important addition polymers**

  (*i*) **Polyethene:** There are two types of polyethene.

> **Low Density polyethene:** They are obtained through free radical mechanism by the polymerisation of ethene under high pressure of 1000 to 2000 atmospheres at a temperature of 350 K to 570 K in the presence of traces of dioxygen or a peroxide initiator (catalyst) and have highly branched structures. They are poor conductors of electricity and this is why they are used in manufacturing of squeeze bottles, toys and flexible pipes.

> **High Density polyethene:** They are obtained through addition polymerisation of ethene takes place in a hydrocarbon solvent in the presence of a catalyst such as triethylaluminium and titanium tetrachloride (Ziegler Natta catalyst) at a temperature of 333 K to 343 K and under a pressure of 6-7 atmospheres. For example, used in manufacturing of buckets, dustbins, bottles, pipes, etc.

  (*ii*) **Polytetrafluoroethene (Teflon):** It is produced under high pressure by heating tetrafluoroethene with a free radical or persulphate catalyst. It is commonly used in the manufacturing of non – stick surface coated utensils.

$$nCF_2 = CF_2 \xrightarrow[\text{High pressure}]{\text{Catalyst}} (CF_2 - CF_2)_n$$

  Tetrafluoroethene   Teflon

(*iii*) **Polyacrylonitrile:** It is produced in presence of a peroxide catalyst. It is used in the making of commercial fibres such as orlon or acrilan.

$$nCH_2 = CHCN \xrightarrow[\text{Peroxide catalyst}]{\text{Polymerisation}} \left. \left[CH_2 - \underset{\underset{CN}{|}}{CH} \right] \right._n$$

Acrylonitrile   Polyacrylonitrile

- **Condensation Polymerisation or Step Growth polymerisation**
  - ➤ **Polyamides:** They are derived from condensation polymerisation of diamines with dicarboxylic acids and also of amino acids and their lactams.

  (*i*) **Preparation of Nylon 6,6:** It is produced with adipic acid under high pressure and at high temperatures. For example, in making of sheets, bristles for brushes etc.

$$nHOOC(CH_2)_4\,COOH + nH_2N(CH_2)_6\,NH_2 \xrightarrow[\text{High pressure}]{553K} \left[N-(CH_2)_6 - N - C(CH_2)_4 - C \right]_n$$

Nylon 6, 6

  (*ii*) **Preparation of Nylon 6:** It is obtained under high temperature by heating caprolactum with water. For example, manufacturing of tyre cords, fabrics and ropes etc.

$$\xrightarrow[\text{H}_2\text{O}]{533\text{-}543K} \left[C - (CH_2)_5 - N \right]_n$$

Caprolactam   **Nylon 6**

  - ➤ **Polyesters:** They are obtained in the presence of zinc acetateantimony trioxide catalyst by heating a mixture of ethylene glycol and terephthalic acid at 420 to 460 K. For example, Dacron fibre (terylene) is used in safety helmets etc.
  - ➤ **Phenol - formaldehyde polymer (Bakelite and related polymers):** It is a condensation reaction of phenol which requires a presence of either acid or base catalyst with formaldehyde. The initial substance produced is known as Novolac which is used in paints.

Novolac

On continuous heating of Novolac, infusible solid mass called Bakelite is produced. It is used in manufacturing of combs, electrical switches etc.

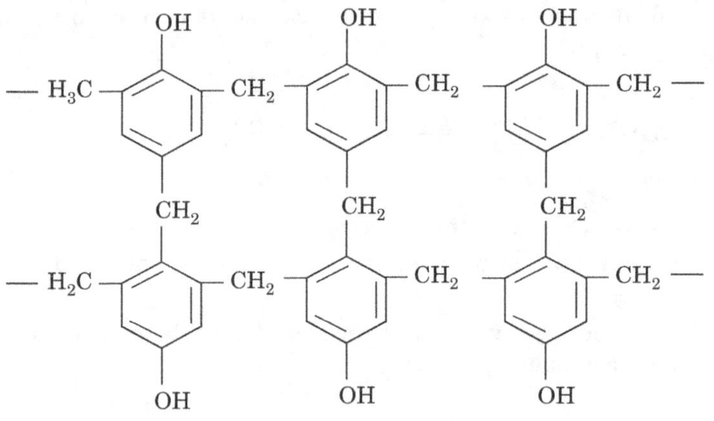

Bakelite

➢ **Melamine-formaldehyde polymer:** It is another condensation reaction of melamine with formaldehyde.

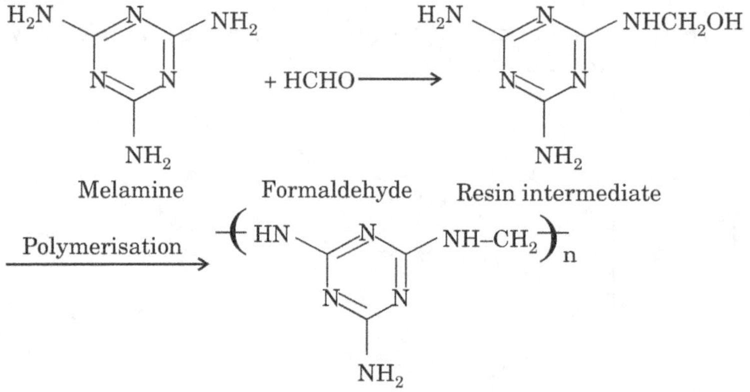

Melamine   Formaldehyde   Resin intermediate

Melamine polymer

- **Copolymerisation:** It is a chain growth polymerisation which consists of many units of different monomers used in the same polymeric chain. For example, butadiene - styrene copolymer is used for the making of auto tyres, floor tiles, footwear components etc.

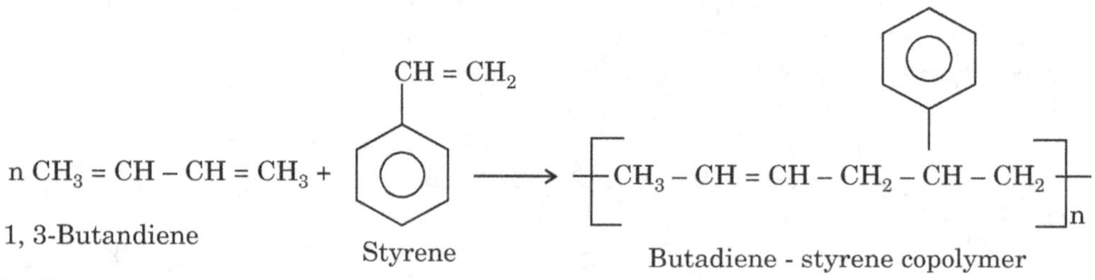

$n\ CH_3 = CH - CH = CH_3\ +$ (Styrene) $\longrightarrow$ Butadiene - styrene copolymer

1, 3-Butandiene

Styrene

- **Rubber**

  ➢ **Natural rubber:** It is a linear polymer of isoprene (2-methyl-1, 3-butadiene) and is also called as cis -1,4 polyisoprene and these chains are held together by weak van der Waals interactions and has a coiled structure and that's why it shows elastic properties. The process of formation of natural rubber by heating a mixture of raw rubber with sulphur and an appropriate additive at a temperature range between 373 K to 415 K is called as Vulcanisation of rubber.

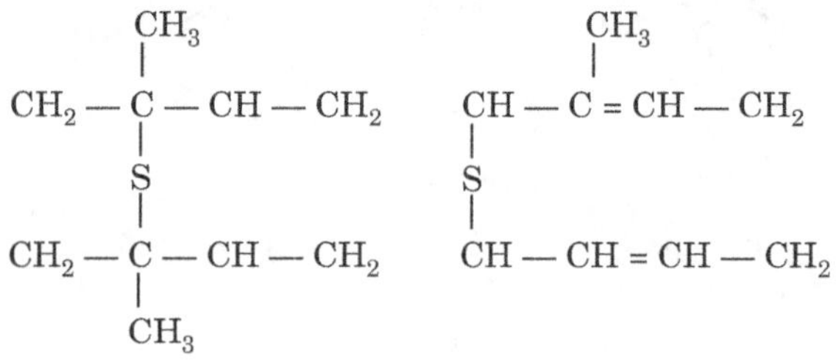

> **Synthetic rubbers:** There are various synthetic rubbers which are obtained from chemical reactions.

(*i*) **Neoprene:** It is obtained by the free radical polymerisation of chloroprene. It is used for manufacturing conveyor belts, gaskets and hoses.

$$nCH_2 = \overset{\overset{\textstyle Cl}{\textstyle |}}{C} - CH = CH_2 \xrightarrow{\textit{Polymerisation}} \{CH_2 - \overset{\overset{\textstyle Cl}{\textstyle |}}{C} = CH - CH_2\}_n$$

Chloroprene
2-Chloro-1, 3-butadiene   Neoprene

(*ii*) **Buna-N:** It is formed in the presence of a peroxide catalyst. It is used in the manufacturing of oil seals, tank lining, etc.

$$nCH_2 = CH - CH = CH_2 + nCH_2 = \overset{\overset{\textstyle CN}{\textstyle |}}{CH} \xrightarrow{\textit{Copolymerisation}} \{CH_2 - CH = CH - CH_2 - CH_2 - \overset{\overset{\textstyle CN}{\textstyle |}}{CH}\}_n$$

1,3-Butadiene   Acrylonitrile   Buna-N

Molecular Mass of Polymers

The molecular mass of any polymer is determined by physical and chemical methods which may vary in their size, mass, synthesis, structure, length and mass.

Biodegradable Polymers of Commercial Importance with their Structures

These are environment friendly polymers.

- **Poly β-hydroxybutyrate – co-β-hydroxy valerate (PHBV):** The following copolymerisation reaction takes place. It is used in speciality packaging.

$$CH_3 - \overset{\overset{\textstyle OH}{\textstyle |}}{CH} - CH_2 - COOH + CH_3 - CH_2 - \overset{\overset{\textstyle OH}{\textstyle |}}{CH} - CH_2 - COOH \longrightarrow \{O - CH - CH_2 - \overset{O}{\overset{||}{C}} - O - CH - CH_2 - C\}_n$$

3-Hydroxypentanoic acid   3-Hydroxypentanoic acid   PHBV

- **Nylon 2-nylon 6:** This copolymer is biodegradable and formed from glycine (H2N–CH2–COOH) and amino caproic acid [$H_2N (CH_2)_5 COOH$]

Polymers of Commercial Importance with their Structures

- **Polypropene:** It is used in the Manufacture of ropes, toys, pipes, fibres, etc.

$$\{CH_2 - \overset{\overset{\textstyle CH_3}{\textstyle |}}{CH}\}_n$$

- **Polystyrene:** It is used as insulator, wrapping material, manufacture of toys, radio and television cabinets.

$$\{CH_2 - \overset{\overset{\textstyle C_6H_5}{\textstyle |}}{CH}\}_n$$

- **Polyvinyl chloride (PVC):** It is used in the manufacture of rain (PVC) coats, hand bags, vinyl flooring, water pipes.

$$\{CH_2 - \overset{\overset{\textstyle Cl}{\textstyle |}}{CH}\}_n$$

EXERCISE

1. Which one among the following is a thermosetting plastic.
   - (a) PVC
   - (b) PVA
   - (c) Bakelite
   - (d) Perspex

2. 'cis-1, 4-polyisoprene' is
   - (a) Thermoplastic
   - (b) Thermosetting plastic
   - (c) Elastic (rubber)
   - (d) Resin

3. Which of the following is not a polymer
   - (a) Gun cotton
   - (b) Perspex
   - (c) Shellac
   - (d) Wax

4. Among the following a natural polymer is
   - (a) Cellulose
   - (b) PVC
   - (c) Teflon
   - (d) Polyethylene

5. Which of the following is a natural polymer
   - (a) Polyester
   - (b) Glyptal
   - (c) Starch
   - (d) Nylon-6

6. Which is a naturally occuring polymer
   - (a) Polythene
   - (b) PVC
   - (c) Acetic acid
   - (d) Protein

7. Which of the following polymer is an example of fiber
   - (a) Silk
   - (b) Dacron
   - (c) Nylon-66
   - (d) All of these

8. Which of the following is a biodegradable polymer.
   - (a) Cellulose
   - (b) Polyethene
   - (c) PVC
   - (d) Nylon-6

9. Which is not a polymer
   - (a) Sucrose
   - (b) Enzyme
   - (c) Starch
   - (d) Teflon

10. Polymerization of glycol with dicarboxylic acids is
    - (a) Addition polymerisation
    - (b) Condensation polymerisation
    - (c) Telomerisation
    - (d) Any of these

11. Polypropylene can be obtained by polymerisation of
    - (a) $CH \equiv CH$
    - (b) $CH_2 = CH_2$
    - (c) $CH_3 - CH = CH_2$
    - (d) $CH_3 - C \equiv CH$

12. Acetate rayon is prepared from
    - (a) Acetic acid
    - (b) Glycerol
    - (c) Starch
    - (d) Cellulose

13. The compound required for the formation of a thermosetting polymer with methanal is
    - (a) Benzene
    - (b) Phenyl amine
    - (c) Benzaldehyde
    - (d) Phenol

14. Discovery of 'nylon' is associated with
    - (a) Newyork and London
    - (b) Newyork and Longuet
    - (c) Nyholm and London
    - (d) None of these

15. The mass average molecular mass & number average molecular mass of a polymer are respectively 40,000 and 30,000. The polydispersity index of polymer will be
    - (a) < 1
    - (b) > 1
    - (c) 1
    - (d) 0

16. In the process of forming 'mercerrised cellulose' the swelling of cellulose is caused by
    - (a) Water
    - (b) Na_2CO_3
    - (c) Aq.NaOH
    - (d) Aq.HCl

17. Molecular mass of a polymer is
    - (a) Small
    - (b) Very small
    - (c) Negligible
    - (d) Large

18. Neoprene is a polymer of
    - (a) Propene
    - (b) Vinyl chloride
    - (c) Chloroprene
    - (d) Butadine

19. Natural rubber is basically a polymer of
    - (a) Neoprene
    - (b) Isoprene
    - (c) Chloroprene
    - (d) Butadine

20. Which of the following in used to make 'non-stick' cookware.
    - (a) PVC
    - (b) Polystyrene
    - (c) Polyethylene terephthalate
    - (d) Polytetra fluoroethylene or Teflon

21. Teflon is a polymer of
    - (a) Tetrafluoro ethane
    - (b) Tetrafluoro propene
    - (c) Difluoro ethene
    - (d) Trifluoro ethene

22. What is the percentage of sulphur used in vulcanization of rubber
    - (a) 5%
    - (b) 3%
    - (c) 30%
    - (d) 55%

23. In elastomer, intermolecular forces are
    - (a) Nil
    - (b) Weak
    - (c) Strong
    - (d) Very strong

Answer Keys

1. (c) 2. (c) 3. (d) 4. (a) 5. (c) 6. (d) 7. (d) 8. (a) 9. (a) 10. (b)

11. (c) 12. (d) 13. (d) 14. (a) 15. (b) 16. (c) 17. (d) 18. (c) 19. (b) 20. (d)

21. (a) 22. (a) 23. (b)

Solutions

1. Bakelite is thermosetting polymer. It becomes infusible on heating and can not be remoulded.

2. Natural rubber is the only addition polymer of nature and is known as cis-1, 4-polyisoprene.

3. Wax is a molecular solid. So wax is not a polymer.

4. Cellulose is a natural polymer. It is present in the cell wall of plant.

5. Starch is a natural polymer and other are synthetic.

6. Protein is a natural polymer of α-amino acids.

7. Silk is protein fiber. Dacron is polyester fiber and Nylon - 66 is polyamide fiber.

8. Cellulose is the natural fiber which is biodegradable polymer rest are synthetic polymer which are not biodegradable.

9. Sucrose is a disaccharides which upon acid or enzymatic hydrolysis gives only two molecules of monosaccharides

10. Condensation polymerisation because loss of water molecule takes place

11. $nCH_3 - CH = CH_2 \longrightarrow \left(-CH_2 - \underset{\underset{CH_3}{|}}{CH} - \right)_n$
Polypropylene

12. Rayon fiber is chemically identical to cotton but has a shine like silk, rayon is also called a regenerated fiber because during its preparation cellulose is regenerated by dissolving it is NaOH and CS_2.

13. When phenol react with HCHO form bakelite which is a thermosetting polymer.

14. Nylon was simultaneously discovered in Newyork and London.

15. Average number molecular weight $\overline{M}_n = 30,000$

Average mass molecular weight $\overline{M}_w = 40,000$

Polydispersity index (PDI)

$$\frac{\overline{M}_w}{\overline{M}_n} = \frac{40,000}{30,000} = 1.33$$

16. Cellulose forms a transluscent mass on treatment with conc. NaOH which imparts a silky lusture to cotton. This process is mercerisation and the cotton so produced is known as mercerised cotton.

17. Polymer always consists of hundreds to thousands of repeating structural units. Hence they have very high molecular mass.

18. $n(CH_2 = \underset{\underset{Cl}{|}}{C} - CH = CH_2) \rightarrow (-CH_2 - \underset{\underset{Cl}{|}}{C} = CH - CH_2 -)_n$
(Chloroprene) (Neoprene)

19. $nCH_2 = \underset{\underset{CH_3}{|}}{C} - CH = CH_2 \rightarrow (-CH_2 - \underset{\underset{CH_3}{|}}{C} = CH - CH_2 -)_n$
(Isoprene) (Natural rubber)

20. Teflon has great chemical inertness and high thermal stability, hence used for making non-stick utensils. For this purpose, a thin layer of teflon is coated on the inner side of the vessel.

21. $n\ CF_2 = CF_2 \longrightarrow (-CF_2 - CF_2 -)_n$
(Tetrafluoro ethane) (Teflon)

22. Vulcanization is a process in which natural rubber is treated with 4-5% sulphur and certain organic compounds which accelerate the reaction between the rubber and sulphur. It introduces sulphur bridges between polymer chains thereby increasing its tensile strength, elasticity an resistance to abrasion.

23. Polymer chain in elastomer are held together by weak intermolecular forces eg. Vulcanised rubber.

CHAPTER 16

Chemistry in Everyday Life

Chemistry influences our daily life and is used in following ways to benefit the human life:

- ➤ Production of cleanliness products such as soaps, detergents, toothpaste etc.
- ➤ Use of chemicals in food as preservatives, artificial sweetening agents etc.
- ➤ Use of chemicals in medicines as antiseptics, antacids, antibiotics etc.

Drugs and their classification

- Chemical substances of low molecular masses which produce biological responses are called drugs. When the effects of these drugs are therapeutic and useful, they are called medicines.
- **Classification of Drugs**
    - ➤ *On the basis of pharmacological effects*: These are the types of drugs that are prescribed for the treatment of particular problem or sickness. For example, antacids bring relief from acidity.
    - ➤ *On the basis of drug action*: These are the types of drugs that have a particular biochemical process for targeted effects. For example, antihistamines that inhibits the actions of histamines that cause inflammation in the body.
    - ➤ *On the basis of chemical structure*: These are the types of drugs that have a particular chemical structure. For example, sulphonamides have common chemical structural feature.

- ➤ *On the basis of molecular targets*: These are the types of drugs that interact with different biomolecules such as proteins and carbohydrates and directly affect the targets.
- **Drug-target interaction**
    - ➤ Enzymes are the proteins that act as biological catalysts
    - ➤ Catalytic action of enzymes: For this action of enzymes interactions such as hydrogen bonding or dipole-dipole interactions are required. The substrate molecule is held by the active site of enzyme by using the strong interactions which is attacked by the reagent and then the chemical reaction is carried out.

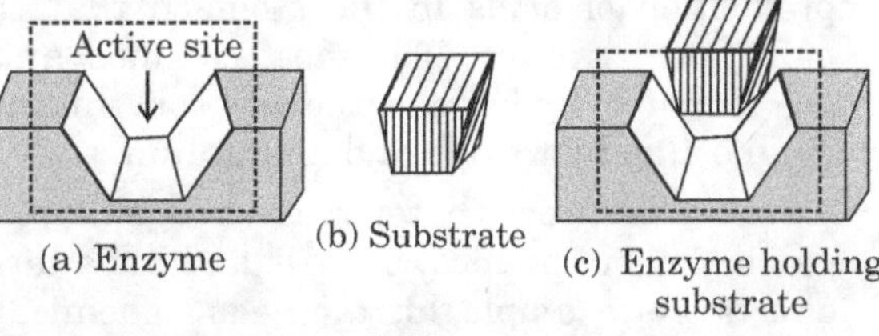

- ➤ Drug-enzyme interaction: Enzyme inhibitors are the drugs that block the binding site of the enzyme and the substrate. There are two ways in which this action takes place:
- (*i*) Some drugs called as competitive inhibitors compete for the active site of the enzyme attachment as shown in the diagram.

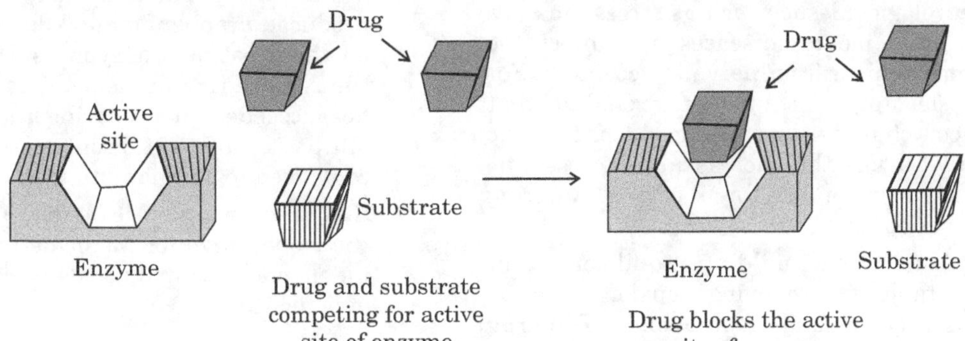

(*ii*) There are some drugs that do not bind with the active site of the enzyme but different site called allosteric site. In this interaction, a strong covalent bond is required which cannot be broken easily.

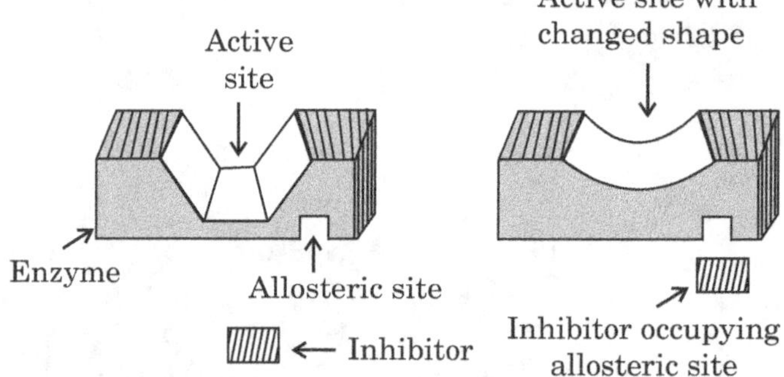

➢ Receptors are proteins that are important for communication in the body. For communication between neurons to muscles, chemical messengers are required which forwards the message to the cell without entering the cell. Different receptors have different binding shapes, structures and composition.

➢ Antagonists are those drugs that bind to the receptor site and inhibit its natural function whereas agonists are the drugs that act as natural messengers by swapping on the receptors.

Different classes of drugs on basis of therapeutic action

- **Antacids:** These are the drugs that stop the excess production of acids in the stomach that causes pain and irritation. The most common antacids are sodium hydrogencarbonate or mixture of magnesium hydroxide and aluminium.

- **Antihistamines:** These are the drugs that have a particular biochemical process and have targeted effects. For example, histamine is a chemical that activates the secretion of pepsin and hydrochloric acid in the stomach. Antihistamines react with the receptors and helps lessen the amount of such acids released in the stomach. For example, common antihistamines are brompheniramine (Dimetapp) and terfenadine (Seldane).

- **Tranquilizers:** These are the types of drugs that act on neurological issues such as stress, anxiety, severe or mild mental diseases and affect the transfer mechanism from nerve to receptors. For example, sleeping pills and nonadrenaline that act on mood changes. Iproniazid and phenelzine are the two drugs that act as antidepressants, which activate receptors for a person suffering from depression.

  ➢ There are some mild tranquilizers that are suitable for relieving tension such as chlordiazepoxide and meprobamate. The drug that helps in controlling hypertension and depression is Equanil.

  ➢ There are some strong tranquilizers called Barbiturates which are hypnotic such as veronal, amytal, nembutal, luminal, valium and serotonin.

- **Analgesics:** These are the types of drugs that minimize or stop pain without actually causing any imbalance to nervous system. There are two types:

  ➢ **Non-narcotic(non-addictive) analgesics:** These are the drugs that have a relieving effect on skeletal pain(joints pain), helps in reducing fever and platelet coagulation and also prevention of heart attacks as these drugs have anti blood clotting action.

  ➢ **Narcotic analgesics:** These are the types of drugs that also have relieving properties but then taken in excess amount can have severe side effects such as coma, stupor and untimely death. This is the reason they are mainly used in child birth, cardiac pain and terminal cancer pain. For example, Morphine, also referred to as opiates.

- **Antibiotics:** These are the types of drugs that stop the growth of microorganisms and kill them eventually these are drugs that are synthesized from chemicals that are low in concentration and they act on metabolic processes.

  ➢ A German bacteriologist, Paul Ehrlich produced arsphenamine, known as salvarsan, for the treatment of syphilis. He was awarded the Nobel Prize in medicine in 1980. In 1932, he succeeded in preparing the first effective antibacterial agent, prontosil, which later was converted to sulphanilamide.

  ➢ H.W. Florey and Alexander Fleming shared the Nobel prize for Medicine in 1945 for their independent contributions to the development of penicillin.

General Structure of Penicillin

Chloramphenicol

- ➢ There are two types of antibiotics, Bactericidal and Bacteriostatic. Bactericidal have killing effects and examples are Penicillin, Aminoglycosides and Ofloxacin. Bacteriostatic have inhibitory effects on microbes and examples are Erythromycin, Tetracycline and Chloramphenicol.

- ➢ Chloramphenicol can be given orally in case of typhoid, meningitis, acute fever, some form of urinary infections, dysentery and pneumonia.

- **Antiseptics and Disinfectants:** These are used to kill or stop the growth of microorganisms.
  - ➢ Antiseptics are used on outer wounds on skin surface. For example, soframicine, furacine, Iodoform and Iodine tincture etc. Dettol is a mixture of chloroxylenol and terpineol.
  - ➢ Disinfectants are the chemicals or drugs that are used in cleaning objects. For example, Phenol is an antiseptic while its one percent solution is disinfectant.

- **Anti-fertility drugs:** These are the drugs that help in the prevention of unwanted pregnancy. For example, Birth control pills contain a mixture of synthetic estrogen and progesterone derivatives. both of which are hormones and known to suppresses ovulation.The commonly used anti-fertility drug is Norethindrone is an example of synthetic progesterone derivative.

Chemicals in Food

- **Artificial sweetening agents:** These are the chemicals added in food to enhance their appeal such as food colouring, flavours and sweeteners. Sucrose is a natural sweetener, whereas Saccharin is the first popular artificial sweetening agent. This is useful for diabetic people. Some artificial sweeteners are Aspartame, Sucrolose and Alitame.

- Food preservatives:They are added to increase the nutritive value of the food since they prevent spoilage of food that happens due to microbial growth. For example, table salt, sugar, vegetable oils and sodium benzoate, C_6H_5COONa are commonly used preservatives.

Cleansing agents

- **Soaps:** These are used for cleaning purposes and are mainly made of sodium or potassium salts of long chain fatty acids.

$$CH_2-O-\overset{\overset{O}{\|}}{C}-C_{17}H_{35}$$
$$CH-O-\overset{\overset{O}{\|}}{C}-C_{17}H_{35} + 3\,NaOH \longrightarrow 3C_{17}H_{35}COONa + $$
$$CH_2-O-\overset{\overset{O}{\|}}{C}-C_{17}H_{35}$$

$$CH_2-OH$$
$$CH-OH$$
$$CH_2-OH$$

| Gylceryl ester of stearic acid (Fat) | Sodium hydroxide | Sodium stearate | Glycerol (or Glycerine) |

- ➢ The process of obtaining sodium salts soaps by heating fat with aqueous sodium hydroxide solution is called Saponification.

- ➢ There are different types of soaps such as toilet soaps, transparent soaps, medicated soaps, shaving soaps, laundry soaps, soap powders or granules.

> Soaps don't work in hard water because hard water contains calcium and magnesium ions which are insoluble in water and separate out as scum in water and become useless. This is the reason why hairs and clothes are not washed in hard water.

$$2C_{17}H_{36}COONa + CaCl_2 \longrightarrow 2NaCl + (C_{17}H_{35}COO)_2\,Ca$$

Soap   Insoluble calcium stearate (Soap)

- Synthetic detergents: These have the same property as those of soaps but they work in hard water as well. They have 3 main categories.

   > Anionic detergents: These are the sodium salts of sulphonated long chain alcohols or hydrocarbons. The anionic part of the molecule is involved in the cleansing action in anionic detergents. They are used in toothpastes.

$$CH_3(CH_2)_{10}CH_2OH \xrightarrow{H_2SO_4} CH_3(CH_2)_{10}CH_2OSO_3H \xrightarrow{NaOH(aq)} CH_3(CH_2)_{10}CH_2O\overset{-}{S}\overset{+}{O}_3\,Na$$

Lauryl alcohol   Lauryl hydrogensulphate   Sodium laurylsulphate (Anionic detergent)

$$CH_3(CH_2)_{11}\!-\!\bigcirc\!-\!\!\xrightarrow{H_2SO} CH_3(CH_2)_{11}\!-\!\bigcirc\!-SO_3H \xrightarrow{NaOH(aq)} CH_3(CH_2)_{11}\!-\!\bigcirc\!-\overset{-}{S}\overset{+}{O}_3\,Na$$

Dodecylbenzene   Dodecylbenzenesulphonic acid   Sodium dodecylbenzenesulphonate

   > Cationic detergents: They are quarternary ammonium salts of amines with acetates, chlorides or bromides as anions. These detergents have germicidal properties. For example, Cetyltrimethylammoniumbromide is used in hair conditioners.

   > Non-ionic detergents: They do not contain any ion in their constitution. The grease and oil are removed by micelle formation. For example, liquid dishwashing detergents.

EXERCISE

1. Soaps are
   - (a) Sodium salts of long chain fatty acids
   - (b) Potassium salts of long chain fatty acids
   - (c) Potassium salts of short chain fatty acids
   - (d) Both (a) and (b)

2. Which of the following is the correct set of food preservatives?
   - (a) Alitame, bithionol and terpineol
   - (b) Sodium benzoate, sugar and table salt
   - (c) Iodme, sugar and of loxain
   - (d) Table salt, seldane and sugar

3. Receptors help in
   - (a) Communication of the cells
   - (b) Killing of the cells
   - (c) degradation of the cells
   - (d) None of the above.

4. Substances used in bringing down the body temperature in the high fever are called
   - (a) antiseptics
   - (b) pyretics
   - (c) antibiotics
   - (d) antipyretics

5. Arsenic drugs are mainly used in the treatment of
   - (a) Jaundice
   - (b) typhoid
   - (c) syphilis
   - (d) cholera

6. Which of the following can possibly be used as analgesic without causing addiction and modification?
   - (a) Morphine
   - (b) N-acetyl-para-aminophenol
   - (c) Diazepam
   - (d) Tetrahydro catenol

7. Asprin is an acetylation product of
   - (a) p-dihydroxy benzene
   - (b) p-hydroxybenzoic acid
   - (c) o-dihydroxybenzene
   - (d) m-hydroxybenzoic acid

8. Which of the following is an antidiabetic drug?
   - (a) Insulin
   - (b) Penicillin
   - (c) Chloroquine
   - (d) Asprin

9. Which of the following is used for inducing sleep?
   (*a*) Paracetamol
   (*b*) Chloroquine
   (*c*) Bithional
   (*d*) Barbituric acid derivatives

10. A broad spectrum antibiotic is
   (*a*) Paracetamol   (*b*) Penicillin
   (*c*) aspirin   (*d*) Chloramphenicol

11. Which of the following is used as a " morning after pill"
   (*a*) Mifepristone   (*b*) Ethynylestradiol
   (*c*) Northindrone   (*d*) Bithional

12. An ester used as medicine is
   (*a*) ethyl acetate   (*b*) methyl acetate
   (*c*) methyl salicylate (*d*) ethyl benzoate

13. A drug that is antipyretic as well as analgesic is
   (*a*) Chloropromazine hydrochloride
   (*b*) Para-acetamidophenol
   (*c*) Chloroquine
   (*d*) Penicillin

14. Barbituric acid and its derivatives are will known as.
   (*a*) tranquilizers   (*b*) antiseptices
   (*c*) analgesics   (*d*) antipyretics

15. The drug given during hypertension is
   (*a*) streptomycin   (*b*) Chloroxylenol
   (*c*) equanil   (*d*) aspirin

16. Which of the following is used as an antiseptic?
   (*a*) Phenol   (*b*) Benzaldehyde
   (*c*) Benzalamine   (*d*) Maleic anhydride

17. Betadine is
   (*a*) antiseptic   (*b*) tranquilizer
   (*c*) antibiotic   (*d*) disinfectant

18. Which of the following will not enhance nutritional value of food?
   (*a*) Minerals
   (*b*) Artificial sweetners
   (*c*) Vitamins
   (*d*) Amino acids

19. The safest and most common alternative of sugar is
   (*a*) glucose   (*b*) dulcin
   (*c*) cyclodextrine   (*d*) aspartame

20. One of the mst widely used drug in medicine iodex is
   (*a*) methyl salicylate
   (b) ethyl salicylate
   (c) acetyl salicylic acid
   (d) O-hydroxy benzoic acid

Answer Keys

1. (*d*)   2. (*b*)   3. (*a*)   4. (*d*)   5. (*c*)   6. (*c*)   7. (*b*)   8. (*a*)   9. (*d*)   10. (*d*)
11. (*a*)   12. (*c*)   13. (*b*)   14. (*a*)   15. (*c*)   16. (*a*)   17. (*a*)   18. (*c*)   19. (*d*)   20. (*a*)

Solutions

1. Soaps are sodium and potassium salts of long chain fatty acids.

2. Sodium benzoate, sugar table salt are used as food preservatives.

3. Receptors help in communication of the cells.

4. The chemical substances used to bring down the body temperature in case of high fever are called antipyretics, e.g. analgin.

5. Arsenic drugs such as arsphenamine known as salvarsan, are mainly used in the treatment of syphilis.

6. N-acethyl-Para-aminophenol is non-narcotics, i.e. not habit forming analgesic.

7. Asprin is the acetylation product of o-hydroxy-benzoic acid.

$$OCOCH_3$$

Aspirin

8. Insulin is an antidiabetic drug.

9. Derivatives of barbituric acid (viz luminal and seconal) are used for inducing sleep.

10. Broad spectrum antibiotics are the medicines, effective against a large number of harmful microorganisms, e.g. tetracyclic, chloramphenicol.

11. Mifepristone is used as a morning after pill.

12. An ester used a medicine is methyl salicylate.

13. Para-acetamido phenol is used as an antipyretic as well as analegesic

14. The drugs given to the patients suffering from anxiety and mental tension are called transquilizers e.g. barbituric acid and its derivatives.

15. Equanil is widely used during depression and hypertension.

16. 0.2% solution of phenol acts as an antiseptic and its 1% solutions is a disinfectant

17. Betadine is an antiseptic because it does not harm living cells and destroy the microbes only.

18. Vitamins doesn't enhance nutritional value of food.

19. Aspartame is the safest and the most common alternative of sugar. It is methyl ester of dipeptide formed from aspartic acid and phenylalanine.

20. Methyl salicylate is widely used in iodex it is also known as oil of winter green.